REITs

By Brad Thomas

A Wiley Brand

REITs For Dummies®

Published by: **John Wiley & Sons, Inc.,** 111 River Street, Hoboken, NJ 07030-5774, www.wiley.com

Copyright © 2024 by John Wiley & Sons, Inc., Hoboken, New Jersey

Published simultaneously in Canada

For general information on our other products and services, please contact our Customer Care Department within the U.S. at 877-762-2974, outside the U.S. at 317-572-3993, or fax 317-572-4002. For technical support, please visit https://hub.wiley.com/community/support/dummies.

Wiley publishes in a variety of print and electronic formats and by print-on-demand. Some material included with standard print versions of this book may not be included in e-books or in print-on-demand. If this book refers to media such as a CD or DVD that is not included in the version you purchased, you may download this material at http://booksupport.wiley.com. For more information about Wiley products, visit www.wiley.com.

Library of Congress Control Number: 2023944357

ISBN 978-1-394-18535-1 (pbk); ISBN 978-1-394-18537-5 (ebk); 978-1-394-18536-8 (ebk)

Contents at a Glance

Table of Contents

Introduction

It never occurred to me back in college that I should become a virtual landlord — which is what owning shares of real estate investment trusts, or REITs (pronounced "reets"), entails. It never occurred to me after graduation when I was working my first job, either. In fact, it didn't occur to me for the first two decades of my professional experience.

It's not that I had anything against being a landlord. Quite the opposite, actually. I wanted to become rich by owning real estate since I was about ten years old. Truly. And most of my adult life was spent developing commercial real estate — hands-on and from the ground up. I also studied many of the well-known *Forbes*-list billionaires with that goal in mind. This included Donald Bren (founder of Irvine Company), Stephen M. Ross (founder of Related Companies), Leonard Stern (founder of Hartz Mountain), and Sam Zell (founder of Equity Group Investments). That latter individual happened to be a REIT chairman — three times over! And all of them built their considerable fortunes on real estate. They directly owned and rented properties out, collecting that income and watching their bank accounts soar as a result.

That makes it sound easy-peasy, I know, so let me start out with a very firm clarification. I can attest from personal experience (in real estate construction and management, not in being a billionaire) that it takes a lot of blood, sweat, and tears to generate that kind of wealth. The individuals just mentioned took on considerable work and risk in order to achieve their success stories. There's a reason why only 1.1 percent of people in the world are millionaires, much less anything higher.

With that said, there's a way to generate significant wealth in real estate by becoming a virtual landlord. It might not make you a billionaire (unless you have a lot of money to start out with), but it also comes with almost no blood, sweat, or tears.

About This Book

That's what *REITs For Dummies* is all about — helping you safely create generational wealth and sustainable cash flow by investing in companies that invest in commercial real estate. I'm extremely honored to write it since I know the positive impact it can have on millions of readers around the globe. My more than three decades of experience as a real estate developer, investor, and analyst provides me with a unique perspective about REITs that I'm more than happy to pass on to you.

Some of that experience was extremely rough — even traumatic. Back before I realized the power and long-term profit potential of REITs, I made a lot of mistakes. I built up a fortune that was ultimately unsustainable: a house of cards that the 2008 crisis toppled in an astonishingly short amount of time. I had to build myself back up from that; it was a journey I now recognize as an immense blessing in disguise. It taught me so many invaluable lessons that not only benefit my life but my readers' and followers' lives as well.

That's why *REITs For Dummies* covers as much as it does, from how these assets got started to how they operate to how to analyze them to how to include them in your portfolio.

I don't for one second or sentence advocate REITs as a perfect investment. You'll see me repeat that caution over and over again throughout the following pages. For that matter, anyone who touts anything as a perfect investment is either grossly misinformed or trying to take your money without making you any in return. But REITs do offer benefits that other assets simply don't and can't. This means they can complement your larger investment portfolio in unique ways that promote both wealth creation and wealth preservation.

Foolish Assumptions

I have a very well-established REIT–analyzing presence through platforms such as Seeking Alpha (a site that allows individual experts to distribute their investment findings) and Wide Moat Research (a company that publishes both free and paid articles on dividend-paying opportunities). Through those, various investment conferences, and personal interactions, I'm used to discussing REITs with a wide range of people, from those who've never heard of them all the way to industry experts and insiders.

I understand that everyone comes to the table with varying amounts of information and finances to work with — not to mention different goals, personalities, and tolerance levels. With that said, I did write this book for a specific set of people. It's a pretty broad set, mind you, but I'm still assuming that if you want to read *REITs For Dummies*

>> You know the basics of investing, such as what a dividend-payer is.

>> You've got enough money to invest without having to take a loan out, destroy your emergency fund, or sell a kidney on the black market.

>> You already have an investment portfolio of some kind, just one that doesn't feature REITs or doesn't feature enough of them.

Admittedly, that last assumption isn't going to ruin this read for you if it doesn't apply. I would just suggest that you perhaps start with something like *Investing All-In-One For Dummies* by Eric Tyson (Wiley). Then come back to this after you're done.

Icons Used in This Book

Speaking of such, the *For Dummies* brand of books aren't actually made for dummies. They're made for intelligent people who recognize a lack of knowledge in some area they'd like some knowledge about. Moreover, they're made for intelligent people on the go. (However, you can still easily benefit from them if you're retired with nothing but sweet, sweet time on your hands.) That's why each one includes a list of icons to help you digest the information at hand in a way that best benefits you and your schedule. This REITs addition to the *For Dummies* universe is no different. Here are the icons you'll encounter and a brief description of each:

TIP

Whenever you see this symbol, it signifies some way to make your life easier. This might be with additional information or an insight into how to implement previous information as best as possible.

REMEMBER

Let me be blunt: There is some information in this book that you don't necessarily need to know, depending on exactly what you're looking for (more about that in a minute). The sidebars — those shaded boxes — for example, can be considered extra-curricular reading or fun additional facts. However, when you see the Remember icon, it's something you want to zero in on and commit to memory.

TECHNICAL
STUFF

This one's pretty obvious but let me explain it all the same. The Technical Stuff icon marks information of a highly technical nature that you can skip over if you don't want to get into the weeds.

WARNING

As I've already stated and will state again, there is no such thing as a perfect investment. But you can make REITs a lot closer to that ideal by avoiding dangers such as the ones highlighted by the Warning icon.

PROPTECH

The appeal and importance of real estate doesn't change, but the way we interact with that real estate certainly has over the millennia — an evolution that's sped up immensely in recent decades. That's why I make sure to highlight facts and figures that show the ever-increasing blend between property ownership and technology.

Beyond This Book

If you still want more after you're done reading everything I've got here, don't worry. I've got your back with a bit more information over at www.dummies.com, where I've added a few more pages of details you might want to know. Search for "REITs For Dummies Cheat Sheet" in your favorite search engine.

Where to Go From Here

Since you've made it this far, I'm guessing (another assumption, I know) that you're ready to read further. In which case, have at it!

Naturally, I think everything in the following pages is worth reading. (It's an amazing body of work and so well-written, didn't you know?) But feel free to disagree. I imagine you have a better idea of what you're looking for than I do. So if you saw chapter headings in the table of contents that zero in on your particular needs, jump right to them. There's no standing on ceremony here.

Each chapter is largely meant to stand out by itself and for itself. This allows you to save some time and skip over sections you already know or that don't pertain to you. However you choose to read the book, I hope you find both happy reading . . .

. . . and happy REITing!

1

Getting Started with REITs

Chapter **1**

Who Wants to Be a Virtual Landlord?

B eing a landlord can make you rich. That's what you want to hear, I know. And fortunately, it's true. Owning buildings and renting them out can be extremely rewarding as you collect income from the property you own. All the same, I wouldn't call being a landlord an easy road to wealth.

There's a lot involved in renting out property on a legal level and perhaps even more so on an ethical one. So many issues can (and do) come up, from structural considerations regarding the actual buildings and properties they sit on to weather-related hazards that can literally hit your holdings, to general nuisances and differences of opinion with tenants. For those who manage entire apartment buildings, those differences can present themselves on a daily basis.

But suppose you could bypass all that by being a virtual owner instead. Suppose you could be almost entirely oblivious of the day-to-day details of dealing with rentals and renters — yet still receive steady income from them every month or every quarter. Suppose you could go online, click a few buttons, and put a few hundred dollars down (or more, if you so choose) to become an almost instant virtual owner of commercial real estate.

Would you be interested? If so, this book about real estate investment trusts, or REITs, is for you.

Commercial Real Estate for the Masses

For centuries and even millennia, owning property was a wealthy person's venture. In fact, land was one of the biggest signifiers of wealth, with kings and lords fighting wars over who was entitled to what. Peasants and even noblemen stayed on land at the will of their superiors. And while that arrangement wasn't always the brutal, one-sided affair Hollywood likes to portray, it obviously was a far cry from an easy road toward wealth independence.

Even as global societies advanced and individuals started owning their own homes, commercial real estate and its benefits (potential pitfalls as well) remained firmly a resource for the rich. It wasn't until the mid-20th century that REITs (pronounced "reets") were introduced and we "little people" had a solid chance of benefiting from sizable property ownership, too. This game-changing category gives the average investor the same access to property-based money-making potential as the rich. I'd even go so far as to say that REITs exist to even out the playing field. (For more detail on when and where and how they were created, turn to Chapter 3.)

REMEMBER

REITs are companies that own, manage, and/or finance real estate holdings. These holdings can be in the form of apartment buildings, hotels, shopping centers, self-storage facilities, warehouses, and even billboards, data centers, and woodlands. And that's the short list — a list that keeps growing every decade. In Chapters 6 and 7, I go through each REIT sector in detail, discussing their pros and cons, because there are definite positives and negatives to know about.

TIP

As I continuously stress throughout this book, there is no such thing as a perfect investment. So the more you know about REITs — or any other asset you want to put money into — the better off you'll be.

REITs Do the Work for You

You probably don't have the finances, time, or desire to start your own real estate investment trust. Which is perfectly fine. Even reasonable. But if you're reading this book, you probably do have the finances, time, and desire to buy into REITs that someone else started, developed, and continues to successfully run.

As I previously state, it takes very little money, comparatively speaking, to buy a few shares. And when it comes to publicly traded REITs — the ones you see listed on the stock market — it takes just a call to your broker or a series of clicks on your keyboard to get the deal done. That's all you need to become a landlord.

And not just any landlord, but a no-muss, no-fuss one. Because, again, you're a shareholder owner, not a hands-on owner. That means you don't have to deal with collecting rent, fixing roof leaks, paying insurance, or evicting problematic tenants and finding better ones.

Take it from me. I have more than three decades of experience in building and brokering over $1 billion of income-producing real estate transactions. I've been a landlord to drugstores, auto parts stores, casual-dining restaurants, fast-food restaurants, tire centers, grocery stores, movie theaters, bookstores, discount stores, warehouses, billboards, cell towers, office buildings, and fitness centers. So trust me when I say there's a lot involved.

Regular landlords have to deal with things like high leverage, partnership disputes, recessions, tenant bankruptcies, and even tornadoes. (My neck of the woods in South Carolina isn't part of Tornado Alley by most definitions, but we still get these forces of nature more often than I'd like.) In Chapter 3, I explain the three Ts most landlords wish they didn't have to deal with: toilets, trash, and taxes. By this, I mean all the parts and pieces they're responsible for — the physical structures complete with pipes, electrical wiring, windows, and doors — as well as services and those pesky obligations to Uncle Sam.

This all adds up, taking significant chunks out of the money landlords make.

REMEMBER

Of course in a capitalistic society, they're not supposed to add up more than your profits. If you do it right (with perhaps a little bit of luck added in), you can make a really decent living. There are specific advantages to owning direct real estate, such as depreciation and lower volatility, as I explain in Chapter 2. But doing it right entails a lot of time, effort, and financing.

There's also the fact that even if you were making a seven-figure salary, it would still be difficult to personally buy up such properties as

>> Caesars Palace in Las Vegas

>> The Empire State Building in New York City

>> The Hilton Waikoloa in Hawaii

The same goes for 195,000 acres of farmland, 226,000 cellphone towers, or over 12,000 free-standing properties worldwide — each set with a single purchase. And that's to say nothing about strings of properties in more than 40 countries and regions around the globe.

Yet REITs allow you to do exactly that. You don't get to own the entirety of those portfolios, of course. You're just one of hundreds, thousands, or even tens of thousands of other investors. But as I note in Chapter 3, fractional ownership still matters. Plus, you still get a piece of the rental profits, not just through share price appreciation but also through dividend payments multiple times per year.

This is because REITs, by law, have to pay out at least 90 percent of their taxable income to their shareholders in the form of dividends. As Chapter 3 details, this allows them to avoid taxes themselves. Shareholders still have to pay taxes on any gains you make, mind you. But they get higher dividends as a result of this corporate-level deal.

Get Paid While You Sleep

One of the reasons I decided to get into the real estate rental industry (so many moons ago) was because someone told me the best way to make money is while you're sleeping. It sounded like good advice, and I took it to heart along the way.

Being a landlord certainly helped me generate significant wealth by leveraging the most powerful tools of appreciation and compounding, as I discuss in Chapter 2. What I didn't know at the time though was that REITs provide all those benefits, plus the benefit of liquidity, along with transparency and diversification.

This is what makes so many REITs *sleep well at night,* or SWAN, investments. While I didn't coin the term, I use it to describe a high-quality stock that pays out dividends while you're sleeping . . . like so many of the REITs I explore in this book.

Size Does Matter

Here's another factor to appreciate about these commercial real estate assets: their sheer size. This is a big deal for a number of reasons. For one thing, the publicly traded U.S. REIT sectors magnitude makes it liquid, allowing investors to trade in and out largely at will. Another point to consider is how the wide, wide world of real estate investment trusts provides investors with considerable diversification benefits.

For instance, tech-centered investors who want something more affordable and less volatile than Facebook can look to Digital Realty, a massive (and growing) network of data centers around the world. Or if you think that brick-and-mortar retail isn't going away, you can consider my favorite REIT, Realty Income. This means that you (the investor) can design and build your portfolio based on your individual tastes and preferences. In Chapter 10, I provide a blueprint to consider strategies I've used over the years.

There are also basic REIT categories to consider above and beyond which properties they tend to buy, which means the larger asset class provides even more opportunity to diversify. I break them all down in Chapter 4 if you want to see what I mean.

Basically, commercial real estate in general and REITs in particular are enormous investment categories that offer something for just about every investor, no matter what their interests and goals are.

Focusing on Fundamentals

I'm sure you're familiar with the board game Monopoly, where you use play money to buy real estate, utilities, and railways. The goal is to dominate the board and have scale advantage — the point where a company has a big enough presence that it gets better banking and business deals than the competition. The issue is how to go about it. Which properties should be picked up and which ones should be passed over?

The same questions apply to income-producing real estate in the real world. When you invest in it by buying up REIT shares, you're buying (portions of) portfolios in high-quality, well-placed real estate operated by professional, ethical management teams. That's the ideal, anyway, and the ideal is very often true. But it's not a guarantee, so you do have to research and analyze what you find.

At least you really, really should.

If that sounds daunting, don't worry! That's what Chapter 8 is there for — my favorite chapter in this book. It's where I show you how to choose your REITs wisely by understanding how to calculate property values and earnings metrics, as well as balance sheet basics. The key to unlocking their value is rooted in their cost of capital: how much money they're spending in order to make money.

REMEMBER

You need to know that REITs thrive when their return on invested capital (ROIC) is greater than their opportunity cost of capital. If the former is at or below the latter, growth may not create value and can lead to a *value trap* or *sucker yield* scenario. More about those in my favorite chapter.

TIP

I also use Chapter 8 to fill you in on REIT-specific financial terms such as funds from operations (FFO) and net asset value (NAV). These can help you understand the margin of safety concept further as you start analyzing potential portfolio picks for yourself. In which case, always keep in mind that the subjects of risk and cost of capital are essential and inseparable. So while you're free to read this book in whatever order you'd like, picking and choosing topics as you see fit, I recommend that you not skip over Chapter 8. It's got way too much important information in it.

REITs on the Street

If you've read this far, feel free to stop for a little bit. I've got some homework for you.

Get out of the house. Go for a drive. See what you can see. Or, if you're perfectly content reading on right away, at least think about your daily commute to work, the grocery store, church, the gym, or wherever else you tend to go. No matter where you're headed locally (in the United States, at least), there's a good chance you'll find yourself in close proximity to a REIT-owned property. That workplace, grocery store, church (yup, even some churches), or gym you frequent might even fall under that category.

As I reference in Chapter 4, REITs own approximately one out of every ten institutional-quality buildings in the United States. And that percentage continues to grow with investor demand.

A Slice for All Types

While REITs were designed for the average investor, I explain in Chapter 11 that institutions, such as pensions and endowments, buy them up too. These are the big fish. The whales. And boy, but do they like to eat up shares of whatever they fix their appetite on, including REITs.

Don't be hating on these big-time players, though. They're not stealing from your pool of potential. If anything, they're helping your investments grow both in recognition and price. This category of investors is important to the growth of the sector in ways that I'm more than happy to lay out.

There are now 29 REITs included in the S&P 500 (as of May 2023). That could not have occurred without enormous firms like Vanguard, Cohen & Steers, Green Street, BlackRock, and State Street getting involved. For decades, that wasn't the case, which was to REITs' detriment. Institutional investors chose to allocate funds elsewhere, deeming REITs to be too new and risky. And I'm not saying they were wrong in displaying caution.

But REITs evolved into something worth putting big money into. I detail their historical progression in Chapter 3, including how 150 million Americans now live in households that invest in REITs through their 401(k)s, IRAs, pension plans, and other investment funds. You can also own REITs through vehicles such as exchange-traded funds (ETFs), mutual funds, and closed-end funds. These can be extremely powerful options to consider, which is why Chapter 12 gives you facts, figures, and important insights into what they are and how you can use them.

I personally prefer to buy up individual stocks instead of baskets of them. But I very well understand that everyone is different. Some of us prefer to play it as safely as possible. Some of us can afford to take greater (though not unreasonable) risks. And some of us choose a middle path between the two.

Whichever category you fall into, this book seeks to give you the kind of guidance you need to make it work for you.

Chapter **2**

It All Starts with Real Estate

Real estate is the oldest asset class in the world, and one that's just as relevant today as it ever has been. Profitable too. According to Savills World Research, all the property in the world is worth an estimated $228 trillion. No other asset class comes even close to matching real estate in this regard, much less beating it:

» U.S. banks — $19.6 trillion

» Gold — $9.3 trillion

» Oil — $1.7 trillion

Why? What's so great about it? The answer is surprisingly simple. It's captured in the definition of real estate: "The land and any permanent structures, like a home, or improvements attached to the land, whether natural or man-made." That makes real estate a commodity that can accommodate shelter, commerce, food production, collaboration, and so much more. In fact, as I show throughout this book, real estate is necessary for doing just about anything on Earth.

As such, it's easy to break this massive asset class into several categories and subcategories. The largest of these, however, is *residential property:* houses that are used as homes. It's valued at around $169 trillion. *Commercial real estate* (property used to make money, such as office buildings, shopping centers, and apartment buildings), meanwhile, comes in at around $35 trillion.

The point is that real estate is the glue that holds the worldwide economy together. In this chapter, I explain why real estate is a dependable asset to have in your portfolio. Its growth over time is steady and remarkable. I also introduce you to some fundamental real estate concepts.

Land: They're Not Making It Anymore

Whether you believe it was Will Rogers (1879–1935) or Mark Twain (1835–1910) who said it, this statement is absolutely true: "Land: They're not making it anymore."

Because the world has all the land it will ever have, experts can put a value on it and use that number to measure other assets against it. In the following sections, I explain how supply and demand drives the value of real estate, look at the relationship between real estate and the gross domestic product (GDP) of countries around the world, and remind you that we'd be nowhere without real estate.

Supply and demand

As I point out in the chapter introduction, there's $228 trillion worth of real estate in the world. And that valuation will almost certainly climb further considering how it's such a finite asset class. It's a matter of supply and demand.

Supply and demand depend completely on the relationship between buyers and sellers. The former has to have something the seller wants, and the seller has to be willing to pay the price the buyer wants. Otherwise, it just doesn't work.

REMEMBER

When demand for a service or product is high, sellers have more control in setting the prices. A particular population wants it, and so a particular population will get it. That's what *demand* is: desire and the ability to act on that desire combined.

And when that desire and ability comes up against *low supply* — a limited amount of said service or product — sellers can really amp up the price. The wealthy win out in those cases, as do those willing to buy on credit, while the poorer and more prudent do without. Either way, the seller tends to win.

When demand is low, that's when discounts enter the picture, as any retailer in a recession knows full well—or as any office landlord in this pandemic-inspired work-from-home paradigm knows full well. And, obviously, low demand and high supply is a bad thing. That means there's a lot of inventory to push at the lowest prices possible.

It's easy to see then that supply and demand are directly correlated. They work against each other until the product, service, or property in question reaches an *equilibrium:* the best estimate of what it's really worth in that moment. Figure 2-1 illustrates this principle.

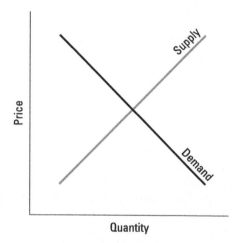

FIGURE 2-1:
Supply and demand have a direct relationship.

Let's apply this to real estate. When demand for housing and commercial properties is high in a particular neighborhood or market, prices rise. We all saw this happen in the real estate market of 2020–2022, where the numbers of homebuyers skyrocketed. That prompted them to bid up home prices almost everywhere, which in turn, raised prices across the larger economy.

However, consider what happened after 2008 when the housing bubble burst and the Great Recession set in. Just like that, demand dropped, leaving a large unwanted supply of houses. Prices fell in order to attract the remaining buyers, who all of a sudden could be much more selective than they were before.

Decline in demand for real estate can also happen when a bull market overdoes it in general. Basically, sellers begin taking buyers for granted until buyers put their foot down and say "enough is enough. It's not worth the price. I'll rent instead." Again, this back-and-forth, push-and-shove, give-and-take dynamic always brings about a healthy balance. Eventually. And as it does, it keeps the real estate market ever changing.

Commercial real estate is just as susceptible to that kind of dynamic. When there's a limited number of a particular kind of property in a particular place, prices can easily go up. This can then encourage builders to come in and boost supply.

DON'T FEAR RECESSIONS, EMBRACE THEM

One of the reasons I became a real estate analyst is because of the period known as the Great Recession. I was a real estate developer for over two decades. I made my living building shopping centers, warehouses, and free-standing buildings, and then leasing them back to credit-worthy customers.

I was making money hand over fist in that climate, right up until the housing market crashed in 2008. The following downturn was called the *great* recession because of how far off kilter property prices had gotten — and how very connected land is to everything in the economy.

The definition of a recession, according to the *Oxford English Dictionary,* is "a period of temporary economic decline during which trade and industrial activity are reduced, generally identified by a fall in GDP in two successive quarters." This interpretation became popular in 1974 after economist Julius Shiskin introduced the *two consecutive quarters* rule based on the fact that healthy economies expand over time. In which case, two quarters in a row of contracting output suggests there are serious underlying problems.

The National Bureau of Economic Research (NBER) then came up with a more flexible rule: "A significant decline in economic activity spread across the economy, lasting more than a few months, normally visible in real GDP, real income, employment, industrial production, and wholesale-retail sales." And while most laypeople recognize Shiskin's authority, the professional — and therefore, official — nod in the United States goes to NBER. That caused a lot of disagreement in 2022. But nobody disputes that the Great Recession was, indeed, a recession.

Downturns always affect real estate, whether through rental prices, vacancy rates, property valuations, or all three. Certain features are common to nearly all economic downturns, including overbuilding and a relaxation of risk standards by builders, lenders, and investors. I get more into the hows, whats, and whys of that both further into this chapter and in chapters to come.

For now though, I think we can agree that recessions don't come out of nowhere. The so-called "great" one, for instance, was sparked by a whole range of issues, including what I refer to as a severe lack of banking integrity — or intelligence — which led to a housing market that was less than perfect. Many financial institutions suffered as a result, including ones that had profited handsomely while the bubble grew.

Plenty of smaller businesses, entrepreneurs, and mom-and-pop investors suffered, too, me included. I lost my whole business and almost my entire net worth. But I built myself back from there, stronger and smarter with REITs. As you find out in this book, volatility can lead to opportunity. You just have to know where to look.

One of my good friends was a commercial real estate appraiser in the 2000s. He was able to take advantage of the chaos in 2008–2009 to purchase millions of dollars' worth of distressed real estate. As a result, his net worth soared. The key is to spot trends as early as possible and look for property sectors that are in danger of overheating: things like a steady rise in construction and sustained increases in property prices. Then get ready, or shall I say, *get greedy*.

To be a successful real estate investor, you must be able to recognize what's hot and what's not. Always remember that real estate is critical infrastructure to most every business, every household, and every intelligent investor. So there is always a profit to be had somewhere.

When you're acting on those opportunities, keep leverage — borrowing — in mind. Most real estate investors use leverage, or debt — unlike the friend I mentioned earlier. For my part, I had to learn the hard way to avoid excessive debt.

Every business uses real estate

As I mention earlier in this chapter, real estate factors enormously in how an economy runs. Here are just some of real estate's many sectors and subsectors:

» Apartments

» Campus housing

» Casinos

» Cell towers

» Data centers

» Free-standing buildings

» Hospitals

» Hotels

» Industrial buildings (for example, warehouses)

» Malls

» Manufactured housing

- » Medical office buildings

- » Office buildings

- » Outlet centers

- » RV parks

- » Self-storage

- » Senior housing

- » Shopping centers

- » Single-family rentals

- » Skilled nursing

- » Vacation rentals

Up until 1960, it was almost impossible for the average person to invest in this type of institutionally-owned property. However, as you find out in Chapter 3, real estate investment trusts, or REITs, were formed to provide access to all these categories.

Introducing Homer Hoyt and Real Estate Cycles

Homer Hoyt (1895–1984) was a land economist who researched the business cycles of real estate. His findings have influenced the study ever since. Hoyt got the idea to research this topic back when he was working as an appraiser and consultant in the 1930s. He specifically targeted neighborhoods in Chicago, Illinois, studying how their market values had ebbed and flowed over the decades. What he found is crucial in understanding the world of real estate investment, including where REITs are concerned.

Recognizing the cycles most businesses go through

Most stocks follow the business cycles of boom to bust to boom to bust. This only makes sense. It also makes sense that there are stages between the two extremes, just as winter freezes don't come right after summer heat waves. In the same way, economists usually recognize four distinct phases of a business cycle:

>> **Expansion:** Demand is strong, giving producers and sellers every reason to increase their efforts. Consumers are willing and able to pay, and business is good.

>> **Peak:** Everything is as good as it's going to get — to the point that it's extreme. Prices are too high, demand is too strong, and something has to — and will — give.

>> **Contraction:** Demand begins and continues to fall and so do prices. Both businesses directly and indirectly involved cope by cutting costs where they can, including by laying employees off.

>> **Trough:** Everything is as bad as it's going to get. Prices are too low, demand is too weak, and something has to — and soon will — change. This might mean a rethinking of the original product or a new product being introduced altogether, depending on the industry and situation.

If that sounds simple, it is. To a degree. Sometimes it's obvious when a new stage has been reached. Then again, both sellers and buyers are often so caught up in the moment that they fail to see what's staring them right in the face. As the saying goes, they can't see the forest for the trees.

TIP

To get a good (though not perfect) understanding of where prices are headed, investors can study general economic activity, income levels, employment, industrial production, retail sales, housing inventory, and the like. While business cycles can be brief — lasting mere months — or more than a decade long, the average length of larger GDP growth is less than five years.

Looking at the long cycles of real estate

Real estate cycles follow the same four stages as their regular business counterparts (detailed in the preceding section). However, real estate cycles are over three times longer than stock market cycles. This is mainly because of construction (development) considerations. Most buildings aren't built in a day or even in a matter of months.

Typically, it takes three years for a real estate project to be completed, from picking out the site to collecting the first rent check. Homer Hoyt and his successors have offered solid professional proof of these phases. But I also know about these phases from personal experience, having been a real estate developer myself for over two decades. I completed over 100 projects in that time, ranging from free-standing stores leased to retailers like Advance Auto Parts and Sherwin-Williams, to mixed-use properties leased to companies like Walmart and PetSmart.

Whenever I built a new project, I would spend almost a year assembling the land, hiring civil engineers to design the site, employing architects to do the actual building, and preleasing the space. It would also take time to seek out financing and obtain zoning approvals (sometimes zoning takes months or even years). Hiring a contractor was particularly time consuming because I would always seek out multiple bids to make sure that I was getting the best price. Then, when construction commenced, there were always delays to deal with due to weather, change orders (amendments to construction contracts), and other considerations.

Some projects can take two years to complete. Others can take up to four depending on their complexity and level of difficulty involved with city planning departments. In contrast, other businesses can adjust their production schedules in a matter of weeks or months.

Keep all that in mind as you study Figure 2-2, which illustrates the four broad phases of the real estate cycle. These phases can be easily matched up with the four business cycle phases mentioned earlier.

These phases are essentially what Homer Hoyt discovered. His 18-year real estate business cycle shows that the brick-and-mortar asset class over the long term can have a high degree of predictability. Table 2-1 outlines the cycles for various aspects of the real estate industry between 1818 and 2008.

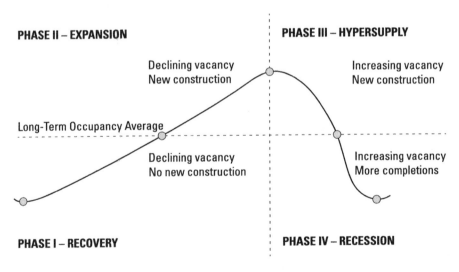

PHASE II – EXPANSION

Declining vacancy
New construction

Long-Term Occupancy Average

Declining vacancy
No new construction

PHASE III – HYPERSUPPLY

Increasing vacancy
New construction

Increasing vacancy
More completions

PHASE I – RECOVERY

PHASE IV – RECESSION

FIGURE 2-2: The four phases of the real estate market.

TABLE 2-1 Cycles in the Real Estate Industry, 1818–2008

Peaks in Land Value Cycle	Interval (Years)	Peaks in Construction Cycle	Interval (Years)	Peaks in Business Cycle	Interval (Years)
1818	—	—	—	1819	—
1836	18	1836	—	1837	18
1854	18	1856	20	1857	20
1872	18	1871	15	1873	16
1890	18	1892	21	1893	20
1907	17	1909	17	1918	25
1925	18	1925	16	1929	11
1973	48	1972	47	1973	44
1979	6	1978	6	1980	7
1989	10	1986	8	1990	10
2006	17	2006	20	2008	18

Source: Adapted from Fred E. Foldvary, "The Depression of 2008."

The Concept of Appreciation and Depreciation

Appreciation and depreciation are two sides of the same coin, and understanding both can help you better appreciate value creation. I remember studying these terms when I was taking my first accounting class in college. While I have never been fond of crunching numbers, I've found that digging deep into financial statements can be rewarding in the long run.

Ultimately, the nature of what you own (real estate, airplanes, art, jewelry, stocks, and so on) dictates how often you'll have to deal with these topics. The key to wealth creation is to own assets, whether hard assets like those listed in the previous parentheses or liquid assets like stocks, that increase in value due to appreciation.

REMEMBER

Short-term assets like stocks can fluctuate on a daily basis, a phenomenon that's less common with long-term assets like real estate. But it's important to keep an eye on both so that you can keep an eye on your future cash flows!

Appreciating appreciation

The term *appreciation* has two distinct meanings. Let's start with the noun, which means a feeling or expression of gratitude. For instance:

I want to express my appreciation of the readers of this book.

In finance though, *appreciation* has an entirely different meaning and is essential to the concept of real estate. It means an increase in the value of an asset over time. And there are several reasons for that to happen:

>> Increased demand for an asset

>> Reduced supply of an asset

>> Inflation

>> Changes in the interest rate

See the earlier "Supply and demand" section for more about how supply and demand are interrelated.

Appreciating depreciation

I'm sure you've heard the saying "What goes up must come down." It applies to gravity, and it applies to real estate as well, though perhaps to a lesser degree.

Depreciation is the opposite of appreciation: It is what happens when an asset's value decreases over time. Depreciation can happen for various reasons, many of which are outside the property owner's control. For instance, market fluctuations and declines can reduce values. Neighborhoods that are seeing a lot of growth and development will see their home values increase; those that stagnate or decline in growth will see their home values decrease.

Whether you ultimately benefit or lose out from that metric, it's just the way it works. This is why it's extremely important to always remember the real estate maxim: location, location, location. That single factor can make an enormous difference in value.

Of course, regular maintenance and upkeep can prevent at least some depreciation. And it can definitely keep the property looking fresh and up to date. That's why most landlords try to upgrade their properties at least every five years, giving them a minimum of new paint and landscaping.

REMEMBER

Depreciation does still happen, regardless. Over time, it's inevitable.

However, many don't understand that it doesn't have to be a liability, especially when you consider the after-tax advantages of owning real estate. You see, buildings on top of properties lose their value. But the land they're built on comes with a fixed cost and does not usually decline in value. Many wealthy billionaires own real estate because of those powerful depreciation advantages.

One example is former President Donald Trump, whose tax returns went public in late 2022. Love him or hate him, and justified or not, his filings show exactly how the wealthy can work their books. Because of how accelerated depreciation is viewed under the law — which allows for deferral of income, conversion of ordinary income into lower-taxed capital gains, and artificial tax losses — he paid little to no income taxes.

For that same reason, many entrepreneurs purchase or construct buildings so that they can obtain depreciation deductions, together with deductions for mortgage interest on the loans. As a real estate developer in my prior life, I used similar means to accelerate depreciation deductions that allowed me to limit my tax liabilities.

Essentially, by using what's called cost segregation, serious real estate investors can accelerate their depreciation deductions—sometimes to extreme levels. And there are other levers real estate owners can use to reduce their IRS obligations further. One of those is through a 1031 exchange, which defers capital gains by selling a property and replacing it with another one within a certain set of time.

This is why depreciation is a crucial concept in real estate investing. You can create positive cash flow by purchasing property while simultaneously reducing your taxable income through depreciation losses — even though the investment also appreciates.

There is no other type of asset that can do this.

Rental Income Is the Key to Value Creation

As I remind my children, income is the key to financial freedom, and there are many ways to generate income. Here are just a few:

» Working a full-time job

» Working a part-time job

- >> Owning stocks that pay dividends (including REITs)

- >> Receiving royalties from books (like the one you're reading; thank you)

- >> Receiving brokerage income (from selling houses)

- >> Having high-interest savings

- >> Offering short- or long-term rentals through rental companies such as Airbnb

Most people have a job, of course, where they get the majority of their income. Beyond that, they might make investments to generate passive income (like stocks, real estate, and so on).

One of my good friends owns a life insurance business where he generates millions of dollars every year in fees. He then reinvests in income-producing commercial real estate. And by that, I mean he's a landlord who gets money every month from his business tenants. I have known this gentleman for over 30 years, and I suspect his real estate portfolio is worth well in excess of $100 million.

The key to his success is that he decided early in his career to invest in real estate that generated sustainable and increasing rental income over time. He also never used debt to fund his real estate investments, so he never had to worry about the added cost of interest. That's what I call sleeping well at night!

REMEMBER

SWAN stands for *sleep well at night*. It's a term I use again in the book, so don't be surprised when you see it from time to time.

It's difficult to make all-encompassing statements about rental income when there are so many different properties to rent to so many different clients on so many different terms. For example, the 2020s popularized many short-term lease concepts, such as pop-up stores and trial contracts. In the first case, these rental agreements can last mere days or weeks, and in the latter, usually a few months (after which, a longer lease may or may not be signed).

But most commercial real estate offers at least year-long rental commitments. Some are signed for decades at a time. And most of them are extremely stable, with evictions and other rental issues being anything but the norm. Therefore, rental properties can lead to very satisfying levels of wealth.

Lease durations range from nightly (for hotels) to more than 20 years. Given that leases lock in specific rate (or rate increases) for the duration of the lease, longer lease terms generally provide greater income visibility (see Table 2-2).

TABLE 2-2

Lease Duration by Property Type

Property Type	Average Lease Duration
Hotels/lodging	Daily
Self-storage	Monthly
Apartments	Annual
Manufactured housing	Annual
Single family rentals	Annual
Student housing	Annual
Retail (shopping centers)	3–5 years
Industrial	3–7 years
Office	5–7 years
Data centers	3–15 years
Retail (malls)	5–6 years
Retail (anchor stores)	10+ years
Healthcare (triple net)	10–20 years
Net lease	15–20 years

When it's a corporation involved instead of a mom-and-pop operation, there's often even more potential for financial advancements. That's nothing against individual or family operators, mind you. And there are even instances of families who built their small-time landlord operations into REITs. But for the most part, REITs and other larger business entities have better resources to promote *value creation*. And by value creation, I mean selling something others want to buy. REITs are (usually) better staffed and better financed with better resources to buy worthwhile properties, update older ones, seek out reliable tenants, deal with unreliable ones, and so on. And that's a very big deal.

Rents and pricing power

When I graduated from college many moons ago, I became a leasing agent for a small-town real estate developer. One of my first assignments was to lease up a brand-new power center anchored by Home Depot, TJ Maxx, and Michael's.

TECHNICAL
STUFF

I bet a lot of you have shopped in a *power center*. Power centers are large (250,000- to 750,000-square-foot) outdoor shopping malls that usually include three or more giant retailers or big-box stores, like Sam's Club or Target. This type of property might also include smaller retailers and restaurants that are either free-standing or located in adjoining strip plazas, surrounded by a shared parking lot.

I spent a lot of time prospecting for tenants to lease space in that first shopping center. And I landed a few: companies such as Dunkin' Donuts, Check Into Cash, and Rock-Ola Café. As a young single dude, I was quite happy with the money I made by being the middleman. But the overall experience also made me want more.

My next leasing assignment was a 50,000 square-foot flex building that was around 90 percent vacant. *Flex space* involves lightly zoned properties that are usually used for industrial or office purposes. The term came into existence after small warehouses were converted into office space instead.

I was able to fill that building up to 90 percent occupancy and generate some additional leasing fees for my services. Once again, I was happy to get paid in the process. But also once again, I knew a better way to create wealth was to start collecting rent checks for myself. That's why, a few years later, I decided to venture out and become a landlord.

I started small with a few rental houses. And then I landed my first big account with Advance Auto Parts in Laurens, South Carolina. I'll never forget that first rent check — the first step in creating a portfolio that would eventually peak at just under $100 million.

TIP

Rental income can be an enormous key to wealth creation. Whether you're a small single-family landlord or a big-time developer, one tried-and-true (though hardly bulletproof) secret to getting rich is to own real estate and let your tenant buy it for you.

Supply and demand are extremely critical to being a successful landlord. Smart landlords should evaluate the subject property (and competitors) and determine whether it has pricing power. By *pricing power,* I mean the change in a firm's product price determined by the quantity demanded. It's linked to the price elasticity of demand.

REMEMBER

Scarcity of real estate can generate high pricing power. The rental price increases — sometimes intensely — because there's insufficient supply to meet demand.

This is something we all saw between 2020 and 2022 in hot markets across the Sunbelt, including Texas. I even experienced it personally, and not on the profitable end of the equation. I have an apartment in West Palm Beach, Florida, that

I'm usually very happy with. But in 2021, the landlord increased the rental price by 60 percent. Sixty percent!

That might sound enormous (and it was) and even insane. But it was directly correlated to the acceleration of people moving to the area. The landlord had pricing power, and he knew it. Which is why I renewed the lease. Reluctantly, mind you, but still renewed.

The power of compounding

One of the secrets to owning real estate (and REITs) is that you can magnify your wealth by allowing the power of *compounding*. It's a very simple but important practice. Albert Einstein once called compound interest "the eighth wonder of the world," adding that "he who understands it, earns it" and "he who doesn't, pays it." This definitely applies to REITs.

Most people are familiar with the concept of the so-called *snowball effect*. It's the idea that a small sphere of snow rolling down a hill gets bigger and bigger as it hoovers up more of the white, sticky stuff. That's also a good description of how compounding can help you grow more money in a savings account, the stock market, or real estate (and not under a mattress). Compounding boosts the growth of that initial deposit through what people call *interest on interest* or the *future value of money*.

Put simply, compounding happens when interest (or dividends) gets added to the principal amount (or investment account). Over time, this can lead to exponential growth.

REMEMBER

Compounding is not a get-rich-quick scheme. It happens over time, and it requires a good degree of patience to eventually enjoy. But when investors determine to wait it out, they can create a mountain of wealth for their efforts.

TIP

When it comes to the stock market, unlocking the magic of compounding requires that you

>> Choose healthy, well-suited dividend-paying stocks, including REITs.

>> Reinvest the dividends they offer.

>> Give the stocks time to grow.

For stocks, compounding is like getting free money out of the ATM. The more you reinvest your dividends into the same stocks over time, the more you're able to accelerate the income potential of your original investment. Your portfolio then amplifies your working money and maximizes its earning potential — just as long as you keep your hands off both the principal and dividends. And because REITs tend to offer higher dividend yields than other stocks due to how they are structured, they can make compounding even more attractive.

Now, not everyone is in a position to make it work. Retirees, for instance, might need whatever extra income they get when they get it. But those who use the power of compounding this way while they're working can expect a much shinier golden-year era once they hit it.

WARNING

You should also be aware of who may be benefitting from compound interest when it comes to your debts. If you're constantly trying to pay off loans or credit cards but the balance never seems to go down, this is because of compound interest that your loan provider is adding to your debt. The amount you owe grows because you're only paying the interest on the debt. Be very cautious about debt that you take on as compound interest. When you're on the receiving end of that income, it can be a SWAN experience. When you're on the giving end, it's much more likely to keep you up at night.

My mother told me as a child that I could make money while I was sleeping, which seemed like a pretty strange concept at the time. But she was right. You just need to understand the power of compound interest first — and put it into action.

IN THIS CHAPTER

» Exploring the development and
evolution of REITs

» Discovering the ins and outs of what
makes a REIT a REIT

» Contrasting REITs with two other
high-income alternatives:
BDCs and MLPs

Chapter **3**

Unlocking the First Level of the REIT Universe

You don't have to understand what REITs are and where they came from in order to make money from them. There are plenty of investors who own shares of these companies and reap at least some rewards without a clue of how the larger REIT sector came to be.

But I believe that the more you know about your investment assets, the more you benefit from them. That's why in this chapter, I outline the history and formation of REITs and the evolution they went through to become the respected money-making machines they are today. I also discuss the rules they must abide by, what they're best known for, and how they stack up against other investment alternatives you may have heard of.

How REITs Came to Be

For starters, let's all acknowledge a perhaps less-than-flattering (but completely understandable) fact about real estate investment trusts: REITs were created so that multi-property owners could avoid paying taxes. Plain and simple. (However, Uncle Sam does get a bite of the apple as REIT investor dividends are taxed.)

Moreover, they eventually succeeded in that goal to a large degree, as I describe shortly. But getting to this point took time, perseverance, and some rebranding to make it happen.

The early years

The rebranding, as I first mention in Chapter 1, came in the form of making a case for the proverbial little guy. Initially, only the rich could afford to enter the money-making world of commercial real estate ownership. But the law behind REITs uses already existing business trust rules to give *all* investors the chance to participate in large-scale investments in commercial real estate. It was a concept that stuck.

The REIT Act of 1960

REITs were born in 1960 when President Dwight D. Eisenhower signed the REIT Act into U.S. law on September 14, 1960. It wasn't stand-alone legislation, mind you. The REIT Act was just one piece of the larger Cigar Excise Tax Extension legislation that landed on Eisenhower's desk. Nonetheless, with a stroke of his pen, he authorized these intriguing investment assets into existence. Just like that, the "little guy" could participate in large-scale, diversified portfolios of income-producing real estate via liquid securities, or stocks.

TECHNICAL STUFF

Getting back to that idea about not paying taxes, one of the details of the REIT Act is the sector's tax status. Approved companies don't have to pay corporate income tax on qualifying income just as long as they pay their shareholders a common dividend that equals at least 90 percent of their otherwise taxable income. Because REITs avoid double taxation this way at the corporate level, their dividends aren't reduced like they are for so many other companies. This makes them tax-efficient conduits for real estate income.

However, this hardly made them perfect investments right from the get-go. (And, like any other money-making opportunity, they're not flawless today.) In the early years, REITs were somewhat restricted, mostly providing investors with a non-taxed, passive, flow-through form of income. This was still a tempting enough idea that the first U.S. REIT — American Realty Trust — was formed very quickly in 1961 by Thomas J. Broyhill. It was run as what we now know as a *mortgage REIT,* or mREIT, which I detail in Chapter 4.

Other early REITs included Washington Real Estate Investment Trust (now Elme Communities), Pennsylvania Real Estate Investment Trust, and Bradley Real Estate (which was bought out and taken private in 2000). And not too long after in 1968, big banks got involved after realizing how much potential there was in this new investment category. This was to the sector's detriment, however, since those financiers had eyes that were bigger than the economy could stomach.

Big banks created a whole slew of mREITs to lend out money to construction and development companies, feeding into a building frenzy that was too fast and too furious to be sustainable. All told, these new entities lent out more than $20 billion — in 1960s and 1970s dollars — to the commercial real estate creation craze. The results were disastrous, with demand crashing and contractors walking off the jobs of partially finished messes.

The growth of the new funds stretched demand and of course, when there's adversity, there's opportunity. In 1971, REITs had a market cap of just $1.5 billion (representing 34 REITs).

Tax Reform Act of 1976

The Tax Reform Act of 1976 helped sift through the rubble left behind by overzealous banks overlending to construction and development companies. The Act authorized REITs to be operated as corporations as well as the business trusts they were initially regarded as, which definitely helped tamp down the excess.

There was still work to be done, however. The Tax Reform Act of 1976 did nothing to change just how passive these flow-through investments were or the rule that they couldn't manage their own properties, two specifications in the original law. That wouldn't change for another decade with the passage of the Tax Reform Act of 1986.

In the same way, REITs still needed to figure out how to be more organized by focusing their efforts on specific property types and/or geographies, and how to be clearer and more precise in their financial calculations. At the time (and still today), publicly traded companies tended to report their quarterly and yearly figures according to generally accepted accounting principles (GAAP). But that understanding of net income just doesn't cover real estate investing in all its nuanced glory, in large part because of the treatment of depreciation in real estate property.

Something still needed to be done.

Tax Reform Act of 1986

The deficiencies highlighted by the difficulties in reporting a REIT's earnings led to the Tax Reform Act of 1986. This one included the provision that REITs didn't need a third party to manage their assets; they could run their own operations after all. This was enormous, as it enabled REITs to retain control over the ins and outs of who they rented to and how. It also meant they were spending less money in the process.

Naturally, it took some time before those changes could be implemented, which was made more complicated by the broader real estate market collapse of the late 1980s. Savings were destroyed in that debacle, the loan industry was badly damaged, and banks and insurance companies stopped offering financing to commercial real estate companies.

But by 1991, the sector was looking at the dawn of a new day, and what many consider to be the start of the modern REIT era.

Modern REITs and UPREITs

Starting in the early 1990s, the industry began to transform from a relatively small group of companies — and mostly mREITs, at that — into a much larger marketplace consisting primarily of publicly traded equity REITs that offer space instead of loans to clients.

In 1993, another breakthrough happened when umbrella partnerships were allowed. These umbrella partnership real estate investment trusts (UPREITs) helped turn what had been a trickle of REIT initial public offerings (IPOs) into a veritable flood. Simply stated, prior to creation of the UPREIT structure, most commercial real estate was owned in partnership form. Selling your portfolio to a public REIT for cash or trading it for stock was considered a sale, which therefore triggered a tax on the gain.

UPREITs, however, allow REITs to own controlling stakes in limited partnerships that owned real estate. This indirect ownership allows them to exchange units of partnership, which is not considered a sale and so doesn't trigger a tax on the transfer of ownership, at least not to a new partnership controlled by the REIT.

REMEMBER

The UPREIT concept means that REITs don't have to actually *own* properties directly. Instead, they can own a controlling interest in an operating partnership that does. Usually what happens is that the other partners supply properties and the REIT — which is typically the general partner and majority owner of the operating partnership units — supplies cash to operate those properties. Owners of the limited partnership units can be members of management and/or large shareholders of the REIT. They have the right to convert those units into shares, to vote as if they already own shares, and to receive the same dividends as if they did. In short, they enjoy virtually the same attributes of ownership as public shareholders.

DownREITs, which are joint ventures between real estate owners and REITs, are structured similarly, though members of management aren't usually allowed to be limited partners. Also, both corporate structures can exchange operating partnership units (OP units) for interest in other real estate partnerships that own properties the REIT wants to acquire. That enables sellers to defer capital gains taxes and diversify at the same time. And that, in turn, can give UPREITs and DownREITs a competitive edge over regular REITs when it comes to making deals with tax-sensitive sellers.

REIT Modernization Act

The next major milestone came in 1999, when President Bill Clinton signed the REIT Modernization Act (RMA). The REIT Modernization Act enables REITs to form and partially or entirely own taxable REIT subsidiaries (TRSs). They can develop and quickly sell properties this way, as well as provide substantial services to their property tenants without jeopardizing their legal standing — a major issue in the past.

The law also greatly expanded which businesses a REIT can engage in. For example, it allows landlords to offer concierge services to apartment tenants, invest in merchant property development (condominiums constructed to sell instead of held), and engage in other real estate-related businesses such as landscaping. TRSs can also form joint ventures with other parties to provide additional services.

REMEMBER

Certain limitations did and do still apply, mind you. For example, no more than 20 percent of a REIT's gross assets could consist of TRS securities at first. That changed to 25 percent with the REIT Investment Diversification and Empowerment Act of 2007 (RIDEA, typically pronounced Rye-Day-Uh), which I discuss later in this chapter. For now though, just know that loan and rental transactions between a REIT and its TRS(s) are also limited by the REIT Modernization Act. Plus, any transactions that aren't conducted on an arm's-length basis incur substantial excise taxes. And income from the TRS is subject to taxes at regular corporate income rates.

TECHNICAL STUFF

Doing business on an *arm's-length basis* refers to an unaffiliated seller and buyer hashing out a deal that seems to suit them both. Neither has any contractual, personal, or any other kind of connection with or commitment to the other, but they both have what the other wants. For the buyer, it's a service or good, such as a property. For the seller, it's financial compensation.

The RMA also very specifically affected the service-intensive hotel and lodging sectors. Before, these REITs weren't allowed to lease properties to a captive, or controlled, subsidiary. That's now changed, provided that each TRS-held property is operated by an outside manager or independent contractor. This way, they can capture more of the economic benefits of ownership for their shareholders.

The National Association of Real Estate Investment Trusts (Nareit) suggests there are several other benefits involved in the legislation as well. These include better quality control over offered services, which can now be delivered directly by a REIT's controlled subsidiary. Plus, the sector has an opening to earn substantial nonrental revenues.

Housing and Economic Recovery Act of 2008

The next significant milestone was the Housing and Economic Recovery Act of 2008 signed by President George W. Bush. It allowed REITs to change the way they accounted for healthcare real estate income under RIDEA — which provides REITs with more certainty and flexibility relating to

- ❯❯ The purchase and sale of assets
- ❯❯ The size of the TRS relative to a REIT's total assets
- ❯❯ Overseas investments and foreign currencies

Simply put, RIDEA allows REITs to participate in the actual net operating income, as long as there's an involved third-party manager. But the Bush administration took it a step further by also giving healthcare REITs the same ability to lease properties to a TRS as their hotel and lodging REITs received under Clinton.

The 21st century

In addition to the gains made in the 1990s and early 2000s, some setbacks occurred along the REIT evolutionary timeline. For instance, in late 2015, President Barack Obama signed a law (Protecting Americans from Tax Hikes Act of 2015) that restricts tax-free REIT spinoffs. In effect, the law banned companies from spinning off their owned real estate into separate REITs tax-free. Previously, businesses such as Darden Restaurants, Sears, Caesars Entertainment, MGM Resorts International, and Penn National Gaming had all strengthened their businesses through this tax-free opportunity. But not anymore.

The law also means that C-corporations (C-corps) now have to write a sizable check to Uncle Sam if they want to separate their real estate in this regard. And dissatisfied investors and activists can no longer encourage management teams to drive shareholder value so quickly and efficiently. That loophole has been closed, keeping companies like Target and McDonald's from depriving Uncle Sam as well.

With that said, 2016 saw a real REIT breakthrough, too. The S&P Dow Jones Indices and the Morgan Stanley Capital International (MSCI) investment research firm moved public equity REITs and other listed real estate companies from the Financial sector of their Global Industry Classification Standard to a new Real Estate sector. This excludes mortgage REITs, which remain in Financials under a new mortgage REITs sub-industry — though there are no mortgage REITs in the S&P 500.

The Global Industry Classification Standard (GICS) is the industry classification methodology that both companies rely on for their proprietary stock market indices — and it serves as one of the main global classification systems for equities. GICS had never added a new headline sector since its inception in 1999.

Table 3-1 lists the 11 sectors of the GICS.

TABLE 3-1   **The GICS Sectors List**

Rank	Sector	Equity Market Capitalization (in Billions)	Equity Market Capitalization (Percent of Total)
1	Information Technology	4,451	20.7
2	Health Care	3,017	14.0
3	Financials	2,759	12.8
4	Consumer Discretionary	2,744	12.8
5	Consumer Staples	2,195	10.2
6	Industrials	2,178	10.1
7	Energy	1,393	6.5
8	Real Estate	814	3.8
9	Utilities	731	3.4
10	Materials	697	3.2
11	Telecommunication Services	502	2.3
Total	**All 11 sectors**	**21,487**	**100.0**

Source: Adapted from S&P Dow Jones Indices, MSCI, FactSet.

This new category acknowledges that there are fundamental differences between real estate companies and other businesses. And it validates the increasing global appeal of the REIT corporate structure. As you find out in Chapter 5, numerous countries have created their own forms of REITs, some of the latest being Portugal, Sri Lanka, and China.

This increased attention and capital investment to the sector has incentivized more private real estate companies to go public or merge into existing listed REITs.

REITs Were Made for You and Me

REITs have been around for well over half a century. They were a great idea to begin with and have been improved upon over the decades so that they're better, stronger, and even faster than ever. The result: They're now somewhat uniquely positioned stocks that appeal to a wide range of investors.

Don't forget that they were fashioned with the average investor in mind. Yes, institutions and wealthy individuals can and do make more money off them, as I describe in Chapter 11. But the main provision of the REIT Act — the one that says REITs must pay out at least 90 percent of their taxable income in the form of dividends — makes these publicly traded companies especially appealing to income-oriented investors who are seeking reliable and predictable income.

REMEMBER

Traditional dividend-paying companies often offer small dividends that only add up if you're able to buy large amounts of stock at a time. But REITs open the door for mom-and-pop investors to generate wealth with small share positions that can add up significantly over time. As I detail in Chapter 2, the power of compounding is enormous — even for those with modest means.

But that's not the only way average investors can benefit. They also get to participate in the high-maintenance commercial real estate business without being bogged down by the 3 Ts: toilets, trash, and tenants. As someone with years of experience as a landlord, I can attest to the aggravation of owning income-producing real estate. I ran quality properties, mind you. Yet almost weekly I would get phone calls from tenants concerning broken toilets, roof leaks, loud neighbors, and a host of other complaints. But with REITs, I don't have to bother with any of that.

REMEMBER

Whenever you purchase even just one REIT share, you're essentially paying for a professional management team to oversee the property and make sure rents are collected on time. And when the tenant doesn't pay, the REIT management team deals with it accordingly. You don't have to lift a finger.

That arrangement alone makes for a compelling reason to consider acquiring these assets. Not to mention how even one share represents ownership in not just one property, but dozens of properties, which gives the investor diversification protection.

So it shouldn't come as any surprise that, according to Nareit, approximately 150 million Americans live in households that invest in REITs directly or access them through REIT mutual funds or similar exchange-traded funds (ETFs). And, as already referenced, institutional investors like pension funds, endowments, foundations, insurance companies, and bank trust departments take advantage of

REITs as well. In addition, millions of Thrift Savings Plan (TSP) participants have access to REITs in their stock choices. And nearly 100 percent of target date funds, which are prevalent in 401(k) plans, have REIT allocations.

The REIT rules

Legally, for a company to be considered a REIT, it must follow these rules:

>> A REIT must distribute at least 90 percent of its annual taxable income, except for capital gains, as dividends to its shareholders. (Most REITs pay out 100 percent.)

>> A REIT must have at least 75 percent of its assets invested in real estate, mortgage loans, shares in other REITs, cash, or government securities.

>> A REIT must derive at least 75 percent of its gross income from rents, mortgage interest, or gains from the sale of real property. And at least 95 percent must come from these sources, together with dividends, interest, and gains from securities sales.

>> A REIT must have at least 100 shareholders with less than 50 percent of the outstanding shares concentrated in the hands of five or less shareholders.

REITs' primary investment attributes

Remember that, in exchange for paying out so much in dividends, REITs can deduct these distributions from their taxable income. Shareholders instead eventually bear the tax burden, but that still works in their favor. This pass-through structure means REITs typically have higher yields than the broader U.S. market.

TIP

With that said, dividends are taxed as ordinary income, so REITs are best held in tax-advantaged accounts like IRAs or 401(k)s, which I talk about in Chapter 10.

I discuss rental income in Chapter 2, which is another enormous part of what makes a REIT a REIT. These leases can lock in future cash flows for years to come, just so long as tenants continue to make payments, and most of them do. Most REITs are far from slumlords and have sophisticated management teams running them. They select their lessees very carefully, knowing they have reputations to uphold and investors to keep happy.

The former chief investment officer of Yale University and bestselling investment author, David Swensen (who is mentioned again in greater detail in Chapter 11) suggests that this feature causes them to be more stable than the overall market.

However, this doesn't mean REITs are automatically less risky than ordinary stocks. Their prices can still come under pressure for logical and illogical reasons alike. And some individual companies are still mismanaged or fail outright due to factors outside their control.

Remember, REITs are not perfect investments. But they are built around a superior concept.

Diversification

A major advantage to owning REITs is diversification. Though they trade as stocks, they're corporately managed collections of real estate. And real estate typically offers low correlation with other stocks and bonds. By that I mean that REIT returns tend to zig while other assets zag, smoothing a diversified portfolio's overall volatility.

In addition, REIT-owned properties are everywhere. More than 500,000 properties are owned by REITs in the United States alone. And because there are almost 900 REITs around the world, as I discuss in Chapter 5, you can imagine the global figure. They're spread across every state and major metropolitan area in the form of retail venues, apartment complexes, office buildings, healthcare facilities, and so much more — sectors I discuss at length in Chapters 6 and 7.

Going back to Yale's late but great David Swensen, he helped popularize the notion that REITs own real assets and therefore share some of their characteristics. Because they hold physical property, he says, they're able to better maintain value and perform well during short periods of unexpected inflation.

TECHNICAL STUFF

There is some historical evidence to support this idea. Between January 1975 and December 1984, for example, the FTSE Nareit Equity REIT Index outperformed the CRSP 1-10 U.S. Total Market Index by an annual 7.1 percent. U.S. inflation during that time averaged 10 percent per year. Moreover, real estate in general boasts a historically strong performance when inflation is higher, as illustrated in Figure 3-1.

Transparency

Speaking of real estate in general, publicly listed REITs offer another advantage over buying up individual properties: transparency. Like other stocks, they're legally required to report on business details, including purchases, sales, earnings, and other company developments. This is all governed by the Securities and Exchange Commission (SEC), whichever stock exchange the REIT is listed on, and according to GAAP regulations.

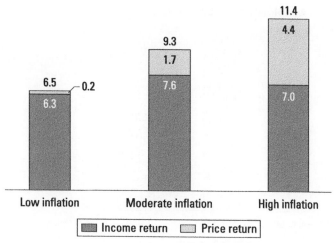

Source: National Council of Real Estate Investment Fiduciaries (NCREIF),
Bureau of Labor Statistics, and Cohen & Steers.

FIGURE 3-1:
REITs rise to
the occasion
when inflation
acts up.

Liquidity

Liquidity is another important consideration when comparing REITs to regular real estate ownership. In the United States, over 200 REITs are traded on national exchanges. They have a combined equity market capitalization of more than $1.4 trillion. And as previously discussed, they're held by both institutional and individual investors, as well as by mutual funds and ETFs (which I discuss more in Chapter 12).

Thanks to that combination of details, REITs are bought and sold on major U.S. stock exchanges every day. There's no need to wait years to save up tens or hundreds of thousands of dollars to buy them, or to convince a bank to lend you that money. Therefore, there's no need to wait weeks, months, or more to find a buyer. Many REITs can be traded in a matter of minutes, depending on the day and how specific (or unspecific) you want to be about the trade details.

Performance

REITs are also noteworthy for their performance. They have a well-recognized track record of delivering reliable, growing dividends. They also enjoy long-term capital appreciation through stock price increases. Together, those factors have provided investors with long-term total returns that are competitive with those of other stocks — and higher than most fixed-income investments.

U.S. REITs offer solid historical returns, averaging 11.1 percent per year since 1991, as shown in Figure 3-2. This track record is built on the sector's stable business model, which focuses on acquiring and developing high-quality assets that generate recurring lease-generated income.

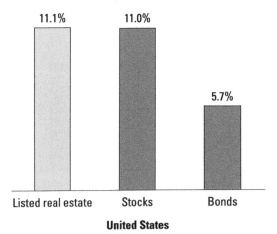

Annualized Returns Since 1991 (US$)

11.1% 11.0%

5.7%

Listed real estate   Stocks   Bonds

United States

Source: Morningstar, Cohen & Steers.

FIGURE 3-2:
REIT returns
versus stocks and
bonds.

Furthermore, all the history discussed in this chapter has fostered a culture of strong investment strategies and corporate governance that generally benefits shareholders. REIT management teams tend to focus on generating long-term stock value rather than fast and flashy gains that can fall apart far too quickly.

Dividends

REITs' real secret sauce is what I refer to as *dividends-a-plenty.* There's a famous restaurant in my hometown called The Beacon, which features the Cheeseburger-a-Plenty, one of its most popular plates. If you travel to Spartanburg, South Carolina, and eat there, you can order this huge cheeseburger buried under a pile of French fries and onion rings, hence the "a-plenty" part of the title.

In the same way, REITs are designed to be supersized dividend payers. They have an embedded mechanism for increasing their payouts. Remember that REITs must maintain a minimum distribution threshold. Therefore, they have to raise their dividends to match any growth in rents and net income. Some individual companies within the sector are lackluster or worse in this regard. Again, I cannot stress enough that there's no perfect investment group or asset. But historically, the REIT sector boasts sustained dividend growth.

Skeptics can (and do) point out that these dividend yields are often below those of many corporate bonds. And that's true. However, bond interest payments don't increase, whereas the REIT industry has a long-term track record of raising its dividends on a regular basis.

REMEMBER

It's the power of REIT dividends that defines the asset class. Their unique business proposition has paved the way for millions of investors around the globe to participate in an exciting and rewarding investment alternative.

BDCs and MLPs: REITs' Kissing Cousins

While real estate pivoted from the Financial sector classification in the GICS, business development companies (BDCs) and master limited partnerships (MLPs) remain there. (See the earlier section, "The 21st Century" for more on the GICS.) Both kinds of companies are pass-through, or flow-through, entities just like REITs. So it's understandable if investors wonder whether they're similarly profitable.

The answer is that it really depends on the specific company and the specific investor involved. The three categories belong in the same family of high-dividend-paying corporate-run assets, it's true. But they tend to deal with vastly different areas of the economy and include different corporate attributes and legal allowances. So here's the rundown on these kissing cousins.

Business development companies

BDCs were created by Congress in 1980 as amendments to the Investment Company Act of 1940. Their intent: to provide small and growing companies access to capital and to enable private equity funds to access public capital markets.

Similar to REITs, BDCs are regulated investment companies (RICs) that are required to pay at least 90 percent of their annual taxable income to shareholders. In return, they avoid corporate income taxes before distributing to shareholders. This drives higher annual dividend yields that mostly range from around 6 percent to 11 percent.

While BDCs are allowed to invest anywhere in the capital structure, the vast majority of them buy up debt. This is because they typically leverage their equity with debt (by up to two times), and fixed-income investing supports their own debt obligations.

Master limited partnerships

MLPs were formed in 1981 (with Congress legislating the rules for publicly traded partnerships in 1987). They're treated as limited partnerships for tax purposes, which is a significant advantage for investors. It means all profits and losses are passed through to the limited partners, who are essentially their shareholders. The same applies to deductions such as depreciation and depletion — which limited partners can use to reduce their taxable income.

To maintain its pass-through status, at least 90 percent of an MLP's income must be realized from the exploration, production, or transportation of natural resources or real estate. In other words, to qualify, a company must generate all but 10 percent of its revenue from natural resources or real estate activities. The vast majority of the time, MLPs exist within the natural resource sphere, though.

WARNING

While they're extremely tax-efficient for investors, MLPs do come with a potential setback. Their filing requirements (income, deductions, credits, and other items) are detailed on a schedule K-1 tax form versus a standard 1099, which is what REIT and BDC investors receive. MLP investors are also required to pay state income taxes on their allocated income in each state the MLP operates in, which can increase their individual costs. MLP dividend yields range from 5 percent to 9 percent.

REMEMBER

Although MLPs and BDCs are terrific income alternatives, keep in mind that REITs have survived (and thrived) through numerous recessions and a global pandemic. They were created over 60 years ago (MLPs and BDCs around 40 years) and continue to gain worldwide acceptance as a highly predictable asset class that offers a compelling risk/reward value proposition for sleeping well at night.

IN THIS CHAPTER

» Gaining insights into how REITs raise money

» Breaking down the equity REIT model and how it operates

» Explaining the confusing safety of REIT preferred stock

» Understanding the pros and pitfalls of mortgage REITs

» Revealing the forgotten side of REITs: private and public non-listed possibilities

Chapter **4**

Understanding How REITs Make Money

Before you can confidently pick which REITs to invest in, it is important to understand how the REIT sector works in general and the different types of REITs available. REITs come in many different flavors, and these categories can make an enormous difference in company profits, dividends, and operations. That's why it's important to understand how the sector works before you start picking and choosing which companies to buy.

In this chapter, I highlight the main ways REITs make money and then examine the major categories they fall into, including equity REITs, mortgage REITs, public and public non-listed REITs, and private REITs. I also unlock the mystery of REIT preferred stock and when it's best to purchase it.

WARNING

Always seek to protect your principal at *all* costs. This means understanding yourself — your tendencies, your capabilities, your finances, your goals — and your investments as thoroughly as possible. Otherwise, your potential shareholder value might not play out the way you would like.

How REITs Raise Money

By raise money, I mean something separate from how REITs make money as typical landlords. As landlords, REITs buy and sell properties, lease them out, and collect rent from those tenants they sign on, as outlined in Chapter 3. But to raise investment funds — funds to be used to enhance profits — REITs have a few different options.

For every REIT that exists and will exist, there are scores of investors willing and able to buy their shares. To make those shares available to the masses and thus, raise capital, REITs generally follow one of two main avenues: taking the company public through an initial public offering (IPO) or raising capital through equity and/or debt financing. (There is a third way as well, which is to issue preferred shares, and I'll touch on this later in the chapter.) The first way is, admittedly, very limited — IPOs are specific events that typically happen once in a company's history. However, they're designed to be extremely powerful specific events, as I explain next.

Initial public offerings

Also known as *going public*, an IPO happens when a private company — any company — first offers shares of itself on a stock exchange. This one-day window allows it to raise capital from a select group of public investors instead of from the typically much smaller pool of private parties it relied on before. Afterward, the company is listed and available for the average investor to buy into as well.

TECHNICAL STUFF

REIT IPOs (or any other IPO, for that matter) serve two purposes: (1) to make immediate money, and (2) to advertise their existence and easily accessible availability to future shareholders. That isn't to say IPOs are the only time REITs (or other stocks) can issue equity. It's not uncommon to see headlines throughout the year or mentions in quarterly reports about new shares being offered.

It's important to understand that issuing shares allows REITs to generate growth. In fact, given that they distribute most of their free cash flow in dividends (as I discuss in Chapter 3) and, therefore, have fewer opportunities to expand on any meaningful level, they have to do this in order to stay competitive on public platforms. When newly issued equity is deployed into *accretive,* or slow-and-steady, investments, every shareholder's profits increase per share. So every shareholder wins when this happens.

REMEMBER

Keep in mind that REITs are more inclined to issue equity when their valuations are near the upper end of their long-term valuation ranges. That's because they can generate wider investment *spreads,* or profit margins. By this, I mean that their shares are trading on the high but still reasonable side, historically speaking.

Ultimately, REITs can use that lower-cost capital to buy up new properties, pay down debt, and otherwise create greater company value, which helps drive future earnings growth. And, naturally, that's precisely what we want to see.

Debt financing

REITs have another way to raise capital outside of issuing equity and that's through debt financing. This is a common tactic in the larger sector, so common in fact that almost all REITs borrow funds. But that hardly means you should take it for granted when a REIT taps into this option.

REMEMBER

When it comes to debt, there are a few things investors need to know. One enormous consideration is that taking on debt comes with interest. You almost never just pay back the amount you borrowed: You pay that much and then an extra amount that's dependent on which interest rate you receive.

Keep in mind that there are two typical types of debt based on the type of interest rate attached to it:

>> **Fixed-rate debt:** In this type of debt, the interest rate used to calculate interest does not change from payment period to payment period. This offers peace of mind to borrowers, who don't have to constantly wonder if their payments will go up. Then again, they won't benefit from lowered payments if interest rates go down.

>> **Floating-rate debt:** In this type of debt, the interest rate is tied to a benchmark rate such as government bonds. (It also tends to involve a premium.) And because benchmark rates are never static, neither are floating-rate debt agreements. As such, borrowers can benefit from lower payments. But they can just as easily be saddled with higher ones as the interest rate winds change.

REMEMBER

The term *debt* includes all short-term or long-term interest-bearing liabilities. In other words, even if a REIT plans to pay off the entire loan in two months' time, it's still considered debt.

In addition, upon the maturity of the loan, debt refinancing is crucial for REITs. They often have to refinance due to their high-dividend payout requirements, which pulls away so much cash that they could otherwise put toward growing their business. It's basically the nature of the beast.

WARNING

Relying too heavily on debt is obviously dangerous. Many REITs found that out the hard way in 2008–2009 after the housing market crashed. To continue making their quarterly or monthly dividend payments, they were forced to cut those dividends — something that's considered very unattractive in the entire dividend-paying universe. This also happened during the COVID-19 pandemic shutdowns in 2020, which was perhaps the biggest *black swan event* (unexpected catastrophe) the REIT world has ever known.

Equity REITs: The Brick-and-Mortar Landlords

Equity REITs are essentially brick-and-mortar investments owned in a securities wrapper. These kinds of companies own and manage income-producing real estate and feature revenues that are generated primarily through rental income.

TECHNICAL STUFF

Publicly traded U.S. equity REITs constitute most of today's REIT market and clearly help power the national economy. As a group, they own more than $2.5 trillion worth of real estate assets in the United States through more than 535,000 structures in all 50 states and the District of Columbia. And an increasing number of these companies also own properties overseas.

Types of equity REITs

The equity REIT category can be broken into numerous sectors and subsectors as well. Some equity REITs own office buildings. Others own apartments. Or shopping centers. Or hospitals, medical office buildings (MOBs), and other healthcare-specific facilities. Then there are the less traditional landlords that still fit into the equity category, including data center REITs, cell tower REITs, timber REITs, and even cannabis and billboard REITs. Yup, there are REITs that own those enormous billboards you might see every day on the road, the vacant ones with (often cheesy) pushes to advertise with them.

All of those are examples of REIT-owned and operated properties. So is the Empire State Building, for that matter. A company fittingly called Empire State Realty Trust has claim to that historic landmark.

The great American REIT rally

Equity REITs own roughly 10 percent of all institutionally owned commercial real estate in the United States (that does not include owner-occupied housing). And again, that's across a whole host of property types. This makes the sector uniquely appealing due to the fragmentation characteristics.

As you drive to work or to the grocery store, think about it like this: One out of every ten buildings you may see (hosting McDonald's, Walmart, Home Depot, Hilton, your local mall or hospital, apartment buildings, self-storage facilities, post offices, and so on) could very well be owned by a REIT. Then again, nine out of every ten are not, which means there's considerable room for REITs to expand.

REMEMBER

As the REIT market capitalization grows, so do shareholder returns. Because equity REITs make most of their money from the physical properties they own, it only makes sense that their valuation — and the valuation of their shares — changes as they buy and sell properties.

As shown in Figure 4-1, equity REITs have a way of surviving and thriving even after the Great Recession (2008–2009) — which was caused by a collapse in real estate demand — and after the COVID-19 pandemic that saw entire buildings shut down for months on end. In fact, at the end of 2021, these corporate landlords hit an all-time record of over $1.3 trillion in market capitalization.

Market Capitalization: U.S. Equity REITs
(Millions of dollars at year-end)

FIGURE 4-1:
U.S. equity REITs' market capitalization.

Given the fact that REITs have so many other potential properties to gobble up still, I see no signs of this long-term trend changing anytime soon. Consider how the number of publicly traded equity REITs has grown from just 20 in 1973 to 182 at the end of 2020 (see Figure 4-2). And that's despite plenty of mergers and buy-outs along the way. Clearly, there's money to be made in this area and people willing to make it.

Helping fuel the growth are many new property sectors that I discuss in depth in Chapter 7. Prior to just 2009, there were no data center REITs, cell tower REITs, cannabis REITs, gaming REITs, or farming REITs, and I expect to see new channels open up in future years. Maybe one day we'll have airport REITs, amusement park REITs, sports stadium REITs, and why not railroad REITs, too?

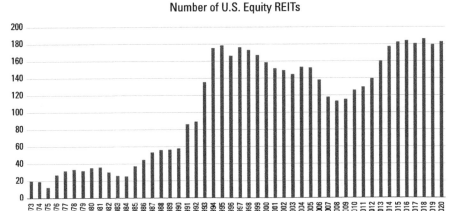

FIGURE 4-2:
Number of U.S.
equity REITs.

U.S. REITS GO GLOBAL

The REIT landscape in the United States has changed in many necessary and profitable ways over the years, including growing on an international scale. By that, I don't mean the advance of REIT adoption around the globe, where more and more countries are including real estate investment trusts into their economies. Instead, I'm referring to the number of U.S. REITs that have been buying up properties elsewhere in North America as well as the rest of the world.

Consider Digital Realty, a data center REIT established in 2004. It spent its earliest years buying up American assets but shifted gears quickly. In July 2016, for instance, it bought eight data centers in Europe. Two years later, it acquired the entirety of Ascenty, a major provider in Brazil. And, more recently, it took on a 55 percent stake in South Africa's Teraco. As of January 2023, it has over 300 data centers in more than 25 countries on all six hospitable continents.

Or take Omega Healthcare Investors. It might operate on a more specific scale geographically speaking. But this senior care facility REIT still had more than 900 facilities combined in the United States and United Kingdom by the close of 2022.

Another example is Realty Income. Known as The Monthly Dividend Company due to its consistent and growing monthly payouts versus the standard monthly dole, it's a popular REIT in the United States. This power player had already been operating in the United Kingdom before 2021. But that September, it announced it was expanding to mainland Europe as well through a €93 million purchase of seven properties in Spain. The company has over 11,700 properties in those three countries as of January 2023.

And consider these other REITs that have the money, the means, and the mentality to take on the world:

- Iron Mountain, a storage and data center landlord that boasts over 1,380 facilities in 59 countries

- Prologis, another data center owner with approximately 1.2 billion square feet of space in 19 countries

- Simon Property Group, a mall REIT with 22 premium outlets and 11 designer outlets in 13 countries; a 22.4 percent interest in European mall maven Klépierre, which has approximately 150 properties across 14 European countries; and an 80 percent stake in The Taubman Realty Group Limited Partnership, which has two Chinese and two South Korean properties

- Tanger Outlets, an outlet REIT with 37 properties in the United States and Canada

- Ventas, which has over 1,200 healthcare facilities in the United States, Canada, and the United Kingdom

- W.P. Carey, which operates over 1,400 properties of various use in the United States and Europe

And this trend only seems set to continue.

Unlocking the Mystery Behind Preferreds

Preferred stocks (preferreds) in general are a bit of a mystery for many investors because they're something between debt and equity, displaying attributes of both bonds and common stock. REIT preferred stocks are no different in this regard.

TECHNICAL STUFF

Preferred stocks are meant to be a safer kind of corporate offering that provides less price-point movement — either up or down — and greater dividend yields. They're not as well used as common shares by either corporations or investors, and therefore they're not as understood.

Preferred equity is essentially the shareholders' equity on a company's balance sheet. Junior in seniority to debt, it's still senior to common equity. This means that preferred dividends must be paid out prior to common stock dividends. Yet, due to the dividend rate typically stated in advance and a lack of voting rights, preferred stock also has debt-like characteristics. You can think of it as in-between capital.

Put a little differently, preferred stock does share some characteristics with common equity. For one thing, it's subordinate to the debt portion of the capital structure. For another, it has equity-like characteristics. Unlike common equity, however, it has a stated dividend rate. Expressed through yield and periodic dividends, this keeps its cash flow transparent on a known and followable daily amount.

But, in return, these investors don't have voting rights or nearly as much say in how the business is run. Preferred stock is often attractive to investors with a low risk tolerance.

REMEMBER

Publicly traded companies have no obligation to offer preferred stock, although many of them do. The kind of companies most likely to are large, investment-grade financial businesses, insurance entities, utilities, and . . . REITs. These companies are typically committed to maintaining strong credit metrics and ratings. But if they do fail financially, preferred shares and the dividends they come with must (almost always) be paid before common stock, though after bonds.

Unlike bonds, preferred shares are not guaranteed to repay a specific amount at a specific date. Under normal market conditions, though, they do have lower volatility than common stocks and usually much higher yields. They also generally offer more downside protection. But, in exchange, they have relatively limited upside potential. Investors tend to buy them because of their stable and superior dividends, not in any hopes that their share prices will add up. The end-result rewards are roughly on a par with those you can expect from REIT common shares. Table 4-1 outlines the differences between common and preferred stock.

TIP

When considering investing in preferred stock, it is important to review the *call provisions* (a clause in the contract for a bond that allows its issuer to pay off the bond before its maturity date) of the securities. Publicly traded preferred stocks are almost always issued with a $25 par value — the face value of a single share when it's issued — and are callable at par five years after their issuance date. The call price is then adjusted for any accrued dividends at the date of the call.

TABLE 4-1	REIT Preferred versus Common Stock Comparison	
	Common Stock	Preferred Stock
Current dividend yield*	4.6%	7.0%
Upside potential	Unlimited	Limited (excluding several convertible issues)
Dividend requirements	Not cumulative	Typically cumulative
Volatility	Higher	Lower
Interest rate risk	Moderate	High
Liquidity	Higher	Lower
Voting rights	Yes	No
Investment lifespan	Perpetual	Limited (typically can be called after 5 years)

Dividend yield: MSCI US REIT Index vs. MSCI REIT Preferred Index as of 4/30/2020.

Consequently, it's also critical to look past the preferred stock's current yield. You want to evaluate the relative *yield to call* as well, which is the return shareholders can expect should the preferred stock be bought back early. This is calculated by simply taking the dividend of the security and dividing it by its market price. When the preferred stock issue is trading above par, the yield to call will be below the current yield. It can even be negative. However, when the preferred stock issue is trading above par, investors should focus on the current yield instead.

TIP

Because of this, investors should seek to purchase preferred securities trading below par value or at a very small premium to par. The hope from there is that the preferred security is redeemed by the issuer at par value at a future date.

To give you an idea of the preferred range of possibilities, there were over 87 REIT preferred issues available from both equity REITs and mortgage REITs according to Bloomberg data from January 2023. The average yield for the group was 8.9 percent.

Welcome to the High-Yield mREIT Club

Mortgage REITs, or mREITs, provide financing for income-producing real estate by purchasing or originating mortgages and mortgage-backed securities, and then earning income from the interest on these investments. Most mREITs choose to focus on either residential or commercial mortgage markets, although some invest in both, making them hybrid mREITs. No matter their targeted customer base, though, mREITs are still REITs that must abide by the same rules outlined in Chapter 3.

Investors primarily find value in them because of their history of relatively high dividends. Long-term, commercial mREITs have traded at an average of 8 percent to 12 percent — tempting returns, to be sure. But with great yield comes greater risk.

REMEMBER

I mention earlier that the more debt you use — for any investment — the greater risk you take on. It's also true that your potential gains are greater this way since you're playing with larger sums of money than you otherwise would be. Essentially, borrowing money (also known as *leverage*) magnifies returns. But your potential for loss also expands. That's why dividends are much higher with mREITs than with equity REITs — to help compensate for the added risk.

If you're wondering whether it's enough compensation — if the higher yields make it worthwhile to invest in them — the answer is *it depends*. It depends on multiple factors that each individual investor needs to assess and determine for themselves.

WARNING

Retirees should avoid mREITs altogether. With all due respect to my older readers (of which I'm slowly but surely becoming), mREITs are a younger person's game. Younger investors have more room to recover from losses.

In general, businesses that use excessive leverage to increase returns rarely provide long-term value. The one REIT-dom exception is during extraordinary periods when commercial real estate can be acquired at abnormally cheap prices. And even that's not necessarily a guarantee. REITs that generate the most consistency — and therefore the most reliable results — are distinguished by modest debt and conservative balance sheet fundamentals.

Of course, when it comes to mREITs, debt is their entire business. They own it instead of property. Yes, they get interest from that debt instead of paying interest on it, but it's still debt in the end and, therefore, a complicated (and volatile) asset to operate and own.

It also means that mREIT profits are very dependent on interest rates. These companies benefit when interest rates come down and the value of the debt they hold rises. So naturally, they suffer when interest rates go up. This reduces their *net interest spreads,* which is the difference between the interest rate they pay to depositors and the interest rate they receive from the loans they hold in return.

WARNING

Net interest spreads are the bulk of how mREITs make their money. When this calculation doesn't fall in their favor, their book values — the cost of holding their debt, in this case — fall, and investors are very likely to lose money. There are other considerations involved, but this is an enormous one. Interest rate changes also affect prepayment rates on the underlying mortgages that they're involved in. An increase or decrease here changes their amortization and accretion and also affects assumptions, which can mean further losses.

Keep in mind that short-term rates tend to rise faster than long-term rates. And that higher long-term rates cause the book value of the portfolio to be marked down.

mREITs also use a variety of hedging methods to try to protect book value. Among these are eurodollar swaps, interest rate swaps, treasury futures, interest-only strips, principal-only strips, swaptions, and the list goes on.

The residential mREIT model

Residential mREITs often engage with U.S. government-sponsored enterprises and agencies such as the Federal National Mortgage Association (Fannie Mae), Federal Home Loan Mortgage Corporation (Freddie Mac), and Government National Mortgage Association (Ginnie Mae). I don't blame you if that makes you pause, filled with fear left over from the Great Recession of 2008–2009 when those institutions had to be bailed out.

I advise extreme caution when it comes to buying up these stocks. I almost never touch them myself due to their track records, which I discuss shortly.

Most people don't know this, but the U.S. federal government is very involved in the residential loan market — so much so that it usually dictates such make-it-or-break-it industry factors as acceptable credit scores, leverage ratios, and down-payment requirements. The private market has far less say in such things.

These agency loans are supported by the three government-operated agencies already listed, though that doesn't mean there aren't non-government entities involved as well. Those private or public institutions — many of which are mREITs — make up a giant market still, even if that is dwarfed by the federal side of the picture.

These institutions are naturally (albeit uncreatively) called *non-agency* mortgage-backed securities. To make up for the fact that the almighty federal government doesn't back their efforts, they often carry insurance or rely on other protective measures.

Stated bluntly, residential mREITs are risky REITs. Investing in them is more dangerous compared with other dividend-paying stocks. Even the best ones suffer from high prepayment leverage, liquidity, and complexity risk — so do commercial mREITs, mind you. You can see as much in Figure 4-3, which compares the larger mREIT segment with equity REITs over a 50-year period. The brick-and-mortar landlords returned an average of 13.4 percent annually versus 8.9 percent.

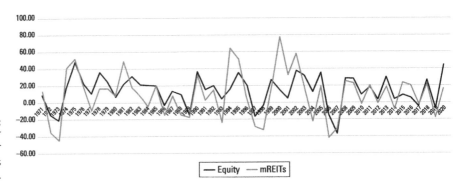

FIGURE 4-3:
Equity REIT
versus mREIT
total returns
(1971–2021).

With that said, commercial mREITs offer loans with shorter durations, which helps them stay afloat at more notable — and more desirable — rates. Residential mREITs' proclivity toward longer-duration loans has given them a history of cutting their dividends, which naturally affects their returns.

The commercial mREIT model

Commercial mREITs focus on financing every other property type not financed by residential REITs, including retail, lodging, office, industrial, and even solar, wind, and cannabis properties. Companies that operate commercial real estate are often less sensitive to government policy and interference. This only makes sense considering how their loans are sourced, originated, and maintained by private (or public) financiers.

While commercial mREITs are still most definitely mREITs and therefore require more caution on the part of investors, they tend to be more stable than their residential cousins. In essence, they are modern-day banks in a REIT wrapper.

The sector can be further broken down into two categories:

>> *Pure balance sheet lenders* originate (purchase) and hold loans for their own balance sheets. They may sell participation units (essentially shares in an investment fund) in those loans for risk-diversification purposes, but they remain the main authority involved nonetheless.

>> *Balance sheet/conduit lenders* mix things up a bit. They originate and/or purchase loans for their own balance sheets or to be sold into conduit securitized vehicles such as commercial mortgage-backed securities.

Table 4-2 outlines the risk associated with three types of mREITs: agency mREITs (those whose mortgages are backed by the federal government), hybrid mREITs (those that hold both residential and commercial mortgages), and commercial mREITs.

TABLE 4-2   ## mREIT Risk Matrix

	Agency mREIT	Hybrid mREIT	Commercial mREIT
Prepayment risk	High	Moderate/High	Low
Leverage	High	Moderate	Low
Investment liquidity	High	Moderate/High	Moderate/Low
Principal risk	Low	Moderate/Low	Moderate/High
Derivative exposure	High	Moderate	Low
Level 3 assets	Low	Low/Moderate	High

Chapter 3 details how commercial mREITs were exceptionally popular in the late 1960s and early 1970s. That's when large regional and money-center banks, along with mortgage brokers, got intensely and foolishly involved. Impressed with the idea of REITs, they saw nothing but dollar signs and opened up almost 60 lending institutions in short order — much to their detriment.

At first, lending funds to property developers (as most of them did) worked well enough and the theoretical dollar signs they'd seen became actual, realized rewards. But then interest rates rose in 1973, and demand for new developments came crashing down. The end results were not favorable for anyone, including the greedy, foolish banks. And most of these mREITs fell apart, utterly failing their investors.

I bring this up again for a reason. While it would be nice to say that banks, developers, and investors learned their lesson after that, that just wasn't true. Around a decade later, a new round of mREITs sprung up to invest in collateralized mortgage obligations (CMOs). And the results, once again, were far from positive.

Fortunately, the quality of commercial mREITs has improved substantially since then. Those disasters left an opening for big, private-equity firms and other companies with more specialized lending platforms to step in. Today, commercial mREITs are mostly externally managed, which means that they're owned and operated by an external manager. That means there is less of a direct conflict of interest, and everyone involved (on the company side) understands the business inside and out.

I cover internal versus external management further in Chapter 9.

Every REIT Isn't Traded on the Stock Market

Thus far, I've been detailing publicly traded equity REITs and mREITs. But they have competitors that operate outside of Wall Street: private REITs and public non-listed REITs (PNLRs). As I point out in Chapter 3, listed REITs benefit from liquidity and transparency — both of which are important attributes worth considering. These benefits should not be taken lightly.

However, private REITs and PNLRs are worthwhile alternatives. That is, they can be if you've done your homework. In which case, they're just like other REITs. They require careful research and understanding to reap regular rewards from them.

REMEMBER

Throughout the rest of this book, I refer exclusively to publicly listed REITs. You can still apply many of the facts, figures, and calculations across the board. But the most common form of investing in REITs is through the stock market.

Private REITs

If you know anything about public REITs, then at least the concept of private REITs is pretty self-explanatory. They still have to abide by the IRS definition of what makes a REIT a REIT, but they don't list on the stock market and therefore don't have to register with the Securities and Exchange Commission (SEC) and do not provide financial or performance data publicly. This does make measuring their performance difficult, admittedly. Public, independent sources just don't cover them. Therefore, it's all on the investor to collect and track private REITs' performance (due diligence is a must).

Then again, their shares are usually offered to institutional investors alone. By this, I mean banks, pension funds, insurance companies, labor unions, and other large investment-oriented organizations that I discuss in Chapter 11. Accredited investors are known to participate as well, with the term usually defined as individuals with net worths of $1 million or more — above and beyond the worth of their primary residence — or with income beyond $200,000 (or $300,000 with a spouse) over the last two years.

Speaking of money, private REITs, sometimes called *private placement REITs*, have minimum investment amounts. If you want to get involved in them, you have to pony up an absolute minimum of $1,000. Most of them have much higher requirements upward of $25,000. That's just the name of the game when it comes to these off-market investments, which is why most mom-and-pop investors don't even know they exist, much less put money into them.

Investors in private REITs also need to be aware of liquidity issues, which may depend on their own financial strength and stability, and that of their fellow shareholders. Although it's theoretically possible for one partner to sell their interest to another, that option comes with potential problems. Trust me on this. It can be like being in business with another person: not so easy to get out of.

In a previous life, I had a partnership valued at just under $100 million. And when it came time to wind down the agreement, my partner wasn't willing to provide an amicable divorce. As a result, I lost millions of dollars (a large part of my net worth), which is one of the reasons I prefer owning publicly traded REITs today.

Private REITs are also typically externally advised and managed. Which, again, I'm typically not a fan of. This doesn't mean they can't be worthwhile investments, only that they can be even more profitable for their shareholders if they didn't have that extra, sometimes self-interested, expense.

Public non-listed REITs

Unlike private REITs, public non-listed REITs (PNLRs) are registered with the SEC; they just don't trade on national stock exchanges. This makes these investments more illiquid, as redemption programs vary by company and the value of the company is less transparent (since they are non-traded). The non-traded REIT market is estimated to be approximately $70 to $100 billion, and according to S&P Global Market Intelligence, there were 35 non-traded REITs (as of April 2023).

As with private REITs, these companies usually are externally managed. They also have a minimum initial investment, though it's a lot more reasonable. Expect $1,000 to $2,500 and a minimum holding period as well.

As with any investment, there are pros and cons to investing in PNLRs. On the pro side, they offer

>> Higher potential payouts (be careful because some pay out more in dividends than they earn)

>> Lower volatility (because they aren't publicly traded)

>> Portfolio diversification

On the con side, PNLRs have these drawbacks:

>> Reduced regulatory oversight

>> High minimum investment

» Lack of liquidity

» Longer holding periods

» Redemption limits

That last con — redemption limits — is a feature PNLRs use to prevent managers from having to liquidate holdings at fire-sale prices. Remember that PNLRs are intended only for investors with the financial means to hold their investments for relatively long periods of time — including during times of market stress and illiquidity.

Chapter **5**

REITs around the Globe

ccording to the *Global REIT Approach to Real Estate Investing,* a 2022 report from the National Association of Real Estate Investment Trusts (Nareit), there are 893 listed REITs around the world today — up from 120 in 1989. And between 1990 and 2022, REITs' market capitalization has climbed from $10 billion to a whopping $1.9 trillion. That's around 1.7 percent of the global equity stock market universe! It's an impressive achievement, to say the least.

Then again, considering the benefits of REITs, perhaps it shouldn't be so surprising. REITs encourage business activity, grow individual wealth, and provide extra sources of tax income for the governments that allow them. So perhaps we should only be surprised that more countries haven't gotten onboard yet.

As of 2022, 41 countries and regions had created their own REIT legislation, some of which are better than others. I go into some of those differences in this chapter, as well as pitfalls to keep an eye out for if you choose to explore the ever-widening global REIT world. There's a lot to know — enough to fill an entire book of its own. This chapter can't give you the be-all and end-all on the subject, but my hope is that it leaves you on more solid footing about the global REIT universe than you had before.

The Long and Short of It

As I detail in Chapter 3, the United States created REITs in 1960, and two countries followed suit nine years later: the Netherlands and New Zealand. In 1971, Australia joined the list, too, which marked the end of the global REIT expansion for a while.

There were no more additions until 1993 when Brazil and Canada began their own programs. This may have been because the United States was still trying to figure out its own situation. But since then, an average of one country per year (at least) has adopted the REIT concept as its own. You can find REITs on every single continent now — minus Antarctica, the one that doesn't count when it comes to commercial real estate purposes. North America, Australia, Europe, Asia, South America, and Africa: They're all accounted for now. Figure 5-1 illustrates the explosive growth in REITs between 1990 and 2021.

Asia has especially gained ground this century. In 2005, only five countries and regions there were allowed REITs, with just a few dozen companies that had taken them up on it. By the end of 2022, those figures had risen to 11 and 233, respectively. While South Korea stands out for growing from three REITs in 2015 to 21 in 2022, I also want to highlight the Middle East here. Saudi Arabia, for instance, had 17 by the end of 2022. And Israel had five.

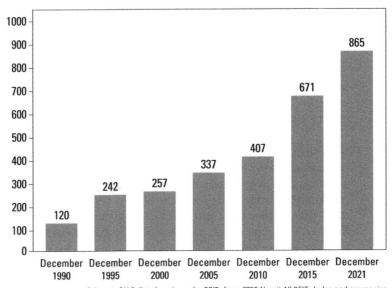

FIGURE 5-1: Number of listed REITs (1990–2021).*

* Count of U.S. listed equity and mREITs from FTSE Nareit All REITs Index and companies listed as equity or mREITs in S&P Global Capital IQ in REIT countries and regions.

Source: Adopted from National Association of REITs (Nareit).

This isn't to say there isn't further room to grow. Clearly there is when there are almost 200 countries in the world, with less than a quarter of them allowing REITs. So this saga is far from over. In fact, the Neuberger Berman Group, an 84-year-old private, independent global investment management firm, deemed the opportunity impossible to ignore due to its intense growth potential — and that was back in 2020. It especially saw Chinese and Indian REITs taking off.

As I demonstrate later on in this chapter, that's already proving true. But even if it wasn't, the international REIT category has already proven itself a force to be reckoned with. According to the Nareit report I reference at the start of the chapter, international REITs easily outperformed their bond, stock, and private real estate counterparts between June 2009 and December 2021.

As illustrated in the graph shown in Figure 5-2, bonds saw a mere 2.73 percent compound annual growth rate while private real estate returned 7.41 percent. Stocks did much better at 8.10 percent, but global REITs still managed to leave them in the dust at 13 percent.

Outperformed International Stocks and Bonds
(compound annual growth rate, June 2009-December 2021)

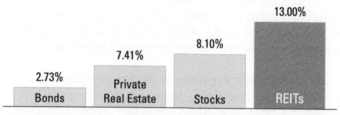

FIGURE 5-2: REITs outperformed international stocks and bonds.*

Source: Adopted from National Association of REITs (Nareit).

Some investors, particularly those in the United States, might point out that a growing number of U.S. REITs are expanding globally. That's correct, and this kind of international investing might be as far as you're willing to explore when your money is on the line. Moreover, that might be as far as you should go: a conclusion you have to come to on your own, possibly with the help of your broker or financial advisor. In which case, I go into greater detail about U.S. REITs with holdings outside the United States in Chapter 4.

Oh, the Places You Can Go and the Money You Can Make

There are three main advantages to investing in REITs outside of your own country. And each one is compelling. Let's start with the risk-management practice of diversification. I know I mention this in Chapter 3 as a reason to like REITs in general, but there's a way to make this good thing better still.

REMEMBER

No market goes straight up. There will always be fluctuations, and some of them can be extreme. But even the smaller stumbles can throw you off your game, prompting you to sell before you've gotten the full benefit of your holdings. And in the case of more significant drops, you can panic-sell and take a serious financial hit. It's human psychology.

Human psychology also explains why people are far more likely to stay in an investment if that investment isn't their only holding when temporary adversity strikes. This applies just as much to investment groups, whether that investment group is small-cap stocks, real estate, or large-cap equities. The more varied your portfolio is, the less volatile it should be, as I explain further in Chapter 10. In the case of national versus international REITs, one country might experience a real estate crisis in any given year — and they all do eventually — but it's much rarer for real estate the world over to crash all at the same time. The 2008 crisis happened, yes, but that was the exception, not the rule.

TIP

Here's another favorable factor to consider: the exact mixture of price point and potential. Some countries — especially emerging markets — will have much cheaper real estate than others. While that might be for a reason (which I discuss later in this chapter), that reason might be set to change in the near future. Getting in early can lead to double-digit and even triple-digit returns at a much faster rate than you would otherwise see in your own backyard.

Speaking of such, there's also a blend of these two reasons (diversification and price point/potential) that's worth pointing out. Different countries allow different property types to become REITs, with each one offering different benefits. It's true that the United States is always expanding its sector range, and it does have an impressive list to its credit so far. But other countries, like China, could have categories we never would have thought of on our own. I call that advantage 2.5.

Here's your official third reason to ask whether international REIT investing might be right for you: global growth. As I'm writing this, the United States just recorded a disconcerting GDP. For the first quarter of 2023, it expanded just 1.1 percent, hardly anything to write home about — and maybe nothing to stay home over either. That's especially true when some emerging economies are recording much, much better numbers — numbers you can access simply and economically through traditional and even many online brokers.

Keeping the "Real" in Global Real Estate

There is a downside to investing in international REITs to consider. Because, let's face it, there always is. Despite their positive qualities, there are many risks to investing in international anything, including REITs. For one thing, it's a constantly changing landscape, with countries and regions making new decisions every year. Sometimes every month.

Some of these changes are positive, of course. Perhaps even many or most of them are. For instance, a number of European and U.K. landlords have been busy enacting reforms to help improve corporate governance, business models, and shareholder returns. The region (or at least large parts of it) now offers simplified sector strategies, less leverage, and greater emphasis on cash flow and active property management.

REMEMBER

Then again, shifting national political issues, political regimes, and political decisions can also lead to undesirable surprises. This can be especially true in emerging markets that are still trying to figure out their REITs or larger real estate situations. And even when investing in well-established nations, it still takes time to figure out how they operate in order to invest as wisely as possible. Heck, it's difficult enough sometimes to figure out what's what in your own country, much less anyone else's.

You'll want to keep currency issues in mind as well. Because if you're investing directly in some other country's stock, you're going to have to do it in that country's currency — which means you have to exchange your own at the going rate. This might be all done online through no-muss no-fuss electronic transactions, but that doesn't mean the potential risk (or potential reward) is lessened one bit.

When you decide to sell that stock and take the profits, you have to reverse the process — once again at the current exchange rate. This can, of course, fall in your favor. But don't expect that double win, especially if you're dealing with an emerging market that's still trying to figure itself out. Your on-fire investment can easily be setting off the smoke alarms by the time you're ready to cash in.

TIP

Taxes, duties, and higher brokerage charges are another area you'll want to know a thing or two about before you put your money into anything international, REIT or otherwise. For instance, you're almost certainly going to have to pay taxes to your own country on whatever money you make. But there are additional fees you'll need to look into in the country you invested in as well.

Quite a few don't have a capital gains tax at all, which is obviously preferable. Others that do have one don't apply it to foreign investors. But you'll also find countries like Italy that take more than a quarter of what non-residents make from selling a stock (the profits, of course, not the losses). Spain levies a high penalty as well at 19 percent.

TIP

This is admittedly not as much of an issue if you're an American investor putting money overseas. The IRS offers ways to protect against double taxation. U.S. investors can choose between claiming a tax credit or a deduction that should cover most or even all the money at stake. But, again, this very much depends on the country you're in and the country you're investing in. So know what you're getting into before you get into it.

The Countries and Regions with REITs — So Far

There are a lot of ins and outs to international investing as a general rule. And there's even more you need to know about when it comes to investing directly in international REITs.

I cover a lot of big-picture information you need to be aware of earlier in this chapter. The rest of this chapter is meant to give you more detailed material by delving into each country that offers REITs. Table 5-1 outlines the countries that offer REITs as of this writing and the year in which they were established. Be sure to explore each country further if you decide that you like what you initially see or already know. To paraphrase American rapper Shwayze, *there ain't no education like a self-education, cuz a self-education don't stop.* (I had to include that reference since I wrote the "Rap Review" column for my high school newspaper. Who knows? Maybe I'll start a REIT rap series soon on TikTok!)

TIP

You might also want to keep an eye out for countries like Cambodia, Ghana, Indonesia, Malta, Poland, Sweden, and Tanzania. They're all considering their own REIT programs at this time. I can't say when their discussions will turn into actualities. But the fact that there's always a number of governments looking into expanding the REIT world speaks to this investment category's power and potential. I, for one, can't wait to see what happens from here!

TABLE 5-1   **Countries and Regions with REITs***

Year Established	Country	Year Established	Country
1960	United States	2007	Italy
1969	The Netherlands	2007	United Kingdom
1969	New Zealand	2008	Pakistan
1971	Australia	2009	Costa Rica
1993	Brazil	2009	Finland
1993	Canada	2009	Spain
1995	Belgium	2010	Mexico
1995	Turkey	2010	Philippines
1999	Greece	2011	Hungary
1999	Singapore	2013	Ireland
2000	Japan	2013	South Africa
2001	South Korea	2014	India
2003	Taiwan	2014	Kenya
2003	France	2015	Bahrain
2003	Hong Kong	2015	Vietnam
2005	Bulgaria	2016	Saudi Arabia
2005	Malaysia	2016	Oman
2005	Thailand	2019	Portugal
2006	Dubai, UAE	2020	Sri Lanka
2006	Israel	2021	China
2007	Germany		

As of 2022.

Combing through the G7 countries

I'm going to skip the United States since you already know that its REITs were established in 1960 and now serve as the model for the rest of the world. Instead, let's get right into six other global powers that have established their own programs since then.

Canada

Canadian REITs operate a whole lot like those in the United States, with a few noteworthy exceptions. For one, while U.S. REITs are corporations, Canadian REITs are mutual fund trusts. They also have to pay out 100 percent of their taxable income instead of 90 percent. And most of them offer monthly dividends instead of the typical quarterly payouts American investors tend to see.

The earliest Canadian REITs — like the earliest U.S. ones — were externally managed vehicles. They had to pay outside executors annual asset management fees, acquisition and disposition fees, mortgage fees, financing fees, development fees, and property management fees — which, suffice it to say, is a lot. That changed over time though as REITs and their investors sought to optimize the cost of running these real estate businesses.

Today, management styles are much more diversified, with external, internal, and hybrid arrangements. The latter involves independent CEOs and CFOs who are supported by the promoter's organization. Moreover, most new REITs with external management structures incorporate a forward-looking concept of internalization in their management agreements. Seeing all of this, I expect the push away from external operations to continue.

As a new-ish investment category to Canada, REITs there don't have much support from institutions yet. They're much more mom-and-pop assets at this time, though liquid enough to warrant consideration both on a national and international level. With that said, they do tend to rely on more leverage than their U.S. counterparts. And you'll probably want to talk to a financial advisor about the Canada-specific tax considerations at stake if you want to invest in them outside of the country.

France

Société d'investissement immobilier cotée, or SIICS, were introduced under Article 11 of the Finance Act for 2003. Real estate is heavily taxed in France, so sole ownership of a commercial property isn't always the best way to go. But SIICS, like U.S. REITs, get special benefits. They must pay out 95 percent of their taxable collected rent-specific profit to shareholders and 70 percent of their profits from realized capital gains. In return, they pay no corporation taxes.

While investors don't get that same privilege, French investment resource Finance Héros notes that dividends paid to individuals are legally classified as income from movable capital. This means that they fall under a flat 30 percent tax unless otherwise requested, which makes SIICs a much more attractive consideration for those in higher tax brackets.

Germany

G-REITs must pay out at least 90 percent of distributable profits to shareholders, and no single shareholder can own more than 10 percent of any one G-REIT. Plus, they're easy to identify because they need to have "REIT" somewhere in their company name.

A minimum of 75 percent of their earnings and assets must be real estate–specific (as in actual properties). Construction and other real estate–related activities don't count. The one exception is for mortgage REITs (mREITs), which are technically allowed. But equity or otherwise, they must be publicly traded by law — a provision that probably won't bother you one way or the other. Other restrictions, however, might not be quite so tolerable.

For one thing, REITs can't invest in residential properties built after 2007. This is over concerns that they would otherwise drive rent even higher than it already is, which is understandable. But this does make it problematic for apartment REITs to exist, to say the least. There's also the issue that none of them, no matter the sector, can trade properties as they see fit. G-REITs can change up to 50 percent of their portfolios every five years or 100 percent of them every ten years. This includes buying as well as selling properties. According to German law, they're pretty much stuck with passive management practices and internal growth.

SOME CUTTING COMMENTARY ON G-REITS (TO TAKE OR LEAVE)

Germany has Europe's largest real estate market. Yet that doesn't automatically mean it's a great place for REITs to flourish. Quite the opposite, in fact, according to GermanReal.Estate (https://germanreal.estate). (And, no, that's not a typo. It's both the business' name and web address.) That source believes REITs are a great concept that should be properly explored and encouraged — with the keyword being *properly*. This, it alleges, has not been done in Germany, where REITs have no flexibility or room to grow.

A 2002 *Real Estate Management and Valuation* publication (volume 30, No. 1) agrees with this assessment. It points out how, "The introduction of legal regulations regarding REITs has not always resulted in successful proliferation," adding that the "market for G-REITs is such an example," with only six in existence today.

(continued)

(continued)

Critics especially object to how G-REITs can't leverage more than 45 percent of their funds at a time. While, as I discuss in Chapters 4 and 8, taking on too much debt can be a major problem for any business anywhere, critics charge that the 45 percent cap is extremely difficult to work with and takes a heavy toll on G-REIT performance.

Those are hardly the most compelling opinions to work with. However, you're more than welcome to look into G-REITs further to see if they're right for you regardless!

Italy

As with G-REITs, the *societá di investimento immobiliare quotate*, or SIIQ — translated as "listed real estate investment company" — isn't common either, though the reason why isn't as clear as with G-REITs. More than 70 percent of Italians owned real estate as of mid-2022, so the national mindset is in the right place to appreciate the REIT model. Or at least it's not in the wrong place.

Commercial real estate is an enormous part of the country's GDP, with less than 1 percent of it being listed. Compare that to Germany's 7.8 percent, though of course very little of that in either case is made up of REITs. Still, this means the potential for growth is significant. More than one source believes the Italian government and businesses should push the concept harder than it currently is, so hopefully SIIQs will grow in popularity from here.

As is, they must invest 75 percent of their capital in real estate, cash, or government bonds. The same amount of their income must come from rent, mortgage interest, and property sales. As with most other REITs, they have to be managed by a board of directors or trustees and have a minimum shareholder count of 100 that's properly allocated. Five or fewer individuals can own 50 percent or more of a SIIQ, which still leaves a lot of room for wealthy investors. And, of course, shareholders must receive a large amount of these companies' taxable income — 90 percent, to be precise.

Japan

Japan launched its actual REIT program at a very rough time, with its first two J-REITs listed just one day before 9/11. Yet as of early 2023, the country boasted one of the world's largest collections of REITs. Admittedly, its 61 listed J-REITs are far, far, far fewer than what you'll find in the United States. But it's still an impressive amount that gets a good bit of international attention.

REMEMBER

J-REITs trade in units, not shares. There are definite differences between the two terms, but they're essentially the same for the purposes of buying and selling them. J-REIT units still pay dividends, with the traditional 90 percent of distributable profits going to unitholders by law.

These companies cannot be family companies and must be externally managed by a member of Japan's Investment Trusts Association. At least 70 percent of their managed assets have to be real estate and at least 95 percent real estate related. They also have to have 4,000 or more units available, with no fewer than 1,000 unitholders.

These companies fall under one of two broader categories: single-use, which hold just one type of property, and the equally self-explanatory multiple-use, which is then split up into two categories as well. Those are combined portfolio J-REITs, which invest in just two kinds of real estate, and comprehensive portfolio examples, which hold three or more. The most popular real estate type by far for J-REITs to invest in are office buildings. As of July 2021, they made up 39 percent of the category's property assets, according to the Tokyo Stock Exchange. Logistics made up 19 percent, retail facilities were at 15 percent, residential at 14 percent, and hotels at 8 percent.

TIP

For those who have already read Chapter 12, those who plan on reading Chapter 12, or those who already know about exchange-traded funds (ETFs) and like the look of them, Japan does offer several J-REIT ETFs. I would also point everyone interested in J-REITs in general to do an Internet search for "J-REIT Guidebook," which is the official source on the subject from the Tokyo Stock Exchange.

TWO PROBLEMS WITH J-REITS

The largest flaw in Japan's REIT law is, unfortunately, a fairly prominent one. It mandates that J-REITs run with external management, which all but guarantees conflicts of interest. This is something I explain in further detail in Chapter 9, but it essentially means that the companies themselves cannot run their own operations. They need an outside business to handle it instead.

For example, Aeon Mall REIT, a J-REIT, is externally managed by Aeon Group. And Aeon Group retailers anchor Aeon Mall REIT's properties. So what happens if an Aeon retailer isn't the best one for a specific space in an Aeon mall? The external manager has to choose between what's best for the Aeon retailer — such as reduce rent below

(continued)

(continued)

market — or the Aeon mall by replacing the Aeon retailer with a third-party retailer that can afford the going market rent.

This is a definite issue those curious about investing in J-REITs need to be aware of. And should you decide it's worth it anyway — which it might very well be — stay on top of the situation. There are external management situations that can work out and even work out well, but they should always be monitored to make sure that shareholders are looked out for.

And here's one more thing to be aware of: Beginning in 2010, Japan's central bank, the Bank of Japan, has made repeated investments into the J-REIT market. That isn't necessarily a good thing for J-REITs in the long run. It certainly boosted their share prices over the last decade. In the event the market begins to worry about REITs for any reason, however, the Bank may begin to sell its holdings.

United Kingdom

In both the United States and Japan, REITs are allowed to own properties outside of the country. UK-REITs, however, are limited to investing on their own turf and must be listed on a recognized stock exchange such as the Main Market of the London Stock Exchange. Like the United States and Japan, though, they have to distribute at least 90 percent of their taxable income to shareholders.

UK-REITs can hold either commercial or residential property just as long as neither is owner-occupied. And, similar to Italy, 75 percent of their assets must be available rentable properties with 75 percent of their profits coming from rental income. They then must pay out the traditional 90 percent of their annual profits to their shareholders.

Laws concerning UK-REITs keep improving, expanding both what these companies can do and how attractive they are to outside investors. The government seems solidly committed to encouraging their existence. I can also point to the country's larger corporation tax increase from 19 percent to 25 percent that went into effect in April 2023. While I doubt British lawmakers had REITs on their mind when they thought it up, it still makes corporate-tax-free REITs look a whole lot more attractive.

The other REIT-permitting countries on parade

You may be more comfortable sticking with international REIT investments presented by well-established, less volatile sources such as the G7 powers. As I say earlier in this chapter, such decisions are up to you. You know your personal situation, from your financial status to your mental tendencies and emotional responses. I do not, so I'm not going to venture what you can and shouldn't handle in this regard.

For those who have the will and the way to be more adventurous with their money, though, there's plenty of REIT space left to play in outside of those seven world powers, as I outline in the following sections.

Argentina

While they've been a legal idea for going on three decades, there simply aren't very many *fideicomisos financieros inmobiliarios* (real estate trusts) in existence in Argentina. This is probably because, as business research website *The Law Reviews* (https://thelawreviews.co.uk) explains, they don't actually offer the same tax benefits as in the United States and elsewhere in the world. In which case, they're REIT-ish or REIT-lite. The biggest fideicomiso financiero inmobiliario right now is Inversiones y Representaciones Sociedad Anónima, which owns offices, hotels, malls, apartments, and land. It's also listed on the New York Stock Exchange.

Australia

A-REITs are either listed on the Bendigo Stock Exchange, Newcastle Stock Exchange, or Australia Pacific Exchange. Most of them are externally managed, on the downside. But a positive aspect is that they're allowed to invest globally. Australia has seen several dozen A-REITs spring up over the decades, some of which might be worth checking out.

Bahrain

Bahrain has only one officially licensed stock exchange, the Bahrain Bourse, which can be found online at https://bahrainbourse.com. The website notes that "the dividend payout of a REIT has to be at least 90 percent of its net realized income [and] unitholders can expect to receive stable distributions." They also have to be authorized and regulated by the Central Bank of Bahrain "before they can be listed on Bahrain Bourse."

Belgium

Belgian REITs stand out because they only have to distribute 80 percent of their post-debt reduction, non-capital gains-specific income. That does give them more room to run, which may or may not work out for their investors. Then again, Belgium does seem to know its REIT business. It's implemented specific tax measures and promoted certain institutions to foster the industry. Belgium has 17 REITs, all of which distribute their dividends annually, not quarterly.

Brazil

Fundo de investimento imobiliário, or FII, are traded in units and must be managed by a financial institution. They also can't qualify for REIT status until they have at least 50 investors. They're required to distribute no less than 95 percent of their capital gains and the same amount of their operating earnings to shareholders twice a year. The concept is very popular in Brazil, with a lot of takers.

Bulgaria

Bulgaria's REITs were enacted in 2021 through the Special Purpose Investment Companies and Securitisation Companies Act (SPICSCA). This replaced the former SPIC regime, though the REITs are still called SPICs. They can only own Bulgarian properties and must be headquartered in the country. Plus, they're required to distribute at least 90 percent of their net profits within 12 months of the end of that financial period. This setup seems to work well enough for them since there are 33 REITs in Bulgaria.

Chile

Chile runs its REIT program through two difference divisions: public investment funds (FI) and private investment funds (FIP). Either way, they must be approved by the Chilean Securities Commission and managed by a Chilean corporation. FI specifically must be managed by a Chilean stock corporation. Both must distribute at least 30 percent of their annual profits once a year.

China

It may have taken a while for China to approve REITs on any level, considering how it began mulling the possibility in 2001. Even now, the Chinese Communist Party (CCP) hasn't actually passed any legislation or determined any official regulations concerning the investment category. As of summer 2023, it was still experimenting with the concept — an experiment that's nonetheless expanding at a rapid clip.

In June 2021, nine Chinese companies debuted on the Shanghai and Shenzhen bourses as C-REITs. This initial round limited real estate holdings to specific categories such as industrial parks and logistics, as well as the more unique toll roads and waste treatment plants. It garnered a lot of attention, both on the national and international stages. The same is true of consequent moves.

The CCP next allowed C-REITs to include affordable rental properties. That was in 2022, with the three resulting IPOs raising CN¥3.8 billion that August, or $740 million at the time. This was a particularly pointed move in the face of the problems Chinese property developers were facing. But the expansions haven't stopped there. Since early 2023, department store and mall REIT models have been approved as well.

Again, this is an ongoing story. So it's difficult to define what exactly makes a C-REIT a C-REIT. But for those interested in global property ownership, it's a story that can be worth following.

Costa Rica

Real estate investment trusts don't exist in Costa Rica, but real estate investment funds (REIFs) do. They invest in real estate and real estate-related opportunities with the specific purpose of producing high fixed returns through long-term leases. They are externally managed by administrative corporations that must be registered, licensed, and supervised by the national securities regulator.

Dubai

There are very few public REITs listed in Dubai — just two at last check — but they must be focused first and foremost on investing in real properties that produce rent income. They also have to be listed and traded on an approved exchange, distribute at least 80 percent of their annual net income, and borrow no more than 70 percent of their net asset value at a time. Dubai REITs can be either Islamic or regular, with the former needing a Shariah Supervisory Board in place to claim the title.

Finland

Finnish rules state that REITs must distribute 90 percent of their funds to shareholders, and no single shareholder can own 11 percent or more of the business. I have to put it that way since there are no Finnish REITs in existence even though they've been legally allowed for well over a decade now.

Greece

Greek real estate investment companies (REICs) started out on shaky ground due to the original legislation, which made more problems than profits according to many businesses. Fortunately, the government accepted that criticism and worked to improve the system. As such, there are four REICs available at the time of this writing — and there might very well be eight by the time you read it. REICs have to be listed on the Athens Stock Exchange. No less than 80 percent of their assets must be in real estate, and no single property investment can exceed 25 percent of their total asset value.

Hong Kong

Hong Kong's first HK-REIT was Link REIT, issued by the Hong Kong Housing Authority. Today, it's one of the largest real estate entities in the world. HK-REITs in general are externally managed and pay out 90 percent or more of their net profits in dividends. They also have to have three or more properties in their portfolio — hardly the most onerous burden. So it's no surprise that there are nine HK-REITs for such a relatively small area.

Hungary

Hungarian REITs follow the standard 90 percent payout model, though any special purpose vehicles (SPVs) they own must pay out 100 percent. They're supposed to be public limited companies with at least 25 percent of their shares available on approved stocks exchanges. And the same amount has to be held by minority shareholders who own less than 5 percent each. Meanwhile, 70 percent of their total assets have to be real estate, and each real estate asset can't account for more than 30 percent of a REIT's total holdings. There were just two REITs in Hungary at last check.

India

India first began seriously considering its REIT program in 2007, legalized it in 2014, and debuted its first listing in 2019. There haven't been many takers since, however, and investor interest hasn't been all that high either, making these stocks less liquid than they otherwise would be. This has surprised some considering how important real estate is to Indians and how key it is to wealth building on a national scale. Yet so far, the REITs that do exist are mainly office-oriented.

According to the Securities and Exchange Board of India, qualifying companies must have trustees, sponsors, and managers — each of which has to be separate entities from each other. Income-generating properties must make up at least 80 percent of their investments, with a minimum amount being under construction. And, as based on U.S. laws, they must give 90 percent of their net distributable cash flow to unitholders either in the form of interest or dividends. These are then distributed at least twice a year.

The Indian system allows for equity, mortgage, and hybrid REITs, as well as private, public, and those that are public but not listed. There is a minimum amount investors must pay in order to buy into them but it's only 10,000 rupees, a recent improvement from the original 50,000.

Ireland

Irish REITs must be listed on an E.U. stock exchange, but they are allowed to hold non-Irish properties if they so choose. They're supposed to distribute no less than

85 percent of their property income (minus capital gains) to shareholders. And they have to maintain a loan-to-market-value ratio of up to 50 percent. Seventy-five percent of their aggregate income and market value should come from property rentals. While there used to be three Irish REITs, there's only one left today.

Israel

These REITs have an interesting rule, in which a solid 75 percent of their assets have to be profitable. The same amount must be invested in real estate within Israel. And the typical 90 percent of their income is paid out in dividends to shareholders once a year. There are six REITs in Israel, a solid number for a country its size.

Kenya

Kenya was the fourth African country to launch REITs, following South Africa, Nigeria, and Ghana. In its case, REITs are regulated through the Capital Markets Authority (CMA) under the Capital Markets Regulations of 2013. Once approved, they can be classified as income REITs, or I-REITs; development REITs, or D-REITs; and Islamic REITs. So far, there's just one in existence at all.

Malaysia

Malaysia was the first Asian country to implement a REIT regime, labeling them "listed property trusts" and forming them as Malaysian registered trusts. Their exact rules and regulations seem to change quite a bit, with amendments in 2005, 2006, 2007, 2008, 2011, 2012, 2018, and 2019. So investors should be aware that more changes could be in the works from here.

Mexico

Mexican *fideicomisos de inversion de bienes raíces,* or FIBRAs, are fairly free to do as they please minus the requirement to pay out 95 percent or more of their taxable income to investors. They have no minimum number of shareholders required and no restrictions on how many shares any one individual can own. That might be why Mexico has a significant number of REITs in play for an emerging market country.

Netherlands

You may think that the first European country to allow REITs may be fairly tolerant of the concept — in which case, you'd be wrong. *Fiscale beleggingsinstellingen,* or FBIs, have to abide by pretty stringent rules, paying out 100 percent of their taxable profits, for one thing. And they can't engage in land and property development. Even so, five FBIs exist today.

New Zealand

At least the Netherlands has clear expectations for REITs. New Zealand, not so much. Its portfolio investment entities, or PIEs, both exist and don't exist at the same time. They essentially use non–REIT laws to operate like REITs despite there not being any actual REIT laws in place. Convoluted though that most definitely is, it seems to work well enough as there are six PIEs today.

Nigeria

Real estate investment schemes, or REIS, might not translate well in American English, but they seem to be working just fine in the country itself. A REIS must pay out at least 75 percent of its income to shareholders no less than 12 months after receiving said funds. It also can't be a financial or insurance entity, has to be overseen by one or more trustees or directors, and has to be either publicly traded or privately owned.

Oman

Omani REITs follow the standard 90 percent payout to their shareholders, but there are some differences from there. For instance, they have a minimum paid-up capital requirement of OMR10 million and can offer as little as 40 percent of their units to the public if they're publicly traded. Omani REITs don't have a minimum number of units that must be owned by citizens. International investors can own all of one if they've got the money and desire to do so.

Pakistan

As usual, Pakistani REITs have a governing body over them — in this case, a trustee structure in place — to encourage the best practices for their shareholders. They're also required to have an external manager in the form of a REIT management company. This isn't as detrimental as it could be, however, since the RMC has to meet certain standards as well. By law, it must have a 20 percent to 50 percent stake in the company. Plus, it isn't allowed to get any management fees. Pakistani REITs distribute 90 percent of their profits to shareholders.

Philippines

P-REITs have some pretty strict guidelines, but those haven't stopped seven companies from signing up under them anyway. They must be listed on the Philippine Stock Exchange as a real estate investment company with a board mostly made up of Filipino residents. One third of directors must be independent, and the REIT itself has to maintain a minimum paid-up capital of PHP300 million. The country is also very suspicious of companies abusing the REIT system and therefore carefully monitors requests that come in.

Portugal

Sociedades de investimento e gestão imobiliária, also known as SIGIs, can be translated as "real estate investment and asset management companies." They must be listed in a regulated market within the European Economic Area and follow strict rules, including about how their portfolios are put together and how much debt they have. SIGIs have to retain their real estate assets and holdings for at least three years, by law.

Puerto Rico

It's been over a half a century since Puerto Rico accepted a REIT model and almost a quarter century since it amended the legal concept — which also happened in 2006, 2011, 2014, 2018, and 2020. So, as with Malaysia, there could be further changes from here. Puerto Rico requires its REITs to be regulated by the Puerto Rico Commissioner of Financial Institutions and managed by at least one trustee or director. At least 95 percent of their gross income must be from qualifying investment income, with 75 percent of it being from approved real estate investment income. And 90 percent of its net taxable income gets distributed to shareholders. There are eight of these REITs in existence at the time of this writing.

Saudi Arabia

As previously mentioned, there are 17 Saudi Arabian REITs, most of which invest across multiple property types. They undergo intense disclosure requirements and are regulated by the Capital Markets Authority, or CMA. REITs formed after October 2018 have to maintain SAR500 million or more in capital, and publicly listed REITs must have 200 public unitholders amounting to no less than 30 percent of the amount available. They're allowed to invest up to 25 percent of their total asset value in international assets, and no more than half of that total can be leveraged.

Singapore

S-REITs are popular entities, with over three dozen of them established and active by the end of 2022. They must be listed on Singapore Exchange to qualify for tax exemptions, and they're expected to get official approval from the country's Inland Revenue Authority and/or its Ministry of Finance. S-REITs can be self-managed, but most of them opt for the external route. Foreign unitholders are treated equally with citizen unitholders, as are residents and non-residents.

South Africa

The SA REIT category has done well for itself, with 30 companies under its banner to date. These businesses must own at least R300 million worth of property and keep less than 60 percent of their gross asset value leveraged. They're also expected to employ a committee to monitor risk. Seventy-five percent of their income must come from rent checks, with the same amount of their taxable earnings distributed to shareholders.

South Korea

The two-decades-old Real Estate Investment Company Act upholds around 20 active REITs so far. These assets can be broken down into three categories: self-managed (also known as REICs), entrusted management, and corporate restructuring. Minimum capital rules and other regulations do exist depending on the category, but foreign shareholders don't have to worry about additional burdens being foisted on them. As such, they're just as free as citizen shareholders to hold up to 50 percent of a South Korean REIT's stock.

Spain

It's much easier to call *sociedades anónimas cotizadas de inversión en el mercado inmobiliario* (try to say that five times fast) by their acronym of SOCIMIs. The English translation is "listed investment companies in the real estate market," which I guess is about as literal a name as you can get. The Spanish government restructured them in December 2012 so that they're no longer directly taxed. As with most global REITs, that burden now falls on the investor, and that tax is higher at 19 percent than you'll find many other places.

In 2021, another amendment added a 15 percent penalty on the SOCIMIs themselves for any profit that wasn't distributed in that financial year. They must maintain a minimum share capital of €5 million with just one class of shares allowed at a time. Oh, and here's a particularly difficult requirement: They have to have "sociedades anónimas cotizadas de inversión en el mercado inmobiliario" in their name. Fortunately, the acronym is also accepted.

Taiwan

These REITs must pay out the normal 90 percent of their income annually. At least 75 percent of their assets must be in real estate assets, and they can invest up to 20 percent in short-term commercial paper, bank deposits, government bonds, and the like. Taiwan also allows for real estate asset trusts. The difference, according to the European Public Real Estate Association, or EPRA (which I mention again in the next section) is that "a REIT will accept funds from investors, which will be invested in specified properties, whereas a REAT will accept properties from a settler and then issue beneficiary certificates representing those properties."

Turkey

Turkish real estate investment companies allocate 50 percent or more of their capital to real estate, which cannot include development projects. They pay their distributions annually and are registered with the Bora Istanbul securities exchange. Their rules and regulations, like several other countries on this list, have changed repeatedly since inception. 2014, 2017, 2018, 2019, and 2020 all saw amendments made to the REIC setup, so there's no guarantee more aren't on their way. This might be because trusts are not recognized in Turkey. Even so, the Turkish real estate market has fostered a lot of interest in the company version that they do allow so that there are now 35 REICs on the market.

Vietnam

V–REITs were first introduced in some fashion in 2010 by a law that's since been rendered null and void. So in one sense, they are the new kid on the block; in another, they've been around for over a decade. The way they stand now is that 65 percent or more of their net asset value must be operated for stable earnings and real estate enterprise–issued securities. And in most cases, 90 percent of their net income per year needs to be distributed to shareholders.

It Ain't Over 'til It's Over . . . and It Ain't Over Yet!

Now that you've seen the list of REIT–allowing countries and territories, I'm sure you see what I mean about it taking an entire book — not just a chapter — to do this topic justice. And that book can only grow from here. Remember that Cambodia, Ghana, Indonesia, Malta, Poland, Sweden, and Tanzania are all considering REIT legislation as well.

TIP

For more information about any of the countries that already have REITs on their books, I suggest looking into the previously mentioned European Public Real Estate Association's latest *Global REIT Survey*. It gives much more detailed information about major REIT regimes around the world, including assessments of how the sector is doing overall. The report is published free online every year. Just do an Internet search for "EPRA Global REIT Survey" and see how much more information you can find!

In Chapter 12, I provide a few easy ways to invest in global REITs via ETFs. For the average investor, this may be the best way to gain exposure to global REITs without having to sift through annual reports or research these stocks one by one. As I point out earlier, the primary advantage of buying into these international landlords is to enhance diversification. But here's a (much) lesser one: It can be kinda cool to tell your friends that you're a landlord of properties in France, Japan, or Israel.

2
Exploring the REIT Universe

Explore the primary REIT sectors, including industrial, apartment, office, net-lease, and retail REITs.

Discover the alternative REIT sectors, including tech-heavy REITs (cell towers and data centers), residential REITs (timber, manufactured housing, and single-family REITs), specialty REITs (farming, billboards, and cannabis), healthcare REITs, lodging REITs, and self-storage REITs.

Understand how property values are calculated through net operating income, cap rates, and internal rates of return.

Gain clarity on the popular REIT earnings metrics available and the basics of a balance sheet.

Recognize the importance of a REIT's management team and its limitations.

Chapter **6**

Exploring the Primary REIT Sectors

There's a good chance that if you live in the United States, you're within easy driving distance of one or more of the 535,000 properties that are owned by REITs. You might work in one, buy your groceries in one, or even live in one if you rent an apartment, home, or plot of land for your manufactured house to rest on.

According to REITs Across America (www.reitsacrossamerica.com), a website run by the National Association of REITs (Nareit), REITs own $2.6 trillion in property value in the United States, and their economic contribution is equivalent to $229 billion in labor income, which comes to an estimated 3.2 million full-time employees (as of 2021). In addition, 44.9 percent of U.S. households invest in REITs in some way, and the combined ownership value of both private and public REITs is in excess of $4.5 trillion. Those are some big numbers!

Much of that investment is made by equity REITs, whose revenues are generated primarily through rental income, as I discuss in Chapter 4. In this chapter, I go into much greater detail on those traditional REIT sectors —industrial, apartment, office, net-lease, and retail REITs — and explain what they do and how they do it.

Understanding REIT Property Classifications

Understanding your own risk tolerance limitations is key to becoming an intelligent REIT investor. In which case, it's important to also understand property classifications, or *sectors,* as each classification comes with its own strengths, weaknesses, and other intricacies that make it more or less stable as a general rule.

REITs invest in a broad assortment of sectors and property types, and that list just keeps evolving. Back when I was in college, I learned about the primary real estate "food groups" such as office buildings, malls, shopping centers, and apartments. However, that was many moons ago. Back then, I would have never imagined I'd be researching 200-foot cell towers disguised as trees, secure data centers powering the Internet, or high-tech distribution hubs that facilitate next-day shipping. And what about biotech research labs, hospitals, casinos, and even cannabis farms? These days, such alternative REIT property types account for over half of REIT holdings (see Figure 6-1)!

REMEMBER

The various REIT property sectors tend to react to market conditions very differently depending on factors such as lease durations, tenant types, economic drivers, and supply cycles. These differences have historically resulted in a wide dispersion of returns in any given period. Take more economically sensitive sectors with short-term leases, such as hotels and self-storage. They can adjust rents relatively quickly in response to ramped up or decreased demand in a cyclical upswing. By contrast, longer-lease sectors like net-lease and healthcare have more defensive cash flows that may be more resilient during economic downturns. There's always a give and take to consider.

There can also be intense differences in performance between companies within the same sector. Just because some companies have low performance numbers doesn't mean you can't find success stories among their competitors. But to understand why some companies work better than others, you still have to understand the economic drivers in which they operate first.

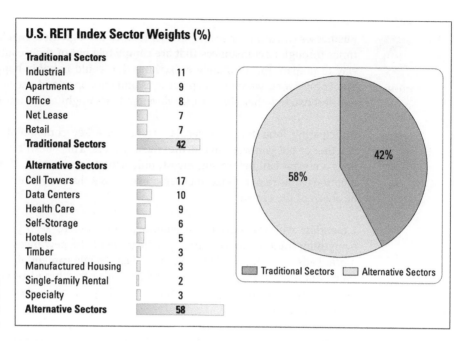

U.S. REIT Index Sector Weights (%)

Traditional Sectors	
Industrial	11
Apartments	9
Office	8
Net Lease	7
Retail	7
Traditional Sectors	**42**

Alternative Sectors	
Cell Towers	17
Data Centers	10
Health Care	9
Self-Storage	6
Hotels	5
Timber	3
Manufactured Housing	3
Single-family Rental	2
Specialty	3
Alternative Sectors	**58**

Traditional Sectors 42% / Alternative Sectors 58%

FIGURE 6-1:
U.S. REIT index
sector weights by
percentage.

Property types, simply put, have different fundamentals. We've learned that many times throughout history, but it was perhaps never in such stark contrast as it was in 2020. Under the shutdown economy during the COVID-19 pandemic, the sectors that fared the best and worst saw a 58 percent difference in profits. Retailers, hotels, and offices were negatively affected to intense degrees as people were suddenly forced to work and shop online. Technology-related REITs (discussed in Chapter 7), meanwhile, rose in popularity thanks to those very same stay-at-home orders.

It's not 2020 anymore, of course. But that year had lasting effects on everyone and everything, the business world included. And investors have had to adjust accordingly. There have been population shifts between cities, states, and regions; more flexible work-from-home and hybrid policies; and that already-mentioned massive shift toward everything online. Based on mounting evidence, I believe much of that won't be reversed.

During the pandemic in 2020, there were plenty of apocalyptic predictions for the death of the office building, traditional retail, gyms, movie theaters, and so on. Today, we see how wrong a lot of that was. Yet it's still safe to say society has changed, and it would be dangerous to pretend otherwise. As I show in the following sections, traditional REITs have had to adapt to these sudden and, in some cases, permanent shifts.

REMEMBER

Businesses will always rise and fall, sometimes through their own fault and sometimes through circumstances that are completely out of their control. There's no way to prepare for absolutely everything that could possibly happen, of course. But as investors, we must keep our eyes and ears open and use our minds to put two and two together about which developments might affect our holdings.

TIP

Anticipating long-term, or secular, trends is a key component of recognizing whether or not you want to buy into these sectors. This doesn't mean you have to have a crystal ball before you invest, only actual data instead of mere fad-based emotions. You're not going to be right every time that way, but you should easily be ahead of the crowd.

I mention avoiding "fad-based emotions" in order to keep you from ditching everything traditional every time you hear about the new investment kid on the block. Fads are a dime a dozen and fade fast. People can and do make money on them, but often through sheer luck, which isn't something I recommend betting on. Ask any casino out there: The odds aren't in your favor when your throw your fortunes to chance.

The urge to jump into innovation — especially when everyone else is hyping it up — can be exceptionally strong. But innovation alone isn't good enough if it's not backed by smart management, proper funding, solid execution, and a successful advertising strategy. In other words, it needs to be sustainable.

Even when all those factors are present, you shouldn't automatically throw out the old for the new. Sometimes both traditional and modern can exist together in significant harmony. Keep that in mind as you explore the traditional REIT sectors: the meat and potatoes portion of this investment class. Together, the following categories represent around 42 percent of the U.S. equity REIT universe.

THE 21ST CENTURY REIT

PROPTECH

One long-term trend you don't want to ignore is the property technology, or proptech, movement. Proptech is simply the use of information technology in the real estate industry. According to real estate software development company Ascendix, it is the intersection of financial technology (fintech), advanced construction technology (contech), smart real estate, and the resource-pooling movement known as the *sharing economy*. Proptech seeks to make buying, selling, researching, marketing, and managing real estate more efficient and effective through computerized offerings and other technological advancements.

In many ways, you've probably already taken advantage of proptech without even knowing it. Have you ever booked a house through Airbnb or VRBO for business travel or vacation purposes? Did you buy a house within the last decade — or simply browse for one — on sites such as Zillow, Redfin, or Realtor.com? In any of those cases, you utilized proptech.

But don't take it for granted just because of those easy-to-come-by examples. Proptech startups are popping up all the time with new ways of addressing real estate in the 21st century. Some of them, no doubt, hope to be the next home-search portal. But they might also seek to revolutionize management software, trading platforms, and the Internet of Things (IoT) in property-specific ways. And that's the short list. This is a constantly evolving area of expertise that will no doubt continue to change our normal ways of doing business for quite some time to come.

Industrial REITs: Warehouses and More

The industrial REIT sector is made up of distribution centers, regular and bulk warehouses, light-manufacturing facilities, research and development facilities, and flex space for sales, administrative, and related operations. Together, they make up around 11 percent of the market capitalization of the U.S. equity REIT universe.

Demand for industrial properties is driven by growth in gross domestic product (GDP), trade, U.S. manufacturing activity, inventory levels, and retail sales trends. And by retail trends these days, I mean e-commerce. That single factor has been the most powerful growth factor for industrial building demand for years now.

As I previously mention — and you already know regardless — online shopping is huge thanks in large part to Amazon. Not only is that behemoth one of the world's biggest and most influential companies, it also inspired many other e-commerce ventures, which necessitates even more warehouse space. Industrial REITs have benefited enormously from these developments. They've built or bought the necessary buildings to house inventory and reaped the profits as they lease out the resulting spaces.

Many investors are content to leave it at that, ignoring the rest of the industrial sector. But other landlords are worth considering under this umbrella, too. For instance, Americold Realty Trust owns and operates cold storage facilities to accommodate food producers, food retailers, and food-service providers. And Innovative Industrial offers specialized facilities for the cannabis industry — a subsector I discuss in Chapter 7.

There's clear diversity within this segment of the REIT world from almost every angle and aspect, including size. For instance, as of early 2023, Prologis stood out as the clear leader with 1.2 billion square feet of leasable space in 19 countries. That's 113 million square meters for everyone outside the United States, Liberia, and Myanmar. On the smaller — yet still substantial — side, is STAG Industrial, which operates approximately 111.6 million square feet (or about 34 million square meters) in 41 states.

It's not unusual for industrial REITs to build new facilities. But they also have plenty of room to buy already-constructed properties considering how, as of early 2023, they owned just 5 percent to 10 percent of the total U.S. market. They are selective though, typically operating only higher-quality assets, not to mention larger facilities. Their average building size is 200,000 square feet.

WARNING

As for sector-specific risks, remember that their fortunes are heavily tied to the economy. While they do feature contracts that lock their tenants in for three to five years at a time, longer stretches of weak retail sales and import issues can work against them. In addition, despite their seeming consistent demand for so many years, these companies can get too big for their britches. Figure 6-2 illustrates the economic sensitivity of different property types versus lease duration.

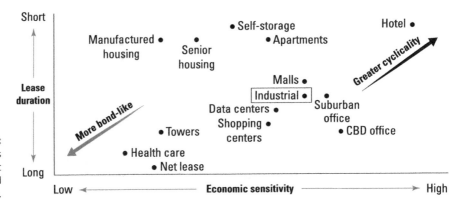

FIGURE 6-2: Property types by economic sensitivity and lease duration.

TIP

Always look into an industrial REIT's building and buying practices. Many acquisitions are made on the assumption that there will be a buyer. And sometimes there just isn't.

Many large REIT exchange-traded funds (ETFs) — a topic I cover in Chapter 11 — own shares in larger-cap industrial REITs like Prologis. That makes sense considering that this sector has performed well between early 2013 and early 2023, returning around 14 percent per year. And the fundamentals backing their story are solid, too. Most industrial REITs have generated consistent earnings and dividend growth, supported by healthy balance sheets and disciplined capital structures.

PROPTECH

Industrial REITs also know how to move with the times, including by utilizing proptech products. Take Symbotic, a revolutionary artificial intelligence (AI)–enabled technology platform built to address supply chains. This industrial REIT enabler — which also has major retailers such as Walmart on its client roster — is essentially a product movement technology platform. It basically rebuilt the traditional warehouse concept with a fleet of autonomous robots operating AI–enabled software. They create a first-of-its-kind physical structure that can power a customer's entire supply chain technology platform. Symbotic is expected to be a hyper-growth company as it disrupts the more than $1 trillion that the retail and wholesale industries spend annually on supply chain functions.

Apartment REITs: Living in a REIT Paradise

The apartment REIT sector is composed of buildings created to house people who can't or don't want to buy a home or who don't want to deal with maintenance. Considering how important shelter is, it only makes sense that the apartment REIT sector makes up around 9 percent of U.S. equity REITs' market capitalization. This category can be further broken down into the following apartment types:

>> **Garden-style:** Ground floor or basement apartments with direct access to private outdoor space

>> **High-rise:** Apartment buildings with 12 or more stories and access to multiple elevators

>> **Mid-rise:** Apartment buildings that have 5 to 11 stories and a single elevator, usually found in urban settings

>> **Low-rise:** Apartments in a community with one to four floors that may or may not have access to an elevator

Again, the REITs that run them offer alternatives to home ownership. So it only makes sense that they perform better or worse based on housing prices, financing rates, and prevailing attitudes toward home buying. With that said, apartments do tend to do well regardless of whether the economy is expanding. This also makes sense considering how new jobs bring in new workers, often from out of town or fresh out of college. People who rent either don't have the money necessary for a down payment, aren't sure that they can commit to a particular location, and/or don't want to bother with the hassle and responsibilities of homeownership.

As with every other kind of REIT, overbuilding is a possibility in the apartment sector. But it's perhaps particularly pronounced here. Moreover, it isn't always completely within these businesses' control. There are competitors to watch out for too, after all.

TIP

It's always a good idea to look into where these investments operate and what the rate of new apartment construction is there. The more competitors there are, the more apartment REITs have to incentivize tenants through lower prices, better amenities, and more advertising — all of which works against their bottom line. I fully recognize that I just stated the obvious. However, it's easy to overlook these considerations when there are so many others to factor in as well.

Another risk is inflation, which can lead to higher operating expenses all around. Paying to keep the grounds maintained; the plumbing, electricity, and appliances up to date; and staff incentivized adds up all on its own. So do higher insurance and interest fees. Some of that can be passed on to the tenant, naturally, but not all of it. Then again, inflation can also bring a few perks in the form of curbing competition. Landlords are far less likely to build anything new when they have to consider all those added expenses.

REMEMBER

Speaking of competition, the U.S. multifamily apartment market — worth $4 trillion to $5 trillion — is very, very, very fragmented. There are approximately 25 million rental units across the United States, and REITs own roughly just 500,000, at last count. That's about 2 percent, leaving lots and lots (and lots) of room to grow.

Apartment REITs tend to choose specific areas of the country to operate in, although some of those areas are fairly wide. For example, Mid-America Apartment Communities owned 101,986 apartment homes across 16 states and Washington, D.C., as of February 2023. It largely focuses on Sunbelt markets such as Atlanta, Georgia; Austin, Houston, and Dallas, Texas; the Raleigh-Durham and Charlotte, North Carolina, areas; Tampa and Orlando, Florida; Nashville, Tennessee; and the Greenville-Spartanburg region of South Carolina.

TIP

The so-called "Sunbelt" is the swath of states across the country's southern border, coast to coast, and includes the Carolinas, Georgia, Tennessee, Nevada, and Utah. It's become an increasingly important hub of economic activity due to typically lower costs of living and doing business. So REITs that are located there can do very well for themselves.

Essex Property Trust, meanwhile, is the only publicly traded multifamily REIT dedicated to West Coast markets. Its properties are located in Northern and Southern California and the Seattle metropolitan area. Then there's AvalonBay Communities, which owns over 88,400 apartment homes in 12 states and Washington,

D.C. It invests in gateway markets in well-placed New York and New Jersey metro areas, the Pacific Northwest, New England, and Northern and Southern California.

In each case, that geography is very strategic. Or at least it's supposed to be. Before the COVID-19 pandemic economic shutdowns, big cities in big states were the place for apartment REITs to be. New York City and Silicon Valley delivered plenty of profits back then. And to be sure, they still can. But the world did change drastically, making it more difficult for those landlords to do business and opening up intense opportunities elsewhere, such as the aforementioned Sunbelt.

The pandemic also brought with it changing housing needs, technological innovation, and cost-of-living differences. All of that accelerated an already existing migration from high-density, high-tax, high cost-of-living locations to more spacious and more affordable alternatives.

REMEMBER

Apartment REITs and other landlords also have to consider the greater focus on live-work-play balances. With so many people continuing to work from home entirely or transitioning to hybrid schedules, tenants are increasingly interested in amenities. This is particularly true of maturing millennials and the aging baby boomers who are moving out of high-density cities. These newly emerged details combined have opened up plenty of proptech opportunities.

PROPTECH

RET Ventures is a leading technology investment firm with a network of over 9,000 multifamily properties and 137,000 single-family rental properties. It identifies and backs cutting-edge technology such as SmartRent, Amenify, Applause, Checkpoint, Fyxt, Kasa, Lexicon, PassiveLogic, Slingshot, and Stake, just to name a few. And several residential REITs such as UDR Properties, Essex Property Trust, MidAmerica Apartment Communities, Centerspace, and Invitation Homes have invested in RET Ventures, in turn. They've gained enormous benefits as a result through technologies that generate operating efficiencies, better engagement with tenants, and quicker responses to customers' ever-changing needs.

Take SmartRent, for one. This RET Ventures portfolio company provides a hub and software solution that enables residents and property managers to control a variety of commercially available IoT devices remotely, enabling operation savings, ancillary revenue, and in-demand amenity for tech-savvy renters.

Also during the COVID-19 pandemic, the leasing process for many apartment landlords shifted to being 100 percent automated. People can now lease apartment units on their smartphones with supporting videos and other ways of seeing what's being offered.

Apartment REITs have returned an average of 8.4 percent over the last decade.

Office REITs: A Diminished Necessity

Office REITs are self-explanatory. These companies rent workspace for traditional nine-to-five employees. They comprise a large grouping that makes up about 8 percent of U.S. equity REITs' combined market capitalization. This sector is typically broken up into two subdivisions that invest in

>> **Gateway markets:** These companies own properties in six large U.S. cities: Boston, Chicago, Los Angeles, New York City, San Francisco, and Washington, D.C.

>> **Non-gateway markets:** These companies own assets anywhere else, often in the Sunbelt and/or other secondary U.S. cities.

Regardless, they tend to operate under longer-term leases, often of 5 to 20 years. These contracts can also include small annual rent increases tied to the consumer price index (CPI) or some other inflationary index, but those terms are almost always fixed.

REMEMBER

Fixed rental increases refer to rent increases that occur every so many years (usually five), generally by 5 percent to 15 percent. A *CPI rental increase* is based on what the CPI is doing, essentially tying rent to national or regional inflation.

In addition, office REIT tenants are often expected to help shoulder the weight of increased taxes or operating expenses that arise in the building. That helps protect and even grow landlords' profits, though they also have to pay pretty high fixed costs — made more burdensome still if the offices are unoccupied — and therefore have higher operating leverage to deal with.

Examples of gateway office REITs include SL Green Realty, Vornado Realty Trust, and Empire State Realty Trust. All three are New York City landlords, with the latter owning the Empire State Building. Boston Properties is another gateway office REIT that spreads out its assets across Boston, Los Angeles, New York City, San Francisco, and Washington, D.C.

As for non-gateway office REITs, they include companies such as Highwoods Properties, Piedmont Office Realty Trust, Cousins Properties, and City Office. All four are primarily focused on Sunbelt states like Arizona, Florida, Georgia, North Carolina, Tennessee, and Texas.

Much like apartment REITs, office REITs had to rethink business as usual after the pandemic shutdowns. Specifically, leasing activity in many markets has been slow ever since and pricing power has been largely absent. There are simply too many national and international companies — the kind that tend to rent space from office REITs — that are still trying to figure out the complex issues involved in allowing remote work or even hybrid models. Other businesses have already made up their minds on the subject one way or the other, and it hasn't always fallen in landlords' favor.

TECHNICAL STUFF

Cohen & Steers estimated in early 2023 that partial and full-time work-from-home (WFH) policies could reduce office demand by 3 percent to 15 percent over the next several years. That depends on various markets' cultural practices, industry mixes, and other economic forces, it's true. But don't underestimate any of those factors. Even in 2023, three years after the shutdowns commenced, gateway markets New York City and San Francisco remained under pressure in this regard. This is true in large part to what I previously mention is impacting apartment REITs: the push away from expensive, crowded areas toward towns and cities that offer less overall stress.

Office REITs generally don't perform well in any downturn, not just in the unmitigated mess of 2020. All but Highwoods Properties cut their dividends during the Great Recession (2008–2009) as well. Yet it's also true that the headaches haven't stopped since pandemic fears eased. Tenant demands for everything from advanced heating, ventilation, and air conditioning (HVAC) systems, to LED lights, digital lighting controls, automatic light switches, energy-efficient appliances, and high-efficiency toilets have put more pressure on office landlords.

According to commercial real estate investor Jones Lang LaSalle, concession packages have eclipsed all-time highs. Take term-adjusted rent abatement periods, which essentially boil down to stretches of free rent. Those grew 26.8 percent since the first dark days of the shutdowns through the end of 2022 and 2.5 percent since the end of 2021. Then there are tenant improvement allowances, which grew 18.8 percent between 2020 and 2023, and 10 percent in 2022. So it only makes sense that REITs with newer properties offering environmentally friendly features and modern amenities can expect better demand and stronger rent growth. Newer buildings are more attractive as a general rule, naturally, but that's even more true today.

Because of these setbacks, office REITs returned a mere 0.40 percent as a group between early 2013 and early 2023.

The More for Less Net-Lease Landlords

Net-lease REITs make up around 7 percent of equity REITs' market capitalization in the United States. They're proven to be one of the most predictable property categories — even during the pandemic shutdowns of 2020 — due to their high-quality, longer-duration corporate rental contracts. This sector is categorized by its triple-net lease structure, a distinctive business arrangement to be sure.

Net-lease refers to a rental situation where the renter pays for some or all of a property's taxes, insurance, and maintenance. These are almost always retail-oriented arrangements and are generally broken down into one of three categories:

>> **Single-net lease:** The tenant pays just one of three expense categories (insurance, property taxes, and maintenance and repairs), and the landlord covers all other costs.

>> **Double-net, or net-net, lease:** The tenant pays two of the three expense categories, usually taxes and insurance.

>> **Triple-net, or net-net-net (NNN) lease:** The tenant pays all three expense categories, typically including roof and structure repairs, and the landlord has zero responsibilities.

This might sound heavily weighted in the landlord's favor, but the arrangement includes lower rents than typical leases offer. So as usual, it's a give and take setup that suits a specific kind or kinds of company. In this case, that kind prefers to operate in stand-alone buildings, a category that includes

>> Fast-food restaurants with drive-throughs

>> Auto parts and garage chains

>> Gyms and health clubs

>> Big-box stores such as Costco, BJ's, and Sam's Club

>> Drugstores such as Walgreens and CVS

>> Home improvement stores like Lowe's, Home Depot, and Tractor Supply

>> Convenience stores like 7-Eleven and WaWa

>> Casinos such as MGM, Wynn, and Caesars

>> Amazon and FedEx for their warehouses

>> Dollar stores like Dollar General or Family Dollar

These places prefer as much autonomy as possible without the full risk of ownership. They want to run on their own hours on their own terms but not on their own property. For them, it's simply easier that way. In fact, these companies consider it to be such a favorable arrangement, they are typically willing to sign 10- to 25-year contracts, complete with contractual rental increases that are either based on fixed terms or the consumer price index.

Some tenants also pay their landlords overage rent on top of their regular rent. This is extra money paid based on how good business has been. If business is booming over an agreed-upon amount, the lessee owes an additional amount in the form of a percentage of gross sales.

REMEMBER

With that said, the rent bumps are typically small and happen only every five years. So most of net-lease REITs' growth comes from new acquisitions and/or developments. To gain an edge, many of the larger ones routinely generate sale-leaseback transactions with larger corporate customers. This entails buying up properties from owners who want to stay there, only this time as tenants.

If that sounds like a cash-heavy way to operate, it is. Fortunately, many of the larger net-lease REITs like Realty Income, VICI Properties, Agree Realty, and W.P. Carey are all investment-grade rated. Their balance sheets are highly regarded by both investors and financial institutions alike, which enables them to obtain cheaper unsecured debt — something I explain in greater detail in Chapter 8.

REMEMBER

In general, the net-lease REIT setup is attractive to well-established, healthy tenants. It's far less a hassle for landlords to operate this way. And it provides stable dividend income for investors. While many other REITs were forced to cut their dividends during the Great Recession and the 2020 shutdowns, most net-lease REITs maintained and a few even grew theirs.

Another appeal the sector holds is its high dividends. Because tenants pay most of the expenses, these landlords can distribute more income to their investors. Plus, they tend to be extremely diverse entities with hundreds or even thousands of properties each — sometimes on an international scale. This means they typically have lower tenant concentrations, which means that if one tenant stops paying rent, it doesn't impact their earnings stream. Knowing all this, it should come as no surprise that three net-lease REITs have increased their dividends for over 25 years in a row: Realty Income, National Retail Properties, and W.P. Carey (see Figure 6-3).

WARNING

On the downside, net-lease REITs don't have the same pricing power as landlords who work with shorter-duration leases. Their profit margins are essentially locked in by 10- to 25-year agreements, with no renegotiations involved — no matter how commercial real estate prices climb elsewhere.

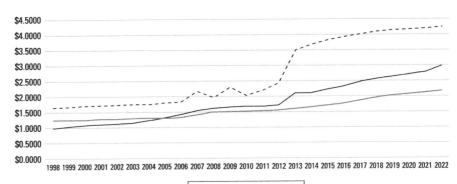

FIGURE 6-3: Dividends paid by Realty Income (O), National Retail Properties (NNN), and W.P. Carey (WPC) between 1998 and 2022.

PROPTECH

Despite their somewhat stodgy details, net-lease REITs are just as interested in keeping up with the times as any other sector. There are plenty of examples I could give here, but I'm going to limit it to one very impressive case involving the aforementioned Realty Income. That company signed a deal in 2023 to help agricultural technology (agtech) firm Plenty develop indoor vertical farming facilities. Their first one is near Richmond, Virginia, and is designed to grow more than 4 million pounds of strawberries every year.

To understand why this venture is so impressive, you first have to understand that vertical farming is exactly what it sounds like. Plenty, for instance, uses vertical grow towers and an innovative lighting, water, and nutrient system in its operations. By growing indoors, it creates an environment that can be fully controlled, delivering just the right amount of everything plants need — and all without pesticides. Its Virginia facility is the largest vertical farm in the world, yet it only covers 120 acres of farmland. That's a fraction of the average 445-acre farm in the United States. So Plenty — and fellow agtech companies — can grow significantly more produce per acre while using just a fraction of the land and water than the conventional competition.

Agtech and vertical farming are estimated to be a $50 billion industry over the next few years. And Plenty's highly automated farming architecture efficiently harnesses scarce natural resources to generate production yields that it believes are up to 350 times greater per acre than conventional farming.

Retail: The Kingdom of Thing-dom

The retail REIT sector is comprised of shopping centers, malls, and outlet centers. Together, they make up around 7 percent of the market capitalization of the U.S. equity REIT universe.

In my prior life (before becoming an analyst), I was a shopping center developer. I created a successful business around building shopping centers and leasing them to retailers like Barnes & Noble, PetSmart, Walmart, and others. So I've witnessed the retail sector transform both personally and literally from the ground up.

I completed my first shopping center in the late 1980s during the so-called golden age of retail. During that time, over 1,000 new shopping complexes were constructed per year. And almost every town with a population over 200,000 people had a traditional mall anchored by major department stores. In 1986, *Consumer Reports* even named the shopping mall one of the top 50 wonders to revolutionize consumers' lives, alongside the birth-control pill, antibiotics, and personal computers.

What it failed to mention was what we would all come to realize two decades later: We were feeding into a trend that was powerful — within reason. Take away that reason with the healthy limits it should have set, and you get something dangerously unsustainable.

We've seen this even with big-box stores, which used to be the crown jewels of strip-mall type shopping centers. That craze was sparked by chains like Walmart, Target, Home Depot, and Lowes. The first Walmart opened in 1962 in Rogers, Arkansas; and Target and Kmart opened their own stores the same year. Today, of course, Kmart is reduced to a handful of assets due to its own negligence. But even the almighty Walmart has been known to close down some of its locations.

We all know how much damage the rise of online shopping has done to brick-and-mortar stores across the board. So I understand why some might think that in-person transactions are a thing of the past. However, face-to-face commerce has been a staple of American retail for hundreds of years. And even though e-commerce is growing in influence, it's still not replacing brick-and-mortar just yet. Traditional retail still owns the obvious bulk of the global retail sales in the United States.

TIP

If anything, the most successful retailers have moved to an omnichannel model that allows merchants to sell through multiple channels, such as online, via a mobile app, and in a physical store. They might go under without their Internet sales, but their traditional transactions are hardly pocket change either.

The once-mighty mall REIT sector

Malls are classified as indoor shopping centers featuring multiple retailers, where at least two of them are *anchors* — businesses that take up a much larger amount of space than the normal tenant. When it comes to mall REITs, these are often department stores.

The mall category, which technically includes outlets (something I discuss later in this chapter), makes up around 3 percent of the market capitalization of the U.S. equity REIT universe. That's just under $50 billion.

The first indoor shopping mall opened in 1956 in Edina, Minnesota, complete with features that really wowed the shopping community. Inside Southdale Center — which still exists today — was a large central atrium with escalators that led to two upper floors. A pair of department stores (Donaldson's and Dayton's) anchored each end of the climate-controlled complex. And the enormous building was surrounded by thousands of parking spaces that were taken up by more than 20,000 people over five days in 1957. That was when famous gameshow host Bob Barker hosted his *Truth or Consequences* live from Southdale.

Many more malls popped up after that. By the late 1980s, America featured about 3,000 of these shopping meccas. Yet as of 2019, that number had plunged to about 1,000 thanks in large part to the rise of online shopping. And, of course, the COVID-19 pandemic didn't help in that regard. Several mall REITs had to file for bankruptcy as a result: CBL Properties and Pennsylvania REIT, one of the very first to form back in the 1960s, as well as Washington Prime. With that said, these REITs were also struggling beforehand thanks to owning too many poorly placed properties that were losing their appeal.

TIP

Today, many malls remain under pressure, and I doubt we've seen the last shut its doors for good. But that doesn't mean that the concept is dead. Plenty of locations are even thriving.

To understand which ones have what it takes, you have to first understand that mall properties are typically classified into several quality tiers based on location and tenant sales productivity:

>> **Class A:** $500 per square foot or higher

>> **Class B:** $300 to $500 per square foot

>> **Class C:** Less than $300 per square foot

Over the last decade or so, Class C malls are especially declining with increasing vacancies as their often lower-quality tenants fail to perform. The bankrupt REITs mentioned earlier had too many of these properties, putting them in stark contrast with competitors Simon Property Group and Macerich. These higher-quality landlords have long since focused on maintaining stronger balance sheets and quality real estate. They're also more willing to adapt, with Simon especially expanding its business model to include mixed-use developments. These properties involve not just retail but also apartments, hotels, offices, and other experiential, or interactive, elements.

All told, REITs own more than 50 percent of current mall space in the United States. That concentration is only second to the cell tower sector, which I discuss in Chapter 7. This corporate ownership, complete with the funding and strategy that comes with it, gives these survivors a better chance of surviving some more — even if mall REITs as a category have returned an average –1.4 percent over the last decade.

PROPTECH

Another factor that can help mall REITs is that proptech concept I keep bringing up. Simon Property Group has been a particular leader in this regard, specifically when it comes to its marketing strategy. It incorporates technological methods that help its tenants drive awareness, engagement, traffic, and sales. This includes collaborating with leading brands on cutting-edge events and promotions to localize digital campaigns to build awareness for in-store initiatives. The REIT has also expanded the use of QR codes at its locations to drive shoppers to deals, sign up for VIP club access, and explore new stores and promotions. In addition, Simon has added functionality to its mobile app for iOS and Android in addition to Simon Search, a new mall-wide product search capability.

EXPERIENCE WANTED (OR MAYBE NOT?)

Before the pandemic, many retail REITs worked hard to bring on experiential anchor tenants. That was in direct response to digitization. The thinking was, if people were turning to the Internet for clothes or books or gizmos and doodads, offer them something that's impossible to duplicate online. Which, when you think about it, isn't a bad business plan.

To be sure, experiential tenants existed long before the rise of e-commerce. This category includes everything from gyms to theaters to tutoring centers, arcades, and bowling alleys. But much more recently, you also have businesses like Topgolf, an indoor driving range that combines the history-laden game with technological advantages. Golf balls are electronically tracked and drives are automatically scored for a hassle-free experience that can end (or begin) with a tasty meal at the same establishment. That company was founded in 2000 but really took off about 15 years later when REIT EPR Properties cut a deal to expand the chain.

Another example of a more recent experiential phenomenon is trampoline parks run by entities like Altitude, AirSpace, Urban Air, and Sky Zone. You can also find indoor skydiving, escape rooms, and Crystal Lagoons. These are definitely some of the most interactive and unique forms to be found. And it's true that rarity alone can create enormous appeal. But none of that was enough during the COVID-19 pandemic shutdowns.

(continued)

(continued)

The more experiential a service was, the less likely it was to stay open after COVID-19 went global. And even before that, I wrote several articles about how there were smart ways to jump on the interactive bandwagon and foolish ways. EPR, for instance, invested far too heavily in movie theaters and at one time had most of its rent checks coming in from that subsector. In order to diversify, EPR expanded into other experiential categories such as TopGolf.

While I enjoy playing games at TopGolf, I would not want to be a landlord of these expensive driving ranges (upward of $20 million each) if the tenant vacates. In addition, TopGolf competitors are sprouting up, which means at some point there could be an oversupply in this niche category.

Unfortunately, EPR has struggled with excessive theater holdings in that regard, which then suffered more as Netflix and streaming services expanded. With that said, the experiential trend, when developed intelligently, is something that can engage communities and increase profits for many retail REITs around the world. People come for the exclusive appeal and end up browsing the regular shops as well.

Outlet centers: Everyone likes a bargain

Outlet centers first appeared in the United States in the 1930s, when factory stores started to offer damaged or excess goods to employees at lowered prices. But it wasn't until the 1980s that the concept really took off. Before that point, there were around 113 outlets. By 2017, there were around 2,576.

The model has also evolved from rural site selection to a tourist-focused business model. For example, the very popular Tanger Factory Outlet Centers has properties in Myrtle Beach and Charleston, South Carolina; Savannah, Georgia; Daytona Beach, Florida; The Dallas-Fort Worth region in Texas; Lancaster, Pennsylvania; and Charlotte, North Carolina. And high-end names like Coach, BOSS, Michael Kors, Adidas, Nike, Kate Spade, Tory Burch, and Vera Bradley tend to rent space on these properties. That's actually why most analysts include Tanger — the only exclusive publicly traded outlet owner —with mall REITs: because they have similar in-line tenants.

Outlets don't enjoy the same sales per square foot as many A and B malls. Tanger's average, for instance, is just $450. But their tenant profit margins are superior due to the lower costs of occupancy, customer acquisition, and logistics. Plus, they provide consistent value for quality merchandise from many sought-after brands.

Outlets increased in popularity after the 2020 pandemic shutdowns because they're a collection of self-contained properties and therefore (in theory) less likely to house germs. It also didn't hurt that many of them are located in Sunbelt markets, where pandemic restrictions were lifted more quickly than in other parts of the country.

As for the landlords and their investors, outlets are easily reconfigured to minimize tenant turnover downtime and capital expenditure (capex) requirements. And while e-commerce is certainly a risk to their business model, many retailers utilize e-commerce as part of their omnichannel strategy. Outlets serve as experiential shopping experiences and tactical means to interact with customers prior to buying. Plus, there's still that instant gratification effect of buying merchandise and enjoying it the same day — especially at discounted prices.

Don't think that they're resting on their laurels, though. Not in Tanger's case, at least. It's connecting shoppers to the brands and value they want through a digital-first platform these days. This way, the outlet operator is leveraging data to unlock greater value for its shoppers and businesses by making investments that drive traffic and improve the average spend and loyalty acquisition. Tanger's technology-focused platform enables its retail tenants to reach high-value customers during key periods.

Shopping for shopping centers

The shopping center REIT sector makes up around 4 percent of the market capitalization of the U.S. equity REIT universe. That's just under $60 billion in market cap terms. And there's plenty of room to expand from there, given that they own no more than 10 percent of shopping center properties, with the private sector owning the rest.

There are several types of shopping centers, each with their own appeal:

» **Neighborhood center:** These range from 30,000 to 150,000 square feet of space and typically feature one anchor store, which is usually a grocery store. The name comes from their small neighborhood-centric primary trade area of about three miles.

» **Community center:** These range from 100,000 square feet to 300,000 square feet and usually feature two anchor stores. They're essentially larger versions of neighborhood centers that offer wider ranges of retail stores and therefore draw in customers from a greater radius.

» **Power center:** These range from 250,000 to 600,000 square feet and have to have at least 75 percent of their available retail space dedicated to anchor stores. With so much featured, they draw customers from a primary trade area of five to ten miles.

Shopping center anchors are usually going to be grocery stores or pharmacies. These are staples that practically guarantee an influx of customers and therefore tend to keep the larger property pretty resilient. About half of the REIT-held shopping centers feature a grocery store for this very reason. Of course, anchor stores such as Walmart, Costco, Target, and Sam's Club can also serve the same consumer-compelling purpose.

REMEMBER

Shopping center landlords tend to offer leases at 5 to 15 years per initial term. And most terms involve CPI-based or fixed annual rent bumps along the way. They can also include the same kind of overage costs that net-lease retailers might see. For that matter, shopping center lease contracts are often triple-net arrangements. So the tenant covers real estate taxes and assessments, repairs, maintenance, and insurance.

Sounds like a nice setup, right? And it is! Just not a perfect one. As with every other sector and subsector, these REITs (and their private-sector competitors) face a number of challenges. The 2020 shutdowns, for one, made shopping center existence more complicated. It hurt some of their renters and sped up the secular trend of digitized everything. Sure, as of 2022, 90 percent of total retail sales were still happening in person. However, about one-fifth of all clothing, sporting goods, books, and electronics purchases happen online. And those are the kinds of things you'll find at a power center especially.

TIP

No shopping center REIT is completely immune to this. Certain retailers will always be rising and falling in favor. But there are tried-and-true tactics landlords can take to protect themselves. One major consideration is the location of their properties. Proximity to considerable residential areas can make or break any REIT, and shopping centers are no exception to that rule. This is probably why they've returned an average of 2.8 percent per year over the last decade.

PROPTECH

There's clearly room to improve in this regard, which brings me back to proptech. The future of the retail industry revolves around technology, and that doesn't just mean a shift to e-commerce. Proptech companies are transforming the brick-and-mortar shipping experience and how landlords run their shopping centers. According to CB Insights, investors are capitalizing new retail formats, in-store technology, supply chain solutions, and much more. Funding in this regard hit $109 billion globally in 2021 — more than double 2020's investment total.

These innovations will be increasingly critical for attracting retail tenants with ambitious sustainability goals. That's why many REITs and retail property owners are transitioning to smarter building management solutions enabled by IoT. This way, they can enable energy efficiency improvements in power, lighting, and HVAC systems. And sensors and other monitoring technology provide granular, real-time data on building performance.

Chapter **7**

Exploring Alternative REIT Sectors

I n Chapter 6, I introduce the traditional REIT property sectors: industrial, apartment, office, net-lease, and retail. Together, they represent 42 percent of the U.S. equity REIT universe. What accounts for the other 58 percent? These days, REITs have become increasingly more diverse, growing to include rental property types that push the landlord boundaries in a variety of exciting directions, including

» Cell towers

» Data centers

» Healthcare

» Self-storage

» Hotels

» Timber

» Manufactured housing

>> Single-family rentals

>> Farming

>> Billboard

>> Cannabis

Some of these property types might sound strange, particularly the first two, considering how the REIT approach to investing centers around land and the improvements made on top of it. Yet within the REIT Act of 1960, the U.S. Congress established a broad definition of what constitutes *real estate* that ended up benefiting REITs significantly. Lawmakers at the time might not have predicted the rise of the digital age, but they did understand that the economy can and does change over time. Sure enough, there are REITs today that own real estate tied to almost all sectors of the economy and hold properties in many different forms. In this chapter, I dive into these alternative REIT sectors, explaining how they got to be where they are today.

REMEMBER

Let me be clear: The definition of real estate has not changed since 1960. It's just that the interpretations of that definition have become more creative along the way.

REITs on the Cutting Edge: Technology REITs

Welcome to the 21st century, where our entire lives revolve around online access. Most of us don't think about it much, if at all, but almost everything we do these days is driven by computers and computerized processes. With very few exceptions, modern society is on *the grid*, whether we like it or not. Our banking systems, water supply distribution, heating and cooling, food distribution and preservation, commercial transactions: It all relies on sophisticated electricity-powered systems. So why should our real estate investments be any different?

I mention proptech — technology centered around improving property ownership and management — in Chapter 6. And this chapter includes even more examples of proptech at work. But what you're about to find out is that there are entire REIT sectors devoted to technology. They don't just use it, they facilitate it and therefore help facilitate all of that banking, water supply, heating and cooling, and so on mentioned in the previous paragraph, starting with cell tower REITs.

Calling all cell tower REITs

There are just three cell tower REITs, yet they account for 17 percent of U.S. equity REITs' market capitalization. And yes, by this I mean companies that own the cell towers your wireless devices use to communicate.

The cell tower subsector began in 2011 when the Internal Revenue Service (IRS) agreed to classify cell towers as real property. After that, American Tower — which was already public — quickly converted from a C-corporation to a REIT. Investors reacted well to the decision, sending the stock price up more than enough to attract the attention of its competitors. Crown Castle joined its ranks in 2014, and then SBA Communications did the same in 2017.

TECHNICAL STUFF

Cell tower companies work off a simple and easy model. Wireless devices such as basic phones, smartphones, tablets, TVs, and connected cars and appliances all contain radios. These radios transmit data over the air via wireless spectrum to cell sites that are often placed high atop towers. The message is then transferred to the core network and on toward the appropriate end user's location via the nearest tower.

Cell towers are considered essential infrastructure because of how important this kind of communication is across so many sectors and aspects of everyday living. And that's not expected to change anytime soon. If anything, the expanding reach and quality of mobile broadband continues to drive worldwide demand for mobile interactions, real-time data and video, a growing number of smart devices, and a wide range of internet of things (IoT) applications.

In 2023, forecasts estimate there will be 5.7 billion mobile subscribers around the world. And mobile networks will support more than 13.1 billion global mobile devices, with 1.4 billion of those being 5G capable. As more people with more devices consume more data, the demands on mobile networks will only get greater from here.

Most REITs offer higher yields compared to other stocks. That's one of their most significant appeals, if not their biggest altogether. But that's not the case with cell tower REITs, which average just about 2.7 percent. To make up for this, they also differ from other subsectors in that they tend to grow their businesses (and therefore their share prices) fairly fast. Between 2012 and 2022, they averaged 13 percent annual growth based on adjusted funds from operations (AFFO) per share — a term I discuss in depth in Chapter 8.

What cell tower REITs do share with every other equity REIT, however, is that they rent out space to tenants. It's just that their wireless carrier tenants such as Verizon, AT&T, and Sprint don't personally occupy what they rent. Instead, they attach their technology to the towers, which typically means a lot less drama for their landlords. It also means a lot less capital spent on advertising, since the big names mentioned are always looking for more leasable space and know exactly who offers them.

Cell tower REITs have it good in so many other ways. After they get proper zoning permissions, all they have to do is spend $200,000 to $300,000 to build a new tower. And if they can't build a new one, especially in big cities, they can use rooftops instead. The elevated structures serve as antenna either way.

TIP

Most towers can host up to three or four wireless carriers at a time. Some can handle as many as five. Once again, this gives them more bang for their bucks. Moreover, they don't do any of the work of installing, maintaining, or removing equipment. That's all on the tenant's end. Cell tower REITs own just the towers. That's it. And they're responsible for just the towers. That's it. This means that there's lots of room to profit.

Put all those factors together, and you get average annual returns of 11.8 percent between early 2013 and early 2023.

PROPTECH

Given everything already mentioned, it should be obvious how cell towers are connected to the proptech movement. In fact, as I previously wrote, there would be no such thing as proptech without cell towers since just about everything it seeks to achieve is done online. So let's give credit where credit's due. As proptech grows and grows some more, so will demand for cell towers and their profits.

Data centers: The digital dynamos

Data centers account for 10 percent of the equity REIT universe in the United States. As of 2023, only two REITs are strictly in the data center business (and a third I discuss below). As with cell towers, this sector came into existence after the IRS accepted a broader idea of what real estate can be.

TECHNICAL
STUFF

Data centers are properties that house computer servers and network equipment on racks in very specialized buildings. These racks, the argument went, are akin to technological apartments. Therefore, REIT status should be granted to interested data centers. And so it was.

Digital Realty and Equinix were two of the first data center REITs to switch from C-corps to REITs. And then you have Iron Mountain, which gets its own sidebar in this chapter. It converted to a REIT in 2014. Although the company's core business continues to be secured storage, it's been expanding its data center holdings since 2017.

Now these aren't simple or cheap businesses to run. To properly house data, there needs to be sufficient mechanical cooling, electrical systems, and network connections. And those can cost a pretty penny. Then again, these landlords rent out space to their customers so these costs are absorbed by the tenant.

Speaking of tenants, there are several different types of data centers out there, each of which appeal to different customers. Hyperscale facilities are owned and operated by the same parties — almost always enormous companies like Microsoft, Apple, and Google. These centers are at least 10,000 square feet and feature 5,000 servers or more.

Wholesale/hyperscale, meanwhile, are owned and used by separate businesses. They offer more room and more potential for tenants to utilize. And they tend to be more exclusive, signing on fewer customers at a time with five- to ten-year contracts.

Colocation and wholesale colocation data centers are also owned by one company and then rented out to others. So clearly, these are categories REITs can fit into. Colocation facilities tend to cater to smaller clients and may even include technical guidance and supervision as a service, whereas the wholesale category tends to be more exclusive in who it takes on, catering to larger, established businesses that know exactly what they want. Operating under five- to ten-year contracts, these tenants purchase more room than they need with every intention of growing from there.

Because data is so important and will no doubt continue to be, data center REITs have a habit of generating above-average annual growth. Between 2013 and 2022, they were sitting pretty at about 8 percent. Their dividend yields, however, are on the lower side in the 3 percent to 4 percent range.

Like cell towers, data centers are considered mission-critical assets. They're also heavily involved in the proptech game by their very nature, given that they host digital information for thousands of proptech uses.

American Tower, the cell tower REIT I refer to earlier, acquired data center REIT CoreSite in 2022 for $10.1 billion. The acquisition was important for American Tower because it provides a one-stop-shop for 5G deployment and enhances interconnection capabilities, cloud on-ramps, and the future network relationships between the cloud, Edge, and mobile.

YOU CAN TEACH AN OLD COMPANY NEW TRICKS

Thanks to the ever-expanding interpretation of what real estate is, Iron Mountain gets to benefit from not one but two unique REIT segments. The company technically began when Herman Knaust founded a mushroom farm in the early decades of the 1900s. Dubbed the Mushroom King as a result of this successful venture, he purchased an old iron ore mine in Hudson Valley, New York — which he named Iron Mountain — in 1936, plus 100 acres around it to expand his operations.

Business was good for well over a decade. But by 1950, the mushroom market wasn't so profitable anymore so Knaust switched gears. Intensely. He had already sponsored a number of Jewish immigrants to relocate in the United States. These people had lost their identity paperwork in the war, posing quite the problems for them. In addition, the Cold War was amping up, complete with fears about all infrastructural harm and loss of intelligence.

The two factors together prompted Knaust to transform his Iron Mountain into a vault. His first customer was a bank that wanted to store microfilm copies, and a lineup of other corporate customers soon followed. Soon enough, he had to buy another abandoned mine to keep up with demand in the New York City area.

I could go on from there, but suffice it to say that Iron Mountain became quite the force to be reckoned with. Today, it serves governments, small and enormous businesses, and individuals alike in 60 countries spread across all six habitable continents. The company boasts 170,000 unique clients, making it the industry leader in storage and information management services. Its mission statement "to be the trusted guardian of assets most important to [its] customers" is an already recognized and continuing reality as it stores boxes and boxes, and shelves and shelves of confidential paperwork, valuables, and other important physical assets.

Knaust's creation was already a global force by the time it decided to convert from a C-corp into a REIT, permission it gained in 2012. It had also been publicly listed for 16 years by that point. Yet it still saw the benefit of advancing and adapting once again on the unique but ultimately successful argument that the steel racking it offered was, in fact, real estate. By late 2014, it had signed all the forms necessary to make the transformation official. And so it began to pay out REIT–sized dividends.

But the company wasn't done adapting and expanding even then. Only a few years later, it was ready to expand its REIT status into a completely different sector — this time data centers. (Admittedly, this makes it even more difficult to classify or compare it to other REITs for evaluation purposes.)

Really though, the move made sense considering how Iron Mountain is all about storage. It simply took that mission to a 21st- century understanding of the concept. Technically, the company had already been dabbling in the idea for a few years, but it got serious about this new business segment in 2017 by acquiring an already established Denver provider, a four-data center U.S. portfolio from another company, and two data centers from Credit Suisse (one in London and the other in Singapore). And it's only grown further ever since.

Many REITs — probably even most of them — don't operate well when they focus on more than one sector of REIT-dom. But there are exceptions to every rule, as evidenced by Iron Mountain.

Essential Healthcare Properties on Parade: Healthcare REITs

Healthcare REITs, which account for 9 percent of the equity REIT universe in the United States, fall into the following categories:

>> Senior housing properties (assisted and independent living facilities)

>> Skilled nursing, or nursing homes

>> Medical office buildings, or MOBs

>> Hospitals

>> Life-science office and lab properties

REMEMBER

Healthcare REITs themselves don't practice medicine. They only lease to those who do. The vast majority of their revenues come from independent lessees that sign long-term contracts with renewal options. And when one of these medical institutions sign multiple leases with a single REIT, they tend to be bundled together in what is known as a master lease.

TECHNICAL STUFF

A *master lease* is a single lease that covers multiple properties leased from a landlord to a tenant. As a single lease agreement, a master lease does not break out rents for individual properties. It gives the landlord an advantage by making it much more difficult for the tenant to cherry-pick the best properties for renewal or to default on some but not others. Also, master leases make it easier (for landlord and tenant) to fully fund the land and building costs for new projects because they can roll them into an existing master lease. This way new locations profit from the existing proven locations in the master lease.

Remember the RIDEA Act I mention in Chapter 3? It allows healthcare REITs to lease properties to taxable REIT subsidiaries (TRSs) as long as those facilities are managed by outside sources. This enables REITs to participate more fully in the properties' upside, though they also experience their tenants' downsides to greater degree. This is why some healthcare landlords don't go this route.

In general, there's a lot of upside potential to investing in healthcare REITs since healthcare services are a necessity, not a luxury service people can survive without during hard times. So it makes sense that corresponding REITs' shares have a fairly strong track record throughout economic cycles. This made the COVID-19 pandemic quite the shock for hospitals and senior care facilities especially. Throughout the pandemic, hospitals canceled elective surgeries across the board out of intense caution, leading to financial chaos for providers and landlords alike. And nursing homes were seen as death traps, a stigma they're still fighting off today.

Different healthcare REITs were affected differently by the pandemic depending on their tenant types. Some, like Ventas, Welltower, and National Healthcare invest in numerous healthcare subsectors. Others are pure-play landlords that cater to just one. Physician Realty, for example, invests in MOBs; Medical Properties owns hospitals; and Omega Healthcare invests in skilled nursing properties. Meanwhile, Alexandria Real Estate invests in essential life-science facilities such as biotech and pharmaceutical labs.

All told, REITs within this sector have returned an average of 2.1 percent per year between early 2013 and early 2023. It would have been higher if not for the pandemic.

PROPTECH

Proptech, however, could be their ultimate saving grace — something they've been working at implementing for years. According to a report on smart buildings by American Council for an Energy Efficient Economy (ACEEE), 69 percent of hospitals had installed a building automation system by 2017. This means they've already taken their first step toward implementing smart technologies that can provide cost savings in a variety of ways.

Proptech's tangible benefits are easy to measure, at least in this case. ACEEE estimates the average hospital can save 28 percent on HVAC energy, 20 percent on water heating, and 30 percent on lighting energy this way. But how can one measure the intangible results? It's much easier to simply list them.

For instance, there are now digital navigation solutions that can help clients and patients find their way to the clinic simply and easily. This reduces the amount of stress they experience while also ensuring smooth operation of the facility. Moreover, this system can be expanded to include hospital equipment. Everything from gurneys, expensive electronic equipment, supplies, and even coffee machines can be tagged and tracked. This means staff can find the piece of equipment they need faster, which helps improve outcomes and reduces time lost to searching for necessary items.

Not only that, but the system collects data from the sensors, allowing hospital managers to optimize and streamline operations even further. Smart systems can also be used to streamline supply chains and deliveries, ensuring better logistics.

Storing Stuff and Lots of It: Self-Storage REITs

Self-storage REITs account for 6 percent of the equity REIT universe, which might sound surprising depending on where you live. Cities, towns, and even more rural areas across the United States often seem saturated by self-storage facilities — an impression I'm not debating. There are about 50,000 of them dotting the country, after all.

Even so, the larger business sphere is dominated by mom-and-pop owners especially. REITs own a mere 7 percent of these properties as of February 2023 (though about 20 percent of available industry space), amounting to $60 billion in market value. They've returned an average of 13.8 percent per year between early 2013 and early 2023.

The reason why this space is such a small landlords' world is because of self-storage's low capital expenditure (capex) requirements. These buildings are cheap to build, cheap to maintain, and cheap to operate. Plumbing isn't an issue, after all. Temperature controls are, but to a lesser degree (pun intended). Employee counts are minimum. And owners don't have to worry about changing the carpet whenever there's tenant turnaround. All they have to do is sweep the floor to prepare for the next lessees to arrive.

And again, those next lessees are very often right around the street corner.

That proximity, admittedly, hasn't always been true. When self-storage facilities were first built in the 1960s, they tended to exist on the outskirts of towns as something of a business experiment. But as the experiment succeeded, these buildings became more and more mainstream. Today, customers tend to demand location convenience. It's now expected every bit as much as conveniently placed shopping centers.

Most of us think of self-storage facilities as something individuals or families spend money on renting. And that is the typical clientele, to be sure, making up a solid 70 percent of contracts. Roughly one in every ten households rents a unit, for that matter. However, small businesses utilize them as well, as do students and military members.

That's why units range from just 5 square feet of space to 20. Some can hold a few stacked boxes of files. Others can fit recreational vehicles like four-wheelers and even boats, not to mention heaps of furniture, equipment, and assorted junk people want to store on a month-to-month basis.

Heck, one of my friends, Gary "Wojo" Wojtaszek, recently launched a new private RV storage REIT called RecNation. During the COVID-19 pandemic, he and his wife traveled across the United States in a camper they had bought. Once back home, they couldn't find a secure, covered storage facility for their camper that suited their needs. When he asked his friends where they stored their toys, they all seemed to have a similar problem. This is when the lightbulb flickered on and Wojo created RecNation.

Other considerations that easily fall in REITs' favor in this highly fragmented sector include superior access to funding, scalability, revenue management systems, and call-in centers. They also have brand value on their side since they run bigger, more widespread operations. There's Public Storage with its orange doors, CubeSmart with its red-lined box logo, and Extra Space Storage's friendly, almost hotel-like green signs.

BEHIND THE ORANGE DOOR

Self-storage facilities essentially offer customers, owners, and investors alike the basics — but modernized basics, in the case of REITs. These companies are high-tech operations on the corporate level, complete with digital marketing, data mining, facilities management, and financial reporting capabilities. Customers can check in online, pay online, and otherwise operate in a contactless self-storage world unless they'd prefer otherwise.

Public Storage, known for its bright orange doors, probably presents the best example of proptech inclusion in the self-storage world. For starters, it uses eRental, a digital lease platform that enables customers to rent online and move in autonomously. This offering accounts for approximately 50 percent of the company move-ins compared to 20 percent to 35 percent for its self-storage peers.

Public Storage even went so far as to enter the proptech field directly by designing Digital Property Access Systems. It provides customers with hands-free digital access through property parking gates, doors, and elevators that can be controlled through its company app. This development came about in December 2020 after the pandemic shutdowns threw business as usual into abject chaos. And it's been well received ever since.

The app has 4.6 stars and 21,000 reviews as compared to an average of 2.3 stars and 130 reviews for the less-comprehensive apps delivered by other REIT peers. It's also important to acknowledge that many privately held self-storage operations don't have those features at all.

Checking Into Lodging REITs

Lodging, or hotel, REITs account for 5 percent of the country's equity REIT universe. There are around 50,000 hotel properties with a total of five million hotel rooms across the United States. But not all of them are owned by REITs. In fact, this sector is one of the most fragmented, owning just 5 percent of the available market.

Perhaps the most unique aspect about hotel REITs is that they look at day-to-day leases instead of year-to-year or even decade-to-decade contracts. In fact, there's a good chance you haven't even thought of hotel fees as being leases. That's how far out of the rental concept they somehow seem to be.

TIP

This is both a boon and a problem for hotel REITs, depending on the day. The biggest reason to own hotel REITs is demand, and demand right now is something worth noting. Global tourism was around $8 billion at the end of 2022, and it's expected to grow by 4 percent per year through 2030.

WARNING

However, rates fluctuate quite a bit based on the time of year and overall economy. This makes their cash flow somewhat unpredictable and a higher risk than other property sectors. Basically, when the economy is doing well and business is booming, the returns can be extraordinary. But when it's down, fewer people travel and there are more vacancies on the books.

Another risk worth pointing out is the rise of competitors such as Airbnb and VRBO. Although major brands such as Hilton, Marriott, and Hyatt have done a good job of staying relevant by adhering to quality standards rooted in customer service — and it's major brands like Hilton, Marriott, and Hyatt that make up a large chunk of lodging REITs' client base — these proptech brands still appeal to the younger generations.

Incidentally, Airbnb is a terrific example of proptech, even if it was created to compete with REITs, not make their existence easier. As part of the sharing economy, it offers travelers someone else's home as a place to stay for the night, the weekend, or some other agreed-upon amount of time. On Airbnb, you can find places to crash on your backpacking trip through Europe or a spot to rent for a month during your internship in Los Angeles. It's also a great way to explore a town you're thinking about moving to or, on the other end, make money on your extra accommodation(s) by allowing a guest to stay the night or several nights.

Back to hotels, though. Smith Travel Research, a leader in data collection for the lodging industry, categorizes the industry into six segments:

>> Luxury

>> Upper-upscale

>> Upscale

>> Midscale with food and beverage services

>> Midscale without food and beverage services

>> Economy

This is based on major chains' system-wide average room rates. Many lodging REITs do cross the line within these various segments, however (minus economy, since REITs in general tend to avoid low-quality facilities). So I usually break them down into these three buckets instead:

>> Limited services

>> Select/full-service

>> Specialty/boutique

Here's another thing you need to know about hotels: They're run under an asset-heavy model, featuring adjusted net operating income (NOI) margins — something I detail in Chapter 8 — of only 10 percent to 20 percent in a regular year. That's the lowest of all REIT subsectors. Basically, these landlords have a lot of real property-related expenses and therefore less actual profit from the sales they make. Moreover, this is true no matter whether business is good or not, making them very sensitive even to small changes in supply and demand.

In short, they're not the most agile investments in taking advantage of opportunities or avoiding danger. And they have slower growth rates than their clientele. Worse yet, they generally have to cut their dividend payments during recessions, which is why they tend to pay higher yields otherwise. They're trying to make it worthwhile for shareholders despite the greater risk involved.

These stocks were loved by investors looking for high yields from the mid-2010s through 2019. But during the 2020 pandemic, every single one of the 18 lodging REITs on record listed on major U.S. stock exchanges had to shut down the vast majority or all of their facilities. As a result, every one of them had to suspend their dividends. It's tough to pay anything out when you can barely support the basics, after all.

Because of this, hotel REITs have returned an average of 2.3 percent per year between early 2013 and early 2023.

Residential REITs: Building the Case for (Rental) Homes and Housing

I discuss apartment REITs in Chapter 6 along with the other traditional sectors. There, I describe the sector as making up around 9 percent of the equity REIT universe. That's a sizable chunk considering how many sectors exist altogether. There's definite power behind these corporate landlords, but they're hardly all-powerful. Nor do they exist within a vacuum.

Chapter 6 describes how the U.S. multifamily apartment market is extremely fragmented. REITs own just about 2 percent of it, and there's competition from similar but separate sectors as well, namely manufactured housing and single-family housing. Each one has distinct appeal in the absolute necessity that is the shelter and housing category. People need proper protection from the elements, and if we can get some perks alongside them, most of us don't object.

Of course, that shelter — extras or no extras — does require certain elements in order to be built. Which is why I start out with timber REITs before delving into the actual housing alternatives that give apartment REITs an even greater run for their money.

Becoming a tree landlord

Timber REITs account for just 3 percent of the equity REIT universe, and they didn't get their own sector until 2010. That was when Weyerhaeuser, which was founded in 1900 as a paper mill and building supply company, got permission to convert. Its share price had been stagnant, you see, and so it thought that selling off half its assets — its operating businesses and most of its papermills — and concentrating on its real estate-specific operations could solve the problem. So Weyerhaeuser kept only its timberlands, its housebuilding, and its wood-product businesses.

Unfortunately, its expectations were inaccurate. Maybe that was its fault. Maybe it wasn't. Many analysts would argue the latter, blaming the residential housing collapse for why Weyerhaeuser didn't take off. Yet one way or the other, two other timber REITs joined its ranks over the years anyway. Combined, they represent around 30 million acres and account for roughly $30 billion in market value.

There are roughly 200 million acres of commercially forested timberland in the United States, mostly found in the Pacific Northwest and the South. But it's a very fragmented industry, and REITs clearly own just a fraction of the total. Yet I'm going to highlight those 200 million acres nonetheless to reassure anyone who's concerned about these companies' environmental effects. You see, despite modernization and the ravages of forest fires over the years, there are still more trees in the United States today then there were a century ago. That's in large part thanks to timberland REITs and their competitors, which are literally invested in literally growing the commodity.

REMEMBER

The lumber industry is intensely important to societal development. Yes, the need for actual building materials ebbs and flows. But the ability to build new houses is always a necessity, and single-family homes in the United States are mostly built from lumber products. We're talking about 150 to 300 trees per house. Multifamily and commercial buildings are incorporating those materials more and more too.

I could therefore make projections about how strong lumber demand will be going forward based on the skyrocketed demand the 2020 pandemic shutdowns inspired. Or I could predict how higher interest rates will drag down homeownership desires for some time to come. Either way, timberland REITs remain mission-critical businesses.

Again, this doesn't always mean their share prices are celebrated all the time. They're not. But also keep in mind that timberland REITs aren't just worth what they sell or even grow. They also offer value as pure real estate plays, which they capitalize on in more ways than one. At times, they lease out areas to miners, energy companies, and recreational groups. They can (and some do) also operate mills to create engineered wood or paper to sell instead of lumber. Plus, you can't forget the dividends they pay.

Timber REITs have returned an average of 3.1 percent per year over the last decade.

Homeownership on the cheap: Manufactured housing

There are only three manufactured housing REITs, which collectively account for 3 percent of the equity REIT universe in the United States. They own just 4 percent of available supply altogether, with a combined market capitalization of just $34 billion. So it's a small sector — but an interesting one with great profit potential.

REMEMBER

The term *manufactured housing* today can include a fairly wide selection of homes, depending on who you ask. But in this case, think mobile homes. And before you go there, please banish visions of dilapidated, crime-riddled communities from your mind. The properties REITs run tend to be the best possible forms of affordable housing. Which, for the record, is very, very nice.

Let's start by discussing cost. According to the Manufactured Housing Institute (MHI), manufactured housing comes with an average construction cost per square foot that's 10 percent to 35 percent less than a site-built home, excluding land costs. The average rental price for a 1,250-square-foot home was $1,018 per month as of February 2023, while it's $1,723 for a traditional 1,000-square-foot rental. And Sun Communities, one of the three REITs that work in this space, says manufactured homes provide 25 percent more space at about 50 percent less cost per square foot.

Moreover, most manufactured home residents own their own homes outright. They just lease the underlying land at varying monthly rates (generally $200 to $500) from the community's owner. In the case of REIT communities, that means they enjoy home ownership and cheap rent (yes, those two go together in this case) in neighborhoods that generally have the quality and appearance of typical suburban living. Homeowners can even enjoy on-property amenities such as clubhouses, pools, tennis courts, putting greens, exercise rooms, and laundry facilities.

According to another such REIT, Equity Lifestyle Properties, there were approximately 50,000 total manufactured home communities in North America by the end of 2022. And data from the MHI shows that approximately 19 million people, or 6 percent of the U.S. population, live in them.

Some of these neighborhoods cater only to seniors; others are open to all ages. It's important to note that the latter has shown a trend in declining occupancy rates. The larger industry has also grappled with a substantial multiyear decline in new home shipments, which is a key indicator of industry health. Then again, turnover rates have been low, leaving the business model itself stable to the point of even being recession-resistant.

REMEMBER

The average tenant stays in a mobile home community for about 14 years, come economic boom or economic bust. If anything, demand can increase during recessions. These homes don't appreciate like traditional houses do, but they're cheap and convenient while still affording permanency. They're cost-effective for community owners too, who do have to worry about keeping up the grounds and common facilities, as well as paying property taxes, it's true. But actual home maintenance falls squarely on their tenants' financial shoulders.

Better yet, overbuilding has rarely been an issue thanks to how difficult it is to get properties zoned. And there are long lead times involved in filling these communities, presenting another barrier to entry that protects existing communities' appeal. Both of these facts also present obvious problems for manufactured housing REITs to expand, but they at least have the expertise to make better inroads.

PROPTECH

Manufactured housing REITs are also in a better position to utilize cutting-edge technology to drive tenant interest and operation efficiencies. Equity Lifestyle and Sun Communities each provide prospective customers with interactive virtual tours to preview their respective communities. They've also implemented online check-in functionality to enhance customer experience with front-desk wait time, reduce contact at check-in and expedite entry to go straight to assigned sites.

Sun Communities has branched out into offering RV parks and marinas. And Equity Lifestyle owns 221 RV communities and 23 marinas in addition to its core portfolio of manufactured housing communities. All told, the sector has returned an average of 12.8 percent per year over the last decade.

The essential shelter play: Single-family rentals

There are just two single-family rental (SFR) REITs. Together they account for 2 percent of the U.S. equity REIT universe. American Homes 4 Rent owns more than 59,000 single-family properties, and Invitation Homes owns more than 80,000.

One of the newest sectors to emerge, SFR REITs were born out of the Great Recession (2008–2009) and the wave of subprime foreclosures it triggered. Seeing an opportunity emerge, a new class of institutional rental operators began buying distressed properties in bulk. And while it initially seemed like a risky idea dependent on a temporary situation, time, complete with the COVID-19 pandemic, is proving it to be very sustainable so far. People who want whole houses in nice, traditional neighborhoods have been able to easily find and rent them instead of facing rejection after rejection from intense competition and mortgage rates.

With that kind of demand in play, it's no wonder the roughly $5 trillion single-family rental market remains highly fragmented. Large-scale institutional rental operators, including REITs, own just 250,000 of the estimated 15 million rental homes across the United States. That's roughly 1.5 percent of the existing stock.

SFR REITs naturally concentrate on markets that are experiencing the strongest economic growth at any given time. This has shown most notably in the Sunbelt region, though even then there are specific qualifications that need to be met. Mom-and-pop landlords can have a second home they rent out anywhere. In that, they're comparable to Airbnb hosts. But that's not the case with institutional owners in this sector. Apartment buildings, yes; single-family rentals, no. Ideally then, they want to buy up or build up entire communities at a time to better achieve scale and keep costs down.

Here are some other contrasts to note between the two very similar yet distinct sector concepts:

>> Typical operating margins for SFR REITs are around 65 percent, largely due to increased maintenance and turnover costs. But apartment REITs incur about 20 percent in common-area expenses and average 70 percent for their operating margins.

>> Annual turnover rates of single-family rentals average roughly 30 percent compared to the 50 percent rate for apartments.

>> Property taxes, which are generally linked to home values, are the single largest (and growing) expense item for SFR REITs. They're lesser for apartment REITs.

In a Class by Themselves: Specialty REITs

In addition to all the diversity discussed in Chapters 6 and 7 so far, the world of equity REITs also includes the following subsectors:

>> **Ground-lease:** A REIT that rents out land to a tenant who is allowed to build and operate on it for a set (typically lengthy) amount of time until the land and everything on it goes back to the REIT.

>> **Sustainable energy:** A REIT that works to meet the needs of the end-user without compromising the ability of future generations to meet their own needs.

>> **RV storage:** A REIT that rents out space for people to safely park their recreational vehicles and boats.

>> **Infrastructure:** A REIT that owns the underlying structure (defined as real estate) a company needs to function.

And who knows? Maybe we'll see REITs someday soon that specialize in airport terminals, jet hangers, sports stadiums, or even railroads. The opportunity set is significant in both scope and size. Already, allocations to listed infrastructure such as solar, wind towers, fiber, and energy have been on the rise in recent years amid growing demand for real assets that offer relatively predictable cash flows and the potential for attractive real returns.

In the meantime, the following sections describe already established sectors and subsectors that are making names for themselves in real time.

Farming REITs

There are two farming REITs, Gladstone Land and Farmland Partners, which represent a combined market capitalization of around $1.3 billion. That's a small fraction of the $2.7 trillion total farm production in the United States, 80 percent of which is privately owned. That makes this sector extremely fragmented.

REMEMBER

That might sound like a negative, but the asset class it's built on is extremely stable. Farming is attractive as a real estate play due to its low volatility, low correlation to other asset classes, and typical hedge against inflation. In other words, it doesn't tend to be as subject to market irrationality as so many other assets, including the ten-year U.S. Treasury bond, S&P 500, gold, and the Dow Jones REIT Index.

Billboard REITs

There are two billboard REITs: Lamar Advertising Company and Outfront Media. They make up a combined market capitalization of around $1.4 billion, with Lamar being the dominant player by far. Both became REITs in 2014, though Lamar was a company way before that point. Outfront, however, spun off of CBS before laws were restructured to prevent such things, as described in Chapter 3.

Clear Channel is another large billboard owner that could very well become a REIT sometime soon. It even began providing REIT-specific metrics in recent quarterly reports. Because it won't be spinning its real estate off, it stands a good chance of achieving that classification if it's really serious about it. But it has another advantage on its side in this space: It already owns and operates billboards.

The legislation surrounding these giant signs creates an almost impenetrable barrier against would-be competitors. Yet it's also very damaging for current owners. Since 1965, this has been an intensely regulated industry that makes it exceptionally complicated to expand. The majority of signage found along federal highways was grandfathered into that onerous legislation. In other words, what exists now has largely existed for decades — almost as long as REITs themselves have been around. Any new construction permits are very difficult to come by.

Even upgrading or improving existing signs can be difficult. It's true that digital billboards have been increasingly dotting the national landscape. Yet there are far fewer out there than there could be due to the legal demands around establishing them. Some cities require landlords to remove two or three existing billboards for every digital asset implemented.

Like cell tower REITs, their billboard brethren own the structures themselves. But they rent the land beneath, often from individual property owners, for 5 to 15 years at a time. Speaking of such, it's not uncommon to find cell tower businesses renting space from billboards.

Cannabis REITs

There are four cannabis REITs: two equity and two mortgage. And yes, by *cannabis*, I mean marijuana.

The Federal Bureau of Investigation still classifies cannabis as a Schedule I controlled substance under the Controlled Substances Act of 1970. Under federal law, possessing, cultivating, producing, and distributing marijuana remains illegal. But states are increasingly ignoring that law — without repercussions — and implementing their own concerning the controversial plant. This has led to a whole lot of businesses beginning, from shops to suppliers to growers . . . to REITs.

As of this writing, 44 U.S. states and Washington, D.C., have legalized cannabis for medical use, adult use, or both. Therefore, a large majority of the U.S. population now has some access to marijuana. Moreover, a majority of Americans reportedly support that access. In 1969, only 12 percent of U.S. adults supported legalization. In 2000, that figure increased to 31 percent. In 2013, it rose slightly above 50 percent. And by most reports, it continues to climb today.

THE C-CORP REIT SPIN LOOPHOLE CLOSED

As I first mention in Chapter 3 and again earlier in this chapter, several C-corporations converted to REITs in the past. These moves helped create entirely new sectors and opened up numerous dividend opportunities for investors to choose from.

Restaurants, casinos, and retailers were especially eager to go for it. They would keep their business operations as-is but spin off their real estate holdings into a separate entity altogether. This helped them make quick money and simplify their operations, but that window of opportunity turned out to be short-lived. On December 18, 2015, President Barack Obama signed the Consolidated Appropriations Act, which contains the Protecting Americans From Tax Hikes (PATH) Act. And that was a game changer.

On the one hand, there were significant reforms included that now make foreign investments in REITs more attractive. And existing REITs won out elsewhere in the legislation as well. It was prospective REITs that lost out. Because companies are now generally ineligible to participate in tax-free spinoffs either as distributing or controlled corporations. There are only two exceptions:

- If both the distributing and controlled corporation are REITs

- If the distributing corporation was a REIT during the entire three-year period (ending on the date of the distribution), the controlled corporation was a taxable REIT subsidiary (TRS) of the REIT during the entire period, or the REIT owned at least 80 percent of the total number of outstanding shares of any class during the entire period

I'll say it again to drive the point home: It's now almost impossible for an existing business to separate its real estate operations into a stand-alone REIT without incurring significant tax liability. The reason: REIT spinoffs were too popular, which was eroding the corporate tax base — just one more example of it always being about the money.

Chapter **8**

Putting on Your REIT Analyst Hat

S o far in this book, I've been helping you build a solid understanding of the REIT landscape and have shown you a road map of how to successfully navigate through it. You've explored whole REIT segments along the way, including the various REIT categories and which REITs are available in which countries.

In this chapter, I provide more information on how to approach and analyze individual REITs, including how to calculate property values, assess REIT earnings metrics, and understand what to look for on a REIT balance sheet. With this information, you'll have the necessary tools to choose the best REIT investment for you and profit from those choices. Admittedly, this chapter includes terms and calculations that might seem complex at first. Don't worry; I walk you through them step by step to help you become not just a REIT investor but a smart REIT investor.

Becoming a Virtual Rent Collector

You can successfully argue that REITs are more than real estate. But it's just as true to say that REITs make all — or almost all — of their money from real estate. Therefore, understanding the value of a piece of land and/or the buildings on top of it is exceptionally important when evaluating a REIT. Let's start by defining a few important terms about property values that REIT analysts throw around all the time, and with good reason.

TIP

I'd love to say that management always knows what it's doing when it makes a new purchase. And I can remind you that most REITs are notoriously conservative in nature when it comes to how they manage their businesses. With that said, they're still run by humans and humans are known for making mistakes — some more than others. So while you want to invest in companies with good to great management, double-checking the facts and figures they publish is rarely a bad idea.

The scoop on net operating income

For one thing, you'll want to know about the very important concept of *net operating income* (NOI). It's used to measure net cash: a company's total cash amount minus its liabilities. In real estate terms, NOI boils down to property-produced income — including recurring rent — minus property-specific operating expenses, such as real estate taxes, landscaping, insurance, utilities, and yearly maintenance requirements.

Here's how it's written out:

Real Estate Revenue – Operating Expenses = **Net Operating Income (NOI)**

What NOI doesn't include is corporate items like general and administrative (G&A) expenses or those expenses that come from interest. Depreciation and unnecessary upgrades (even if they add value) don't factor in either. NOI is supposed to simply indicate how much you should make by owning and leasing a typical commercial property in a typical year.

NOI should usually grow 2 percent to 3 percent annually, keeping in line with normal inflation. However, for the record, if you're reading this during a time of sky-high inflation, try not to laugh at that statement. Or cry.

Understanding cap rates

Net operating income also helps real estate investors figure out a property's capitalization rate, which can then be used to figure out its value.

A capitalization rate, abbreviated *cap rate*, measures a property's yield in a one-year time frame without worrying about any debts it might come with. In short, it provides the property's natural, unlevered rate of return, calculated as:

NOI ÷ Current Market Value = **Capitalization Rate**

If a property is worth $10 million on the market, and it generates $400,000 in NOI the first year, its cap rate is 4 percent. A buyer could therefore look forward to about a 4 percent annual operating cash flow (its as-expected income) under those conditions.

If you're pausing right about now to ask whether 4 percent is a good cap rate, you're no dummy. Though I do have to warn you that the answer is rather obnoxious: *It depends.*

TECHNICAL STUFF

Higher cap rates typically indicate greater risks with greater possibilities of higher returns. But what constitutes an uncomfortably high amount varies from sector to sector, location to location, property to property, and even investor to investor. Economic factors such as inflation, interest rates, and gross domestic product (GDP) all can and do easily affect cap rates as well. That's why you have to expect a cap rate for an apartment building in San Francisco to be very different from a comparable property in Cleveland — perhaps even a whole percentage point off.

I told you it was an obnoxious answer. But here's how to help navigate through it anyway: Compare the cap rate you're evaluating with the cap rates a REIT has paid before and/or those of similar assets in the area. That can give you a much better idea of whether the new purchase or potential purchase is a good one or not.

Internal rates of return on review

Another important term to understand is a REIT's *internal rate of return,* or IRR. The IRR is the annual rate of growth that an investment is expected to generate. This is based on calculating the income you expect to receive until you sell. When each receipt and contribution is discounted to net present value, it should all add up to zero.

The formula used to calculate the IRR looks like this:

$$0 = NPV = \sum_{t=1}^{T} \frac{C_t}{(1+IRR)^t} - C_0$$

Where:

C_t = Net cash inflow during the period t

C_0 = Total initial investment costs

IRR = The internal rate of return

t = The number of time periods

TIP

If looking at that equation makes you relive some particularly painful math classes in high school or college, take a deep breath. You don't have to solve it by yourself as long as you have the required data and a spreadsheet software program. Microsoft Excel, for example, includes a preset feature to calculate IRR, which definitely makes things easier. In fact, most people use modern tech offerings to help calculate IRR; this cheat isn't something you need to hide as your dirty little secret.

What's less convenient is that, unless you're looking back on a real estate asset that you already sold, IRR is based on a series of assumptions. For instance, you have to make educated guesses about future occupancy, NOI growth, and future market value when you go to sell. With that said, let's face it: Life is filled with assumptions. And an educated analysis of what your internal rate of return could and should be is an important part of making REIT investing more predictable.

INTERNAL GROWTH DRIVERS (RENT BUMPS)

Many property owners can achieve above-average increases in rental revenue by focusing on tenants' needs and abilities to pay higher rental rates. These methods include percentage rent; rent bumps; and expense sharing, which is also known as *cost recovery*.

As I point out in Chapter 6, percentage-rent clauses in retail and some healthcare leases allow property owners to benefit from tenant revenues that come in above a preset amount. For instance, a contract could say that a grocery store will pay 3 percent of its annual sales if those sales exceed $5 million. Of course, this is something a sane tenant will agree to only if the property and location are particularly attractive. Market conditions also have to be optimal at the time of signing, base rent needs to be reasonable, and the landlord needs to have a good reputation for keeping its properties relevant.

Rent bumps, meanwhile, provide built-in rental increases at certain points in the lease timeline to add built-in NOI growth. These can be fixed dollar amounts already known at signing or a percentage based on the consumer price index (CPI) or some other inflationary index. Office and industrial property owners are especially known to use this feature, thus providing built-in same-store NOI growth. And some healthcare and retail REITs use them, too.

Finally, expense sharing, or cost recovery, happens when each tenant pays a share of whatever property expenses occur during the year, such as janitorial services or security. It might show up as a *cost-sharing* or *common area maintenance (CAM) recovery* clause in the lease and can sometimes include improvement expenses or advertising as well as maintenance.

These additions improve landlord NOI and therefore earnings, and tend to smooth out annual operating costs into more manageable, anticipated expenses.

REIT Earnings Metrics

You can measure a company's value in several different ways, but most investors want to know about a company's streams of income and cash flows. The Securities and Exchange Commission (SEC) requires that all publicly traded companies file audited financial statements complete with specific details as defined by generally accepted accounting principles (GAAP), the approved U.S. government standard for financial calculations.

Most companies highlight their net income as a key measure of profitability. However, REITs run a different category of business that requires a different kind of calculation. So while REITs still have to report net income, net income per share, and unaudited net income, those terms just aren't as useful in determining their cash flow and dividend safety.

For starters, real estate depreciation is always treated as an expense in accounting. Yet real estate appreciates in value as long as it's in a good location and is well-managed. It generally rises due to

>> Inflation and increasing construction costs

>> Rising rents and operating income

>> Property upgrades

>> The finite nature of available land

REMEMBER

That's why net income under GAAP is meaningless as a measure of cash flow. You have to add back real estate depreciation into the equation to make it matter.

REITs need to make other adjustments, too, like subtracting from their net income any capital gains income recorded from property sales, which, for the record, is usually determined after straight-lining contractual rental income over the term of the lease. By *straight-lining,* I mean that the entire term's base rent is lumped together and then divided by the number of months involved.

Suppose you have annual rent increases of 2 percent a year for a five-year rental contract. By the fifth year, rents will be about 8.25 percent more than they were in the first. So under GAAP, you even it out by showing rents of just over 4 percent more than you actually collected in the first year. This results in an accrued rent receivable (rent that's due but not collected yet) that grows over the first half of the lease and then declines in the second half.

Even then, though, it's not the most accurate of assessments because a dollar in the first year will almost certainly be worth more than in later years due to inflation.

FFO to the rescue

To help deal with how poorly net income addressed real estate realities, Nareit (the National Association of Real Estate Investment Trusts) adopted *funds from operations,* or FFO, in 1991. Quickly popular in the industry, FFO measures cash generated from regular, consistent real estate–related business activities.

Admittedly, FFO still doesn't completely compensate for straight-lined rent, leaving FFO per-share growth lower than cash flows would suggest. The omission of not deducting this clear non-cash inflation of revenue may have been because straight-lined rent GAAP adoption occurred after FFO finally was formally recognized in 2003.

Regardless, here's how you compute FFO:

Net Income + Depreciation + Amortization – Gains on Sales of Property = **Funds From Operations (FFO)**

Again, this works much better than net income. However, it still fails to remove certain seldom occurring items or non-cash occurrences: balance-sheet expenses such as capital depreciation, and investment gains and losses that don't involve cash payments. Many investors came to realize that, despite how much better FFO was than the previous metrics, something more was needed to properly report recurring cash flow – something that can be used to support dividend payments. Recognizing this, many analysts and some companies began to report *adjusted funds from operations* (AFFO).

The dawn of AFFO

Adjusted funds from operations (AFFO) is another way to measure a real estate company's earnings by making several adjustments to FFO, the biggest of which subtracts recurring capital expenditures, also known as *capex,* from the total. This acknowledges that not all depreciation is non-cash in nature.

You see, landlords generally make improvements to their real estate each time they sign on a new tenant. And these improvements generally last the tenant's entire stay. Then again, renewing a lease typically involves an added tenant improvements allowance. This all begs the question then of how much real estate companies have to shell out every year to retain their portfolio quality and tenant occupancy.

AFFO tries to account for that. But, admittedly, it can account for that in different ways. There's no sector-wide definition or calculation I can point to, and it isn't sanctioned by the SEC. Therefore, it isn't always consistently reported or analyzed. That said, AFFO disclosure is very helpful to determine a company's high-level estimate of normalized cash flow per share. Here's a common calculation you can use:

FFO – Straight-Lined Rents – Recurring Capital Expenditure + Equity-Based Compensation + Lease Intangibles + Deferred Financing Cost = **Adjusted Funds From Operations (AFFO)**

I want to point out *lease intangibles* especially. This term emerged around 2004 to reflect the cost of procuring tenants. Prior to that, it was simply chalked up as part of the valuation process.

Deferred financing costs are another non-cash factor. These are the expenses involved in bank or bond financing, such as fees and commissions paid to those involved. In this case, though, they do get paid upfront and are then subject to non-cash expenses in order to qualify for AFFO purposes. Really, this is all about timing. There's a clear cash component involved that reoccurs as bonds and bank notes mature and are replaced.

REMEMBER

Equity-based compensation also qualifies as non-cash, though the dividends allocated to it do not.

A worthwhile "FAD" to keep in mind

Funds available for distribution (FAD) is another way to evaluate a REIT's operations. FAD is the amount of cash a REIT retains to pay its common shareholder dividends, and it accounts for non-recurring capital expenditures.

While there is no standardized method for calculating it, many REITs use the following equation, adjusting the FFO value for straight-lined rents, non-cash items, and recurring real estate-related expenses:

FFO – Recurring Capital Expenditure = **Funds Available for Distribution (FAD)**

REMEMBER

To calculate AFFO, REITs deduct the amortization of real estate-related capex from FFO. But to calculate FAD and CAD (cash available for distribution), REITs tend to also deduct non-recurring, normal, and recurring capex. In addition, they can deduct repayments of principal on mortgage loans.

The biggest problem here is that, once again, there's no definite definition of how to calculate FAD or CAD. So while some might find it superior to other forms of evaluating REIT earnings, it's still not perfect.

Calculating NAV

Still other institutional investors and analysts think a REIT's net asset value (NAV) is the superior assessment to go with. To calculate a REIT's NAV, you first figure out that REIT's standard cap rate, then apply it to a 12-month forward-looking estimate of NOI:

Gross Income – Operating Expenses = **NOI**

This means you're including the following factors into the financial picture:

>> Estimated value of land

>> Development in process

>> Equity in consolidated joint ventures

>> Approximate value of fee income streams, non-rental revenue businesses, and other investments

Next, debt and other obligations are subtracted along with other operating expenses, including adjustments made for government-subsidized financing. If you want to calculate NAV per share — which also considers *in the money* (above-market-price) options, operating partnerships units, and convertible securities — you'd simply deduct the dollar amount of outstanding preferred stock from there.

Here's how you calculate for NAV per share:

$$NAV = \frac{(Assets - Liabilities - Preferreds)}{Number\ of\ shares\ outstanding}$$

TIP

NAV is essentially akin to liquidation value: how much a company would make if it went out of business and sold all its assets in the process. Keep in mind though that this approach is subjective, since anyone can assign any cap rate to the NOI.

WARNING

One issue with that is how REITs are rarely liquidated. So investors should think twice before paying more than 100 percent of NAV per share for a stock — unless there are strong reasons to think the situation will improve from there, such as low cost of capital, robust FFO, or dividend growth forecasted.

Appendix B outlines the four-step process for calculating a REIT's NAV.

Putting Weighted Average Cost of Capital on the Scale

Now that you have an understanding of REIT earnings metrics, let me explain the important and often misunderstood concept known as *weighted average cost of capital* (WACC).

As I point out previously, REITs cannot retain much of their earnings for reinvestment. They have to give at least 90 percent away in the form of dividends. So if they want to grow through acquisitions or new developments, they often have to find the necessary cash elsewhere. They may do this by selling existing assets, contributing some of their properties to new joint ventures, or taking out loans. But for the most part, they usually sell new shares to investors when they want to expand externally. In which case, you need to know the real cost of doing so.

You can evaluate this cost by looking at a REIT's nominal cost of equity capital, which is the REIT's expected per-share FFO for the next 12 months. When issuing new equity, this per-share FFO should be adjusted for the new shares that are issued and the expected incremental FFO earned from the investment (of the proceeds) from such new share issuances.

Or you can look at the true, or long-term, cost of equity capital, which considers such dilution over longer time periods. It estimates shareholders' total return expectations (share price plus dividends) on their invested capital.

WARNING

Either way, understand that the cost of equity capital rises as the REIT takes on more debt (something I discuss later on in this chapter). Financial backers and investors expect higher returns to compensate for higher risk. That's just how it goes.

Despite the importance of determining a REIT's true cost of capital, there seems to be no general agreement on how to calculate it. So here's what I advise: Don't just focus on an acquisition's initial FFO boost but also on its probable longer-term IRR. Ask yourself if the latter exceeds the REIT's estimated weighted average cost of capital, which combines the cost of equity and the cost of debt.

REMEMBER

Cost advantage is a big deal for any kind of business. When a company can manufacture its products or provide its services at lower cost, they can pass those savings on to their customers, who are then more likely to buy more — from them, not their competition. Here's the secret formula to achieving these fatter profit margins:

Capitalization Rate – Cost of Capital = **Spread/Profit**

TIP

REITs should never take advantage of even reasonably attractive asset opportunities if their cost of capital exceeds likely returns. As an analyst, I pay very close attention to WACC and compare it to companies' cap rates on new assets. You should too.

Suppose the fictional XYZ REIT has a 5 percent weighted average cost of capital from a 6 percent cost of equity capital and a 4 percent cost of debt capital. Now it wants to buy a portfolio of properties at a 6 percent cap rate. That looks like an attractive WACC, at least at first glance. You always want to assess other details as well.

But suppose its cost of equity is 8 percent, and the cap rate is 6 percent. This would give it a 7 percent WACC and therefore have a negative investment spread of 100 basis points. So even if XYZ borrows 50 percent of the purchase price at a 6 percent interest rate, the deal makes no sense.

TIP

Generally, higher costs of capital force companies to invest in riskier investments, though you shouldn't automatically shun companies or sectors because they seem to compare unfavorably to others. Again, you don't ever want to see negative spreads. That would almost certainly be a sign of incompetent management.

But cannabis REITs, for instance, work with a sector in which tenants automatically have poor credit or limited credit availability. And skilled nursing REITs work with industry-specific rent coverage that also results in higher WACCs.

Check out Appendix A for more information on assessing a REIT's WACC.

The Cost of Buying In and Buying Up

Truly entrepreneurial management teams are always looking for ways to improve their investment returns. And sale and reinvestment strategies can be highly effective.

There may be short-term costs in terms of temporary earnings reduction, admittedly. Higher-quality purchases, for instance, often trade at lower entry yields and cap rates than the lower-quality assets REITs often sell to raise funds. However, the long-term benefits are usually more than worthwhile when handled properly.

Along those lines, there are "small" investments REITs can make, buying up a property here for $5 million or a portfolio of them for $1 billion. Or they can go big and swallow up entire competitors. As a REIT investor, I tend to evaluate such mergers and acquisitions (M&A) through the lens of an investment banker, not as a REIT analyst.

TIP

While M&A can bring meaningful value to REIT stakeholders, it's often a guessing game. So I don't automatically consider M&A to be a catalyst for future earnings.

That doesn't mean that you should ignore such deal announcements, especially when there have been dozens of these REIT deals over the last decade. In 2021 alone, there was $99.4 billion in activity; and in 2022, that figure was $83 billion (see Figure 8-1). These two years showcase an especially active period thanks to the ripple effects of the COVID-19 pandemic on the real estate markets, low interest rates, private equity's voracious appetite, the acceleration of tech disruption, and activist activity.

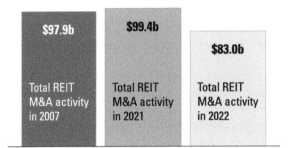

FIGURE 8-1:
Total REIT M&A
activity in 2007,
2021, and 2022.

$97.9b — Total REIT M&A activity in 2007

$99.4b — Total REIT M&A activity in 2021

$83.0b — Total REIT M&A activity in 2022

Here are three of the biggest company-on-company moves from that period just to give you an idea of how large these takeovers can get:

>> Kimco's $20 billion merger with Weingarten

>> Prologis' acquisition of Duke Realty for $25.4 billion

>> Realty Income's all-stock acquisition of VEREIT to create a combined company with an enterprise value of $50 billion

While two of these deals (Kimco-Weingarten and Realty-VEREIT) were between retail REITs and the third came from the industrial sector, the M&A fervor also involved offices, senior housing, residential, data centers, and cell towers.

Looking at REIT Balance Sheets

When assessing a REIT's profitability, it is also important to look at its balance sheet. I already brought up how cost of capital is tied to the cost of equity and its debt. But how does that debt break down?

For instance, many REITs offer publicly traded common equity, preferred equity, and bonds (the latter of which I discuss at the end of this chapter). Each has its own risk-return profile. And each can be used or combined to create a customized risk and return profile for your particular portfolio. Figure 8-2 illustrates the capital structure of a typical REIT.

Personally, I'm a fan of REIT debt in the credit space, which is referred to as *preferred stock*, though the bulk of my investments are in regular stocks. I explore both in the following sections.

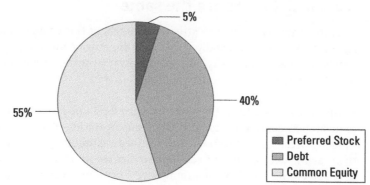

Typical REIT Capital Structure

5%
40%
55%

Preferred Stock
Debt
Common Equity

FIGURE 8-2:
Typical REIT
capital structure.

Conservative and consistent dividends

Earlier I discuss how REITs are known for their dividends. That's partially due to the inflationary nature of rents and property values, but much more so because they must pay out at least 90 percent of their taxable income to shareholders. As a result, REIT common equity, or regular stock, dividends tend to be higher as a percentage of free cash flow than those you'll find from other companies. And REIT shares normally trade at higher dividend yields.

But here's what you might not know. In general, according to Ned Davis Research, "companies that grew or initiated a dividend have experienced the highest returns relative to other stocks since 1973" and "with significantly less volatility."

From 1973 to 2021, dividend income's contribution to the S&P 500 Index's total return averaged 40 percent. And REIT dividends can be even more effective, comprising more than half their respective stocks' returns. From the early 1990s through 2022, U.S. REITs increased their payouts at a 6 percent average annual rate.

It's true that many REITs cut their dividend payouts in 2020 due to the economic shutdowns during the COVID-19 pandemic. However, as conditions — and cash flow — improved across nearly all property sectors, cash dividends made a strong comeback. And U.S. REITs should continue to see their income increase, which means their legal distribution rate remains above the level required by law. Combined, those two factors almost always force REITs to raise their dividends.

It's freeing to see dividend checks hit your account every quarter or even every month, depending on the stock. Knowing that money is on its way regardless of whether you're in the office or not is psychologically soothing, no matter whether you're going to spend it right away or reinvest it.

Not all dividends are the same

With that said, as I hope I've stressed throughout this chapter, not every REIT is right for you. And some really aren't right for anyone until they get their balance sheets in order. That's why you should always consider their dividend-payout-to-AFFO ratios.

TIP

As they issue new equity, the best-managed REITs make sure to retain money for acquisitions, developments, and other opportunities. This is smart, long-term thinking because, in the end, using retained capital for such activities is cheaper than raising debt capital or selling new shares. In addition, it's always good to have something saved up for a rainy day — or an unexpected months-long interruption to business as normal.

That's why a modest AFFO payout ratio is actually a good thing. It acts as insurance against unexpected events and opportunities alike that might cause temporary downturns in free cash flow. While it varies from sector to sector, 65 percent to 75 percent typically suffices just fine. Net-lease REITs do run higher at 85 percent, however, since they're working with longer-duration contracts and require lower tenant improvements and leasing commissions.

WARNING

No matter how traditionally safe REITs can be, it's important to remember that they can run into distressed credit markets and other undesirable situations. Real estate investors also need to understand that there could be unforeseen lawsuits, tenant bankruptcies, and other negatively impactful possibilities. So once again, don't fall in love with any investable company or category. It won't fall back in love with you. It can't.

What happens when hardships come but a REIT doesn't cut its dividend and even raises it? Those stalwart stocks should be commended and perhaps invested in as well. They planned. They prepared. And they came out ahead as a result. That's what I call a SWAN (sleep well at night) stock.

Watch out for sucker yields

The financial crisis of 2008 and economic shutdowns of 2020 came as major surprises to most. I certainly didn't see either coming. Yet there were warning signs, especially with the financial crisis. There usually are.

The same goes for individual investment entities operating under individual circumstances. When a REIT pays out too much of its AFFO in dividends, it opens up more risk of cutting its dividend in the future, with its stock price taking a likely hit as well. I and many of my fellow analysts call this recipe for disaster a sucker yield.

When a company pays a dividend beyond its earning power, it's eroding its own capital. And while each one has its own particular amount that it can or can't sustain, normal REIT dividend yields fall in the 3 percent to 5 percent range. Six percent during a time of rising interest rates such as in 2023 aren't an automatic reason for concern. But if a company pays an 8 percent, 9 percent, 10 percent, or higher yield, there's a good chance it can't sustain it. Moreover, it probably already has a track record of cutting its payouts. And its balance sheet will probably feature considerable debt, or leverage, as well.

REMEMBER

That's not always true, mind you. There are times a perfectly healthy company's stock falls out of favor for some reason, sending its dividend yield skyrocketing. But it's true more often than it's not.

If a REIT earns $1.20 per share in FFO but uses $0.20 for recurring capital expenses, that leaves it with no more than $1.00 for dividend payments. And if it pays out the whole $1.00, it has nothing left — no margin of safety — to expand the business or set aside funds for unforeseen expenses.

As we've already established, that's a problem — a major one.

It's easy to ignore that when the payouts you're promised in the moment are so high relative to the stock price you pay. I am very well aware of how strong the lure of sucker yields can be. But fight it anyway. You don't want any part of them. Not one bit.

REIT preferreds

REIT preferreds aren't as popular as REIT common shares, but they're still well worth considering. They usually come with very attractive spreads and are often unconditionally guaranteed on a senior unsecured basis by current and future subsidiaries.

I first mention preferred stock in Chapter 4, but it's worth discussing in further detail here since they factor into balance-sheet considerations. Preferred stock occupies a unique space between debt and equity, displaying certain attributes of both bonds and common stock. They're almost always senior to their common counterparts — meaning that their holders get paid before regular shareholders in the case of financial difficulty, though after bonds. They offer fixed quarterly dividends but, unlike bonds, aren't guaranteed by the issuer to repay a specific amount on a specific date.

Most preferred stocks have either very long maturities or are perpetual. And, under normal market conditions, they offer lower volatility than common shares, not to mention much higher yields. In addition, most preferred stock is issued by large, investment-grade, stable issuers that don't usually throw their shareholders for any loops.

You'll most often find these offerings labeled as fixed-rate cumulative redeemable preferred stock. With that said, there are plenty out there that are non-cumulative. In those cases, if dividends are suspended for some reason, the issuer isn't obligated to pay back any missing ones. That's why banks like them better and investors do not.

TIP

Another thing to note is how many preferred stocks convert to floating-rate coupons after five years. This provides their shareholders with some protection against rising interest rates. And always keep in mind that preferred stocks may be convertible into common stock, either by the holder's decision or upon maturity.

Here's another thing to keep in mind about REIT preferreds: They have some of the best legal contracts — known as covenants — in the investment-grade debt space. They do a bang-up job reporting on them, too, often focusing on the following metrics:

>> Unencumbered asset coverage of unsecured debt

>> Maximum amount of total debt

>> Maximum amount of secure debt

>> Minimum income coverage of debt service

The financial covenants often contained in REIT bonds help protect investors at all levels of the capital structure by limiting the amount of leverage a REIT can take on while simultaneously helping to ensure that unsecured assets cover unsecured debt. These details — and much more — can be found in each offering's prospectus. So make sure to read them if you're interested in buying any up.

Those writeups are not something to take for granted.

What a Strong REIT Balance Sheet Looks Like

When considering a REIT's overall health, you should keep in mind the following:

>> A REIT should only carry a modest amount of debt relative to its total market cap — the total market value of its assets — or its earnings before interest, taxes, depreciation, and amortization (EBITDA). This is a REIT's debt-to-market cap ratio.

>> Operating cash flows should be more than enough to cover interest payments on that debt and other fixed charges. This is a REIT's debt-to-asset value ratio.

Most of the time, you're going to see the debt-to-market cap ratio calculated by dividing a REIT's debt by the sum of its common equity cap, preferred stock, and debt, like this:

Total Debt ÷ (Common Stock Equity + Preferred Stock Equity + Total Debt) = **Debt-to-Market Cap Ratio**

Admittedly, a few analysts base it on estimated asset value instead of share valuation. In which case, the formula looks like this:

Total Debt ÷ Estimated Value of All Assets = **Debt-to-Asset Value Ratio**

This less common calculation has the benefit of being more conservative, for one thing. REITs generally trade at market valuations that are only slightly above their net asset values, after all. This second approach also avoids the rapid fluctuations that can come with debt ratios, since share prices are more volatile than assets. That makes sense since stocks go up and down, often for no good reason at all. And those fluctuations rarely affect a company's actual property value.

On the other hand, the estimated value of assets can be very subjective. That's why most experts don't bother with debt-to-asset value at all.

Another consideration you should keep in mind is that both debt-to-market and debt-to-asset paint rosier pictures than they should when the economic sun is shining on REIT stocks and properties alike. The unfortunate era of 2008–2009 proved how problematic things can get. As soon as the crisis hit, these valuations dropped dramatically, and debt-to-market cap and debt-to-asset value ratios spiked.

TIP

That's why I advise looking at debt to expected EBITDA as well, particularly for the past 12 months or the 12 months to come. This highlights a REIT's debt levels against its cash flow before interest payments, a ratio that tends to be more stable. If you see debt-to-EBITDA ratio of 4x, that's pretty conservative. Five to seven is typically an acceptable range, and anything above 8x is getting more risky.

Interest coverage ratios

Another way to analyze debt levels is to look at how much a REIT's EBITDA exceeds its debt-specific interest payments. This is known as the *interest coverage ratio*.

Suppose that the fictional Sparkle City REIT has annual EBITDA of $14 million. But it carries $100 million in debt, which costs it $7 million in annual interest expenses. In that case, its interest coverage ratio would be $14 million divided by $7 million, or 2x.

An interest coverage ratio that's significantly below 2x will often be cause for concern. Unfortunately, I can't give you a definitive here, because there are always exceptions to the rule. But a red flag should go up nonetheless if you see something so low. Make sure to analyze it accordingly.

Another focus should be on recurring financial commitments like dividend payment obligations on outstanding preferred stock or scheduled debt repayments. The latter is known as the *fixed-charge coverage ratio,* and it assesses how well a REIT's current EBITDA can cover its debt obligations.

As with the interest coverage and debt-to-EBITDA ratios already mentioned, this means analysts (including novice ones) aren't distracted by periods of stock price or property price volatility. On the negative side, these methods do add unused land, properties under development, and other temporarily non-revenue-producing assets into the picture. They can also inaccurately favor REITs with temporary unusually high rates of return. That's why my suggestion is to examine as many of these formulas as you can to determine how healthy a REIT's balance sheet really is.

Debt maturity

Another important marker of a REIT's health is the length of its debt contracts. REITs will often renew loans once they're due, but sometimes that isn't an option. Sometimes a lender isn't willing or able to accommodate those plans. In which case, the REIT has to look for a new lender. And if a new lender isn't available, they have to figure out how to pay the full amount then and there.

At best, this would mean selling off assets for whatever it can get and/or raising new equity at very dilutive prices. At worst, it can mean bankruptcy. Therefore, the longer the maturity, the less a REIT has to worry about such complications.

And here's another thing to like about long-term debt: It can actually be cheaper to get. This makes sense when you consider the process of financing a car. Your credit rating almost always determines how much interest you pay. And the worse your credit rating, the higher the interest. That's because the lender knows you present more of a risk of not being able to complete your payments.

The same risk factor applies to longer maturities, just in reverse. For one, they give REITs more time to pay back what they owe. But more important, they give

REITs more time to make money off the assets they borrowed in order to pay back what they owe. Add in a company with an excellent balance sheet to begin with, and you've got a situation lenders are willing to reward.

TIP

You'll also want to pay attention to maturity dates and their collective average. As a general rule, it's a bad sign when there are too many loans due at the same time — an indication that management wasn't paying enough attention or was otherwise incapable of keeping things orderly.

BLUE-CHIP REITS: THE BEST OF THE BEST

I'm a big believer in blue-chip REITs — companies that consistently have excellent balance sheets. I can't say there's a dictionary-approved definition of what they are, but here's a checklist of traits they tend to adhere to:

- A track record of effectively deploying available capital to create shareholder value
- A focus on and expertise in one sector
- A deep regional or local market expertise
- A conservative and intelligent dividend policy
- Corporate governance and management worth talking about
- Meaningful insider stock ownership.

Blue-chip REITs don't have to tick off every single one of those items, but they will tick off most. They've been around the real estate block a time or two and had the time to acquire expertise, quality properties, and reputations of dependability. Age might not automatically lend wisdom, but these companies have made the most of their years.

That doesn't mean they'll never experience volatility. They can and almost undoubtedly will. For that matter, they can even fail or fall from their blue-chip pedestals. For example, remember Simon Property Group, a mall REIT I mention in previous chapters? It had an 11-year streak of paying and raising its dividend before the COVID-19 pandemic shutdowns hit. The fact that it had to shut down its properties for months on end was hardly its fault, in which case it wasn't its fault that it had to slash its promised payouts. But the situation still threw the company out of the blue-chip category for the time being. A REIT can't shortchange its shareholders and keep its crown, even if it has no other choice in the matter.

(continued)

(continued)

In other words, don't put your entire lifesavings into a single blue-chip REIT. (Don't do that with any stock, for that matter.) You never know what may happen, even to a company like Federal Realty, which has raised its dividend every year for more than five decades (that's referred to as a *Dividend King*). The past is no guarantee of the future.

It's just that you have a much better chance of making slow and steady stock market gains and getting consistent dividend payouts from blue-chip REITs. And when their share prices do dip or even dive, they tend to recover faster than other-colored competitors. That's why I often advise readers to put unowned blue-chip REITs on their watchlist, because they don't tend to go on sale very often. And why should they when their FFOs and asset values consistently rise over time just like their dividends? Or when they have the respect of not just their peers but also financiers, who are more than happy to court their businesses with great rates?

Blue-chip REITs rarely have the highest dividend yields. And you can usually find other REITs out there that offer better returns in any given year. But what they do provide are total returns that average 7 percent to 8 percent per year. If you're looking for a bedrock to base your portfolio on, you could do a lot worse than a spread of blue-chip REITs.

Variable-rate debt

Variable-rate debt can be a killer on FFO in rising interest rate environments, especially since interest is such a large portion of a REIT's expenses. Yes, interest rates could decline and there are usually indicators of which direction it will go over the short or even mid-term. But there's never any guarantee.

REITs rely on predictable, gradual increases in rental income, so when rates rise too fast, there are limited ways they can deal with the increased debt requirements. These ways can be powerful, mind you. But they remain limited nonetheless. That's why fixed rates are typically the way to go. Exceptions might include times when a REIT wants to open up a short-term line of credit that can be paid off easily through stock offerings, opening up longer-term and fixed-rate debt, or selling assets.

TIP

Out of all the sectors and subsectors, hotels are much better suited to take on variable-rate debt. After all, they tend to perform significantly better when the economy is strong and significantly worse when it's not. And interest rates tend to rise when the economy is strong and sink otherwise. Therefore, variable-rate debt can act as a hedge against downturns, with lower rates partially offsetting lower hotel receipts.

It just depends on how much debt is taken on compared to a REIT's gross asset value or market cap.

REIT credit ratings

Here's one final way to make sure a REIT isn't taking on too much debt: Look at its credit rating, if it has one. Smaller companies might not have one, for the record, and that's okay. It does cost money to get those evaluations done. But seeing a rating by Standard & Poor's, Fitch, Moody's, or some other credible agency does make investing easier. Table 8-1 outlines Standard & Poor's rating hierarchy.

TABLE 8-1   **Standard & Poor's Credit Rating Hierarchy**

Grade	Rating	Comments
Investment	AAA	Highest rating; extremely strong capacity to meet financial commitments
	AA	Very strong capacity to meet financial commitments
	A	Strong capacity to meet financial commitments but somewhat susceptible to adverse economic conditions and changes in circumstances
	BBB	Adequate capacity to meet financial commitments but more subject to adverse economic conditions
	BBB–	Considered lowest investment-grade by market participants
Speculative	BB+	Considered highest speculative-grade by market participants
	BB	Less vulnerable in the near-term but faces major ongoing uncertainties to adverse business, financial, and economic conditions
	B	More vulnerable to adverse business, financial, and economic conditions but currently has the capacity to meet financial commitments
	CCC	Currently vulnerable and dependent on favorable business, financial, and economic conditions to meet financial commitments
	CC	Highly vulnerable; default has not yet occurred but is expected to be a virtual certainty
	C	Currently highly vulnerable to non-payment, and ultimate recovery is expected to be lower than that of higher-rated obligations
	D	Payment default on a financial commitment or breach of an imputed promise; also used when a bankruptcy petition has been filed or similar action taken

TIP

A credit rating of BBB– or above is considered investment-grade. The higher the rating, the easier it is to borrow cheaply. And the easier it is to borrow cheaply, the easier it is to grow.

The Case for Buying Bonds

As I discuss in Chapter 4, when a REIT needs to raise capital, it frequently sells bonds. This form of debt financing comes with a promise to repay the original principal amount, plus interest, over a certain period of time. The exact amount of interest offered directly relates to the company's financial strength and past record of repayment. (This is true of any bond, not just those issued by REITs.)

Take a bond issued by an A-rated REIT. Financial markets and investors have a high degree of confidence that it will repay its loans, and so the company in question can offer a relatively low interest rate as a result. It's a safe play and therefore doesn't need to bend over backwards to attract buyers. On the other hand, a REIT with a high debt load and/or a history of financial problems will have to sweeten its bond offering with more substantial yields.

Those higher-risk, higher-reward opportunities can pay off, mind you. But you want to know everything you can about any investment before you put your hard-earned money into it. Fortunately, there are third-party ratings agencies that assess each one that hits the market.

To get a better idea of what REIT bonds are and whether they're a good fit for your portfolio, let's compare them with REIT common shares. You should be aware of four major differences:

>> **Capital stack position:** Bonds fall into the debt portion of a company's financial factors. Common shares, however, are equity. This means that bonds have automatic priority repayment over them. If disaster strikes and the REIT falls to pieces, bondholders are made whole first on the list of holders. Most of the time, this is a non-issue and everyone gets paid what they're supposed to when they're supposed to. But when extreme circumstances do hit, common shareholders are lucky if they get a penny back since preferred stocks – which I discuss earlier in this chapter – come next on the totem pole.

>> **Returns:** Because bonds present less risk, they also offer less reward. Returns here are mostly made up of income, with little chance for major capital appreciation. Regular REIT returns are much heavier on the income, with capital appreciation being a garnish, not the main meal.

>> **Value drivers:** A bond's value is driven by market interest rates, the issuer's cash flow, and the market's belief that the company can repay its debt as promised. A common share's value can move on sentiment — whether positive or negative — in the moment. But long term, it's all about the cash flow produced from the REIT's portfolio of properties.

>> **Terms and Conditions:** Bonds have a fixed maturity date. The issuer must return investors' capital at that point. Common stock, however, is open-ended. It's bought, held, or sold according to the investor's whims and the market conditions when that whim occurs.

TIP

REIT bonds are quite a lot more boring than REIT common shares. But for the risk-adverse investor who can't bear the thought of losing money, boring can be better. If you're near retirement or are already retired, for instance, you might not be in a great place to ride out stock market volatility the way younger crowds can. In which case, a balance of stocks and bonds might be your best bet.

Chapter **9**

Separating the Wheat from the Chaff

I n Chapter 3, I explain the five most recognized reasons to own REITs: diversification, transparency, liquidity, performance, and dividends. What I purposely don't mention is management, a factor that does so much to hold those five reasons together. In short, the folks who run REITs are pretty important.

You may have heard the phrase *separating the wheat from the chaff* before. It comes from the age-old practice of separating seeds from shells and husks: the edible from inedible. It's a great analogy to what good management does with a REIT: harvesting everything as it comes up, culling what needs to be culled, and keeping what needs to be kept for optimal results.

The same goes for outside analysis of the companies you're considering. Everyone is entitled to their opinions, of course. But you're entitled to fact-check those opinions and determine for yourself whether they're educated, accurate, and/or ethical. In this chapter, I describe why it is important to pay attention to your REIT's management team, including whether it's internally or externally managed. I also explain how to evaluate short sellers and activist investors and why you need to know what the executive team gets paid and its succession plan.

Let the buyer beware! And let this chapter give you ample room for both caution and ultimate confidence.

Management Works for You

Legendary value investor Benjamin Graham and his fellow Columbia University professor David Dodd wrote in their classic book, *Security Analysis* (McGraw Hill), that "a stockholder is an owner of the business and an employer of its officers." Throughout his life, Graham reminded investors that they, not management, were the legal owners of these enterprises. As such, they deserved to be treated with the respect and consideration owners of a private enterprise expect from their management teams. Both Graham and Dodd passed away decades ago, but that insight still stands true today.

Seriously, think about it. When you purchase shares in a REIT, you're helping pay management's salary. And because you're buying shares in a public company, you're also contributing to its board of directors' pay. This isn't like owning a single duplex or apartment complex where any old Tom, Dick, or Sally can be involved. (With all due respect to anyone with those names.) We're almost always talking about individuals with well-tailored resumes who are well paid to produce superior results.

That's not to say they always succeed. As I say repeatedly, things happen. Sometimes serious damage is done by forces that are completely out of a REIT's control. But more often than not, if a company is going to fall apart, it's going to be management's fault because of either greed or incompetence. So never look at someone's resume and automatically think that they're a quality fit. There are plenty of people out there who should know better and choose to do worse anyway.

REMEMBER

That's why I always recommend researching management before buying a stock. I also highly advise keeping an eye on them after the fact. They usually leave clues — if not tell-all signs — that can help you determine if your investments will outperform, live up to expectations, stagnate, or fall hard. In short, it's always important to keep an eye on the management teams you're employing to see if they're doing their job.

Rather than just using hindsight to find out how past decisions panned out, put yourself in management's shoes as new opportunities come up and new decisions are made. See if you agree with their choices. Benjamin Graham's student, Warren Buffett, has said that the best managers think like and "walk in the shoes of owners." But I think you can reverse that and it still rings true.

TIP

This is true of numerous investments, not just REITs. In fact, many of the details discussed in the following sections can be and even should be applied to the larger stock market. So feel free to apply much of this chapter across your entire portfolio!

Minding your management

As I point out in Chapter 8, any publicly traded company is exceptionally reliant on capital markets. That's where success or failure is largely determined and shareholder returns are largely realized. Companies thrive when they create real economic value for their investors, which happens when their rates of return exceed their cost of capital. And that happens under ethical, experienced, in-the-know management.

Chapter 8 more specifically covers the cost of capital, one of the most critical insights into evaluating strategic decisions and determining value creation. Simply put, the capital markets offer funding choices for REITs to grow by issuing debt, buying and selling individual properties, and pursuing larger mergers and acquisitions (M&A) deals.

REMEMBER

But it's management that assesses those options and chooses accordingly. This is why it's extremely important to *follow the money*. You always want to make sure management is making the most of its opportunities to deliver steady earnings and grow dividends.

Here's where there's REIT–specific good news, though. Their income is generated through lease contracts, so it's much easier for analysts and investors to forecast REITs' earnings growth than that of many other businesses out there. Think about how hard it would be to make a solid guess about how many cups of coffee Starbucks will sell in a given year. Then compare this to the ease of determining how many rent checks a REIT will collect from Starbucks that same year.

Of course, even with this high level of predictability, there are hiccups or surprises when it comes to corporate management. This is why you should never completely rest on your investment laurels.

REMEMBER

Always be ready to question a REIT's decisions — and to act accordingly.

Avoiding the bad actors

There will always be bad, incompetent, or otherwise unfortunate actors in the REIT sector, just like there will always be bad, incompetent, or otherwise unfortunate actors in any other asset class. From time to time, you'll even see REIT managers attempt to manipulate financial information by massaging accounting estimates. That happened in 2014 when American Realty Capital Properties executives were charged with manipulating earnings (in the form of adjusted funds from operations [AFFO]) to make it seem like the REIT was meeting Wall Street forecasts. When the truth couldn't be ignored any longer and management admitted that employees had intentionally concealed accounting errors, shares plunged as much as 37 percent in a single day.

The following investigations and lawsuits dragged on for years, leading to jail time for its CFO and plenty of pain and chaos for its investors. As for the REIT itself, it rebranded itself as VEREIT in 2015, a much more attractive entity run by a terrific CEO named Glenn Rufrano. (Yes, he deserves a shoutout!) And, as I mention in Chapter 8, it went on to merge with Realty Income in 2021. So VEREIT its assets are now in a much better place, but its past still remains a cautionary story for all of us to keep in mind.

TIP

Always look for clues about whether a REIT is walking the walk and not just talking the talk. Two examples would be dangerous payout ratios (or sucker yields, as I describe in Chapter 8) and conflicts of interest. What you want to see instead are strong indications of consistency, predictability, and transparency.

REMEMBER

There will always be a few bad apples here and there in REIT-dom. So as I keep saying over and over again, you never want to put your full faith and trust in any one entity. With that said, most REIT executives are well-respected leaders with decades of experience in their respective sectors. A big reason I own REITs is because of skilled management and their ability to manage risk. Those elements are what separate the best from the rest; and there are a strong number of REITs that work hard to keep those elements first and foremost in their business dealings.

Internal versus External Management

Some companies are managed internally, and some companies are managed externally. As an investor of REITs or any other publicly traded stocks, you should know the difference.

Internal management is how a normal company is run. It's by far the standard way of doing business, where all executives and other employees work directly for the company. In the case of a publicly traded company, the board of directors of an internally managed company and its shareholders decide who runs the firm and how those individuals are compensated. Management and shareholders are, at least in theory, on the same team. And when there's significant insider ownership (as in company personnel owning shares), that theory almost always becomes hardcore fact.

External management means that the business in question hires a third party to perform all material operations. This includes selecting assets and determining the optimal use of leverage. Typically, an externally managed company has no actual employees; the third party handles that, too. This setup makes investors at least a little less relevant and often a little less profitable.

External managers tend to be large asset managers like Blackstone — a global behemoth with just under $1 trillion in assets under management (AUM) and more than 12,000 real estate assets — and KKR with its $504 billion AUM. They build externally managed companies strictly for the purpose of managing them for fee revenues.

TECHNICAL STUFF

Externally managed REITs and other types of investment alternatives pay base management fees, and they're incentivized to grow AUM. In other words, the more they buy, the more they make. In fact, there's an actual amount of money they need to bring in before they can get any bonuses, known as performance fees. These amounts vary from contract to contract, of course, but they're designed to make sure the external manager isn't slacking off. Unfortunately, they can also push these third parties to do more than they should, making foolish purchases just to get the additional pay.

This isn't to say that all externally managed REITs are bad investments. In certain cases, this setup can provide tremendous value to both parties. One example of an excellent partnership is the aforementioned Blackstone's management of Blackstone Mortgage, a commercial mortgage REIT with a $27 billion global loan portfolio. The latter's relationship with its "big brother" offers it enormous access to proprietary deal flows, as well as property and market information it otherwise couldn't tap into.

TIP

You just need to keep your eyes open. It's critically important to review the terms of the external management contract and to compare every bit of it to externally managed peers, including any potential conflicts of interests. A poorly structured external management contract should make you think twice about investing in a company. That's the nicest way I can put it.

PUT INVESTED CAPITAL TO WORK FOR YOU

Here's one way to tell whether internal management or external management is doing the right thing by you, the investor. Look at return on invested capital (ROIC). It's used to evaluate a company's efficiency in putting capital to work in profitable investments. Here's what the formula looks like.

(Net Income – Dividends) ÷ Total Capital = ROIC

It gives a sense of how well a company is using its money to generate profits. And if you want to dig even deeper, try comparing ROIC with the weighted average cost of capital (WACC). That will really reveal whether invested capital is being used effectively. (See Chapter 8 and Appendix A for more on evaluating WACC.)

If the ROIC is at or below the cost of capital, there might not be much value creation at work. Companies should aim to find the right combination that drives the highest discounted value of their cash flows.

What About Short Sellers?

There are, of course, problems that management has less, little, or no control over whatsoever. One example is short selling, which is when an investor — often a hedge fund — borrows an asset (like a stock), sells it, and then buys it back to repay the loan. If the asset goes down in price, the hedge fund makes the difference between the two price points. Then again, if it goes up, the short seller loses money.

TECHNICAL STUFF

The opposite of short is long, so an investor who is *long* is an investor who owns the asset.

WARNING

To be blunt, short-selling actions can be dead wrong. It's an exceptionally risky practice that relies on market timing. I don't recommend anyone trying it out. This is especially true for investing novices, but it's put plenty of experienced individuals and entities in very bad places, too. The most you can earn on a short is 100 percent of however much you put in — and that's only if the stock goes to zero. But the potential losses are limitless if the stock goes up.

You're also on the hook for any dividends the company pays while the short position is open — which makes the risk even more pronounced with REITs because they tend to pay high dividends. The same goes for the interest charged for borrowing shares. In addition, REITs' real estate portfolios are almost never worthless, which once again makes it more expensive to maintain a short with limited rewards.

Advocates of short selling believe it's beneficial to investors. They say it helps identify overvalued shares and then narrows the price inflation by selling them. And because there are times when that turns out to be true, I wouldn't ignore short-seller analysis altogether. It can end up being an important part of research, bringing serious issues to light such as operating deficiencies and financial fraud.

A REIT short that actually worked

You do have to look pretty hard and far in order to find a REIT short seller who's justified. But it does happen from time to time.

Take Hayman Capital Management's Kyle Bass, who accused Dallas-based UDF Properties of operating a Ponzi scheme in 2016. He raised red flags regarding the REIT's conflicts of interest through its external management. He even went so far as to accuse it of orchestrating a scheme to mislead investors about how well its five funds were performing. (They invested in residential real-estate developers and private homebuilders.)

Once those concerns were out in the public eye, UDF's stock tanked, eventually falling below $5 (the technical definition of a penny stock). And the Nasdaq even delisted it before the year was out. Worse yet, a federal jury found four UDF executives guilty of fraud in 2022 and sentenced them to a combined 20 years. That further vindicated Bass, who had already earned quite the reward from shorting the shares. He pocketed around $34 million for his efforts, showing that even a short seller can be right twice a day.

In "short," if a REIT's fundamentals are solid and the stock price is justified — which again, is usually more true than not in such cases — managers should let their actions speak louder than words. If the fundamentals are weak as touted, though, the management team should focus on fixing them or otherwise be taken to task. Obviously.

A short caught with its pants down

I've been a writer for over 13 years now on Seeking Alpha, a stock research platform that was launched in 2004 by former Morgan Stanley technology analyst David Jackson. The website is crowd-sourced, which means thousands of writers like me produce news on financial markets as we see fit.

Back when I first began writing there, I never imagined how big it would get. Yet the site and the concept it's built on has only gotten more and more popular. A wave of other web-based financial chat rooms have sprung up over the last two decades, including on Yahoo! Finance and Reddit, all of which allow investors to gain insight into varying and sometimes very insightful opinions.

The downside, of course, is that anyone can say anything they want. So there can be pointless trash talk . . . or worse. Many of the writers are strongly opinionated and sometimes irresponsible or even intentionally misleading in what they write. Take the anonymous writer on Seeking Alpha who went by the handle Rota Fortunae. (His real name is Quinton Mathews.) He wrote an article in July 2018 in favor of shorting agricultural REIT Farmland Partners, accusing it of being at risk of insolvency.

As news of the REIT's alleged impending doom circulated further, the stock plunged, dropping by more than 39 percent. It took more than two years for the share price to fully recover — and only after Farmland's management team took legal action to protect its good name and management measures.

Farmland claimed that this was an intentionally inaccurate scheme known as a *short and distort*. That's where someone makes a negative claim against a company in order to spark fears and net an almost assured and significant shorting win. Farmland has already won against Quinton Mathews. But it's still suing Dallas-based hedge fund Sabrepoint Capital Management over the same debacle. Farmland believes that entity worked with Mr. Mathews in spreading misinformation to tank its shares.

WARNING

Whoever was involved could have gotten away with it, too, since there's very little policing or enforcement by the Securities and Exchange Commission (SEC) on Seeking Alpha or its competitors.

One of the best ways to address this is for management teams to rethink the corporate attitude toward financial website discussions. I've seen a few REIT CEOs like Joey Agree, CEO of Agree Realty; Chris Volk, former CEO of STORE Capital; and David Gladstone, CEO of Gladstone Land, engage with readers on Seeking Alpha. That's what I call transparency!

As a general rule, management is content to ignore such postings. It would even be accurate to say that many (if not most) of them look down their noses at them. I do understand where they're coming from in that perspective, considering how, as I said before, there can be a lot of trash talking and ignorant commentary on these sites.

At the same time, uncensored discussions from average investors can be a great way to gauge their investor base's mood and sentiment, not to mention the effectiveness of corporate communications. As I explain in Chapter 10, retail investors can be important stakeholders worth paying attention to — even if they own a mere hundred or thousand shares each. That's why I've recommended to several REIT CEOs that they should rethink their engagement (or lack thereof). And I'm happy to report that a growing number of them are taking my advice.

Activist Investors on the Loose

Speaking of getting involved, we need to discuss *activist investors*. These are shareholders — whether individuals or entities — that buy heavily into companies with the sole purpose of changing them from the inside out. Their intent in this is, of course, to turn a profit by encouraging (some management members would say bullying) a broad range of objectives, including

>> Making corporate governance changes

>> Spinning off properties

>> Restructuring operations

>> Enhancing dividends or buybacks

>> Asserting managerial compensation

This concept is hardly new. It's been used on company after company over the decades (or perhaps longer). But now activist investors have begun looking into the REIT sector specifically, proving themselves just as much a force for corporate change as ever.

One example of a REIT–focused activist investor is Jonathan Litt, CEO of Land & Buildings. He's pushed hard to turn around troubled REITs like Taubman Centers, Apartment Investment and Management Company (AIMCO), and Ventas — two of which have since been bought out. Likewise, in 2016, Land & Buildings successfully campaigned for MGM Resorts to spin off its properties into a REIT, which became known as MGM Growth Properties. (MGM Growth Properties has since been swallowed up by VICI Properties, another gaming REIT.)

Litt is known in general for his sometimes forceful opinion about boards of directors. He believes that REITs should have several independent outside directors who answer directly to shareholders' concerns about capital allocation, expense controls, compensation programs, and the like. These experts should also be able to implement strong financial systems and controls. The way he sees it, the stronger the organization and its financial discipline, the more efficient it will be as a real estate owner and manager. Therefore, the more it should be able to increase its market share.

COME SEE ABOUT ESG

Environmental, social, and governance criteria, or ESG, is an investing framework that has become a very big deal in the investment community over the last few years. ESG is a system — not an individual investor or investment entity — that seeks to change how companies exist in general. It evaluates how much time, energy, and financing companies give toward protecting the planet and treating their employees and customers according to set standards. This can and does push management to promote more diverse workforces, cut back on carbon emissions, and employ executives who make greater efforts to respect their shareholders.

There's a lot of good that can be done through ESG for everyone involved, including by protecting companies from unethical and unwise investments. And according to the National Association of REITs (Nareit), the REIT industry is increasingly accepting the ESG framework as the way to go. More and more of these businesses are creating departments dedicated to prioritizing these efforts.

Between 2017 and 2021, almost 30 more REITs opened full-time employee positions dedicated to this movement. Moreover, according to Nareit, "all of the largest 100 REITs by equity market cap are now reporting their ESG efforts publicly, including on their company websites and in annual reports, proxy statements, and/or stand-alone sustainability reports."

On the downside, the rapid growth of ESG investment funds has led to growing skepticism and pushback. Many critics claim that some (or most) companies have been ambiguous or downright disingenuous in touting their ESG accomplishments. A mild example of this would be shifting to a paperless system for alleged environmental reasons that are really economic all the way. Obviously, that can still benefit investors depending on how management puts their savings to use. But it's underhanded, nonetheless.

There are also a growing number of analysts who say that ESG funds underperform their non-ESG alternatives. And more political accusations have led a growing number of U.S. states to boycott this investing trend altogether.

Regardless, the movement remains powerful and therefore shouldn't be overlooked. As with everything else that management allows, enacts, or is otherwise involved in, keep a close eye on how well executives are handling the matter to your benefit.

That's not an opinion every REIT shares, and so his presence isn't always appreciated. Then again, activist investors are used to being disliked. That rarely dissuades them from pursuing their goals, anyway. And often, those goals are worth pursuing.

The truth is that market requirements and additional investor expectations — activist or otherwise — can seem nettlesome and costly. But they often end up actually strengthening organizations in the long run. Management should, therefore, welcome outside opinion, like it or not.

Following the Money: Executive Compensation

For my part, as a non-activist but still pretty opinionated investor (you can call me a *suggestivist*), I know what concerns me and what makes me nod in satisfaction. And really, it boils down to management again. I prefer to see executive cash compensation based on metrics that motivate leadership teams to invest in value-enhancing and moat-enhancing projects.

Management and boards of directors should always recognize and act on the recognition that they must be low-cost providers — just like Walmart and Coca-Cola — in their respective spaces in order to generate predictable profit margins. Some of the most successful REITs over the last 10- and 20-year periods have been able to consistently generate superior returns because of the disciplined capital market practices they were financially and ethically motivated to put into place.

REMEMBER

Properly compensated REIT executives also find themselves in better positions to recruit, motivate, and retain effective personnel, who can then help add to the company's growth story. This is part of the reason you should always pay close attention to executive compensation. They're your employees, for all intents and purposes; and happy, motivated employees are most effective.

This is why I don't automatically object when a REIT CEO earns millions of dollars between salary and incentives (cash and equity). Then again, sometimes executives make that money without earning it. Each one needs the proper combination of checks and balances.

To (hopefully) make that assessment easier, the SEC adopted pay-versus-performance disclosure requirements with passage of the Dodd-Frank Act in 2022. The regulations outlined in this act require companies to provide a new table disclosing specified executive compensation and financial performance measures that previously didn't have to be reported to the same degree.

These days, executive compensation, shareholder voting rights, and composition of boards are highly transparent and scrutinized by shareholders. A 2019 study by Goodwin Proctor showed that 17 percent of REIT boards are classified, with 59 percent separating the CEO and chairman roles.

Passing on the Crown

Management succession is another important issue that should be addressed but isn't nearly as often as it should be. In a CEO's defense, the topic can be very sensitive. Nobody wants to talk about their potential ousting or death, of course. And some people don't like to think about retiring either. (They're going to be moving and shaking forever, don't you know?) But everyone has their limits, even high-powered, highly paid executives.

When we're dealing with poor management, that inevitable change can be a godsend. But what about when a company's reputation and success are built around a single name? The stock market doesn't like to be spooked, and news that a well-respected CEO will no longer be leading the way can send it panicking. So REIT investors need to know who will likely replace a top executive and what tools that person will have at their disposal when the time comes . . . as it always does eventually.

The ultimate objective, of course and as always, is to ensure that the stakeholder and manager are aligned.

3

REITs for All Investors

Understand the different types of REITs — growth, value, and income — and find out what type of investor you are.

Gain clarity on the tax situation when investing in REITs.

Explore why institutional investors love REITs.

Get the scoop on REIT exchange-traded funds (ETFs) and other bundled packages like mutual funds and closed-end funds and find out if they are right for you.

IN THIS CHAPTER

» **Identifying the type of investor you are**

» **Understanding the different types of REITs**

» **Building a properly diversified portfolio**

» **Figuring out your tax situation when dealing with REITs**

» **Weighing IRAs versus Roth IRAs**

Chapter **10**

Building a Smart REIT Portfolio from the Ground Up

You've covered a lot of ground so far in this book — the history of REITs, the types of REITs, the various property sectors, basic REIT fundamentals, and REIT management. Now you're ready to put it all into practice and learn how to build a REIT portfolio from the ground up.

My hope is that if you've read this far, you're pretty enthusiastic and ready to join an estimated 150 million Americans who already own REITs (directly or indirectly). That's roughly 45 percent of American households! REITs can be — and I would argue almost always *should* be — an important part of any preretirement or in-retirement portfolio.

Remember that REITs not only offer income, they also protect it thanks to how different they are from so many other investments. In Chapter 3, I mention how portfolio volatility can be reduced by holding a diverse range of assets that feature low correlations with each other. And it's worth reiterating that fact here. When one category goes down, another will go up or stay steady, keeping your nerves steady and preventing you from panic-selling at a loss.

If that's something you want to avoid like I do, let's delve into the question of where you should begin in constructing a healthy REIT portfolio.

What Type of REIT Investor Are You?

TIP

The first thing you need to do when thinking about adding REITs to your investment portfolio is ask yourself two questions:

>> How should REITs be weighted relative to other investments?

>> How should they be weighted relative to each other?

How you answer the first question very much depends on two things, with one of them being your individual risk tolerance — how much uncertainty you can handle calmly and rationally. That's something I cover further in the next section. For now, let's concentrate on the second aspect, which is how unique you consider REITs to be. Personally, I advise you to think of REITs as their own separate category altogether: as a core asset class in and of themselves. The very influential Global Industry Classification Standard (GICS) agrees with me, as it gave publicly traded real estate companies their own classification in 2016 (see Chapter 3).

Former chief investment officer of Yale University and bestselling investment author David Swensen pointed out in *Unconventional Success* (Free Press) that investing in equity real estate can produce "inflation protection at a lower opportunity cost than other alternatives." He argued that this core asset class results in bond-like rental streams and equity-like residual values — some of the best of both worlds. In other words, it's its own world altogether.

In reference to the second question — how REITs should be weighted against each other — remember that REITs offer fixed-income characteristics that stem from their sometimes very different lease contracts. So once again, the answer depends on what type of investor you are.

You can help determine what type of investor you are by reviewing the property sectors I cover in Chapters 6 and 7. For instance, sectors with short-term leases such as self-storage facilities and hotels exhibit much greater inflation sensitivity. Other sectors explicitly allow landlords to pass higher costs on to their tenants. And in the case of retail properties like shopping centers, landlords can even receive a percentage of sales, as discussed in Chapter 6. That helps their value increase, not decline, with inflation.

This kind of information can help you better determine what to put into your portfolio and what to leave out.

Know your REIT psychology

Understanding your personal details can also help you better determine what to put into your portfolio and what to leave out. In college, I majored in business and minored in psychology. I admit, at the time I wasn't thinking rationally about that secondary focus since I never thought it would be helpful. (Although now that I have five kids, I have found child psychology to be quite helpful!) Fortunately for me, though, I was proven very, very wrong when I became an investor. Psychology plays an enormous part in determining what and when you buy; what and when you sell; and, therefore, what kind of profit or loss you end up taking and when.

TIP

Unless you're willing to honestly acknowledge this reality and force some logic into your biases, failure awaits. It's critical you spend time thinking about your goals and objectives instead of just acting on them. Don't just ask what you want. Ask why you want it. And if the answer isn't a good one, perhaps reconsider your original desire. Successful investing doesn't happen by fulfilling your every whim.

At the same time, you don't want to force yourself into some one-size-fits-all alternative (which I address in Chapter 12) about what you should do. A custom-tailored portfolio that takes your available finances, goals, and temperament into consideration all but guarantees greater results than the alternative. You'll also want to pay special attention to your time horizon. How long you have to reach your goals (usually until retirement) represents one of the most influential variables in structuring your REIT portfolio.

REIT temperament

I'm going to stress that temperament issue I mention in the previous section. Knowing your own unique personal risk tolerance is essential, since panic-selling is one of the key factors in why individual investors fail to meet their goals. You might think a stock looks good because of its intense growth story, celebrity status, or somebody's very certain suggestion. But when volatility hits and shares lose some value, your natural instinct will be to bail out. That's nothing against you personally. It's just human nature.

We all want to make a lot of money quickly and effortlessly. So when we think we see an opportunity to do so, it can be like a siren's call. But, to paraphrase Frank J. Williams, an influential 1920s Wall Street writer, this doesn't work any better with stocks than it does anywhere else in life. So always tread carefully, look twice, and think three times before buying. At least.

For my part, I vet REITs for a living. It's easier for me to spot a good one versus a bad one right away. Yet I still spend countless hours fact-checking my instincts. That's why REITs represent much more than 20 percent of my investments despite how I advise others to consider the 15 percent to 20 percent range. I base my higher figure based on my level of expertise and the amount of time I'm willing to spend expanding that expertise.

I think that's a good idea regardless of what assets or asset classes you're considering. And I encourage you to continue growing your knowledge of what you're buying into.

Basically, it boils down to this: Investors who do their homework can have an edge over ordinary stock pickers.

Looking at REIT Types

REITs can be classified into three different categories: growth, value, and income. After you've determined where particular REITs fall along this spectrum, you'll want to match them up with your personal risk tolerance profile, using this knowledge to grow your portfolio more efficiently.

You don't have to stay tied to a single category, of course. Feel free to mix them up as you see fit. REIT-dom is a smorgasbord where you can take what you want and leave what you don't. Just make sure you get the proper "nutrients" as you decide and don't over-indulge along the way.

Growth REITs

As the name implies, growth REITs have a lot of room to expand in the foreseeable future. They're often already growing at a faster rate than the overall markets, and so they can generate the highest earnings (AFFO per share) and dividend growth, too.

AFFO stands for *adjusted funds from operations*. Calculating AFFO is a way to measure a real estate company's earnings. See Chapter 8 and Appendix C for more about how to do this.

It shouldn't come as much of a surprise that growth REITs are mostly found in technology-based sectors like cell towers and data centers right now. The life science field falls into this category as well. These economic areas have historically seen their earnings rise by 8 percent to 12 percent every year, which makes them very tempting, to say the least.

Clearly then, entire sectors or subsectors can fall into the growth REIT category. But so can individual companies. Newer businesses, after all, have the capability to generate external growth more rapidly. This makes sense since they tend to have smaller denominators to grow earnings. Moreover, that status can last for years and years. For example, VICI Properties, a gaming REIT I mention in earlier chapters, grew annual AFFO per share by around 9 percent from the time it went public in 2018 through 2022.

In short, growth REITs can provide substantial returns. Though you should pay close attention to their costs of capital. It's also worthwhile to monitor their investment spreads, which are key drivers for profit margins. Also keep in mind that sometimes the smaller, less-stable REITs can experience severe sudden price declines.

As always, it's a give and take.

Value REITs

Value REITs can often provide long-term profits for those who do their homework. That's why you want to keep margins of safety in mind when selecting stocks. By this, I mean built-in price cushions that allow you to take some kind of loss without breaking the bank. Obviously, you never want to buy an asset you expect to lose money on. At the same time, you should always understand that the possibility exists.

In the case of a stock purchase, applying a *safety of margin* means buying it below its fair-value price, whatever that may be. The wider the margin, the lower the risk and the greater potential for gain. The further "on sale" an asset is when you buy it, the better your chances are that it will rise from there and make you a profit by the time you decide to sell it yourself. This is true even when you expect dividends as well.

Benjamin Graham, who I first mention in Chapter 1, is considered the father of value investing. It's a title he earned decades before REITs were legalized, but I use his advice all the time in my portfolio-building practices. As Warren Buffett, his famous student, told an audience at Columbia Business School in 1984:

> You do not cut it close. That is what Ben Graham meant by having a margin of safety. You don't try to buy businesses worth $83 million for $80 million. You leave yourself an enormous margin. When you build a bridge, you insist it can carry 30,000 pounds, but you only drive 10,000-pound trucks across it. And that same principle works in investing.

To put it into context, a value REIT is one that trades below what seems like a reasonable price ratio based on FFO, dividend yield, NAV, and other valuation measures I discuss in Chapter 8. These kinds of bargains can happen for a number of reasons, including lack of exposure, lack of understanding about what the company does, or periods of general or specific market panic.

Small caps, for instance, don't get the same attention as their mid- and large-cap compatriots. But as they grow, that changes. Sustainable energy REIT HASI, meanwhile, has gone through bouts of low valuation when investors struggled to figure out what it did. And even blue chips, as described in Chapter 8, have seen their shares fall out of favor here or there due to market crashes or unflattering opinions about their ultimate sustainability.

While those unflattering opinions are occasionally true, that's not the norm. Recognizing that, some investors wait for such momentary disappointments to happen to blue-chip shares. They know those occasions often make for good times to buy in, sit back, and wait for the stock to rebound.

REMEMBER

A company might not start out as a value stock, only to turn into one and then shoot right back up in price a day, week, or month later. Or it might take years for it to come into its own. There's no crystal ball here to figure out price movements ahead of time — no matter how much we might wish otherwise. Again, we can only evaluate where a company should be trading based on valuation and price history. How long it takes the market to correct its error is up to the market.

Determining individual REIT value also involves some consideration of the larger sector and the company in question's current competitive position within its peer group. You want to look at its *economic moat,* the sustainable competitive advantage that helps preserve its pricing power (cost of capital) and dividend growth potential. Does it have what it takes to rebound? If the answer is yes, it can make for an excellent opportunity.

The nice thing is that, even if you turn out to be mistaken, value stocks tend to carry less risk than growth stocks by their very nature. You just can't lose as much when the price is lower. At the same time, don't be cocky; treat them as wisely as you would any other stock.

Income REITs

REITs have the very big potential to bolster your fixed-income portfolios, and that's why most investors buy them up. Their dividend yields typically exceed those of guaranteed instruments such as U.S. Treasury securities or certificates of deposit (CDs), offering attractive income and the potential for price appreciation. That's why almost all REITs are considered income stocks in the end. But in this context, let's narrow down that definition further.

I detail the power of compound interest in Chapter 2. But as a reminder and in REIT-specific terms, this is where you make money by reinvesting the dividends you get into the stocks that gave you those dividends . . . which allows you to buy more stock . . . which allows you to get more dividends . . . which allows you to buy more stock . . . which allows you to get more dividends. The end result is a lot more money than what you started out with.

This does mean the REIT in question has to be reliable, though. Slashed payout amounts slow the process down, perhaps by a lot, depending on how much the dividend is reduced. And the same applies to retirees who don't reinvest their payouts but use them as actual income.

In that light, I'm not going to classify growth REITs in the income REIT category. The former category tends to represent more risk and/or lower dividend yields. With that said, an income REIT can also be a value REIT for the same reasons I list in the previous section concerning how even dependable blue-chip REITs can get discounted. It just happens sometimes.

If the company in question has a solid track record of paying out a rising dividend every year with a decent yield, it belongs in the income REIT category.

Building a Diversified REIT Portfolio

As I point out in Chapter 3, there are plenty of property sectors, investment characteristics, and geographic locations to consider when investing in REITs. And you're only going to be able to invest so much into so many depending on how much money you have to invest in the first place. One easy way for individual investors to diversify is through REIT mutual funds and exchange-traded funds (ETFs), which I discuss in detail in Chapter 12. But for those who like to pick and choose individual companies, like me, here's what you need to know.

If you're working with a limited amount of money or want to ease into REIT ownership slowly, six separate stocks should provide a decent amount of sector diversification. I'd say that's the minimum amount to achieve diversification, but it suffices nonetheless. You can better your odds further by perhaps selecting one (intelligently investigated) REIT from each major sector — apartment, retail, office, and industrial — and one from two newer sectors such as cell towers, self-storage, hotels, gaming, or the like.

TIP

With that said, holding eight to ten REITs would be better, because, of course, the more (intelligently investigated) assets you can hold, the less likely you are to catch a bad break.

It also allows you to expand into other sectors and subsectors. Or you can choose different geographical focuses within sectors you already bought into. Suppose you have one apartment REIT that focuses on the U.S. East Coast. Well then, you can buy another that focuses on the Sunbelt, so that, if some area-specific issue comes up in one place, your "other place" holding will balance it out.

WARNING

You could also diversify by investing in REITs that hold more than one property type. That's another way to achieve diversity. However, I will tell you that those companies tend to be jacks of all trades, masters of none. This means your money is better spent elsewhere.

My anchor-and-buoy model

Now that we've got that covered, let me tell you about my all-purpose anchor and buoy blueprint for getting started in REIT investing. This is my typical response whenever someone asks me which stocks to buy to begin their portfolio.

THREE WAYS TO CONSIDER YOUR REIT DIVERSIFICATION

Some investors model their portfolios on market weightings, which means they look to see how much each sector takes up of the larger REIT world. If data centers make up 3 percent, then 3 percent of their REIT–specific cash goes toward data centers. It's as simple as that. People who go that route operate on the belief that the market is pretty efficient over time, so why try to fight it? Of course, this setup does require that you have more rather than less money.

Other investors prefer certain sectors over others. And they can have very good reason to do so. They take the time to examine which sectors are struggling, which ones are stagnant, and which ones are thriving. Then they invest accordingly.

This is the method I tend to favor myself. However, it does take a lot more time and effort than the let-the-market-decide method. Plus, it can be tricky to find the right combination at the right time. Think about it: You want to invest in REITs at fair value or better. But if you're working with common logic and intelligent evaluations to reach your conclusions, you're probably not the only one thinking along those lines.

It becomes a race from there, with the early bird getting the discounted worm, the not-as-early bird getting the fairly priced worm, and the late bird finding itself with only overpriced offerings. In other words, the price of the stock you want might be too high by the time you get to it. Which means you have to be on top of your analysis game or, at the very least, far from the bottom.

If neither of those methods sounds appealing, there's another way that ignores sectors altogether. It focuses instead on putting together a REIT portfolio with varying qualities, such as those that

- Offer predictable, steady growth

- Have above-average growth

- Are deeply discounted

- Have high yields but low volatility and less impressive growth possibilities

As for which method works best, I can't say. There aren't any studies done on the subject to my knowledge, which might be just as well. Different people with different investing styles, needs, and goals are bound to do better with one over the others anyway.

Just make sure you're diversified regardless.

Using ten equally weighted REITs (10 percent each), I provide something along the lines of the snapshot shown in Figure 10-1 as an example portfolio they can work with. Keep in mind that this isn't a personalized recommendation. As I've said before, I don't know your personal situation and considerations. It's meant to be a model only.

Growth	Ticker	Market Cap	IG Rating	Dividend Yield	Growth Est
American Tower	AMT	93.8	BBB-	3.0%	12.0%
Digital Realty	DLR	29.3	BBB	4.9%	6.0%
Camden Property	CPT	10.8	A-	3.9%	6.0%
Prologis	PLD	108.1	A	3.0%	12.0%
Hannon Armstrong	HASI	2.4	BB+	6.6%	8.0%
Income					
Realty Income	O	41.6	A-	5.0%	5.0%
VICI Properties	VICI	31.2	BBB-	5.0%	5.0%
Federal Realty	FRT	7.5	BBB+	4.7%	5.0%
Agree Realty	ADC	6.2	BBB	4.2%	5.0%
Starwood Property	STWD	5.5	BB	11.5%	2.0%
Average		**33.6**		**5.2%**	**6.6%**

FIGURE 10-1:
A sample
REIT portfolio
with ten stocks.

As you can see in the figure, I selected ten REITs — five growth and five income — that generate an average dividend yield of 5.2 percent. If you were to invest in this sample basket, you would receive dividend income generated from

>> 300 data centers in 25 countries from DLR

>> 225,000 global cell tower sites from AMT

>> 172 Sunbelt-focused apartment communities from CPT

>> 340 climate infrastructure investments from HASI

>> 1.2 billion square feet of warehouses from PLD

>> 12,200 free-standing properties in 50 states and Europe from O

>> 50 high-end gaming and/or experiential properties from VICI

>> 103 properties with 3,300 retail tenant and 3,000 apartment renters from FRT

>> 1,839 free-standing properties across 48 states from ADC

>> A $20 billion loan and infrastructure portfolio from STWD

This REIT basket has generated very stable dividends over the years, which is the key to this anchor-and-buoy strategy.

The exact arrangement can change going forward, of course, and not just because an individual company might fail or be bought out. Consider how cannabis REITs were once considered growth plays, with Innovative Industrial Properties in particular growing earnings (AFFO per share) by an annual average 8 percent in the 2018 to 2021 period. However, cannabis REITs are now value plays based on their slower growth and cheaper valuation multiples.

REMEMBER

That's why this is a sample portfolio, not an end-all-be-all blueprint. The larger takeaway should be how helpful it is to have such a wide range of assets in hand. If there's a hiccup with one company's tenant — or even that entire company — or a geographical event such as a hurricane or earthquake, you shouldn't see much of a glitch in your dividend results, if any at all.

The growth picks (DLR, AMT, CPT, HASI, and PLD) do generate lower yields, with an average 4.3 percent. But their forecasted growth is above average at 8.8 percent. Alternatively, the income picks (O, VICI, FRT, ADC, and STWD) generate an average 6.1 percent yield and 4.4 percent for forecasted growth.

TIP

If you're interested in higher-dividend income, you may want to add a few more income picks to the mix. Those of you who don't mind the extra risk and volatility potential could perhaps even look into one or two mortgage REITs. And the more cautious could consider preferred shares. Just whatever you do, stay away from the sucker yields I mention in Chapter 8.

Ideally, depending on your personal situation, I'd look to own closer to 20 REITs over time. In that case, you may want to sprinkle in healthcare, manufactured housing, malls, self-storage, office, farmland, and single-family rentals.

Your house doesn't count

REMEMBER

Speaking of single-family spaces, your house does not count in this REIT portfolio for the simple reason that it's not a REIT.

Personal residences do represent valuable nonfinancial assets on many personal balance sheets. And there's no doubt that they insulate individuals from changes in the cost of renting. Inflation-sensitive habitation costs constitute a significant portion of most household budgets. So homeownership reduces the need for inflation-hedging assets in investors' portfolios.

But income-producing commercial real estate is very different than owner-occupied residential real estate. Analysis shows that REIT long-term returns outpaced home ownership returns. Moreover, the National Association of REITs (Nareit) has shown a correlation of just 0.46 over four years, meaning they're not nearly as similar as you might think.

They certainly face different economic drivers than residential housing. This makes sense since owning a home is primarily about having a place to live. It can produce capital gains over time, but it doesn't generate current income — quite the opposite considering such burdens as mortgage interest, real estate tax, insurance payments, and maintenance costs.

Figure 10-2 shows how homeownership long-term investment returns generally lag REITs, even taking into consideration the value of having a shelter.

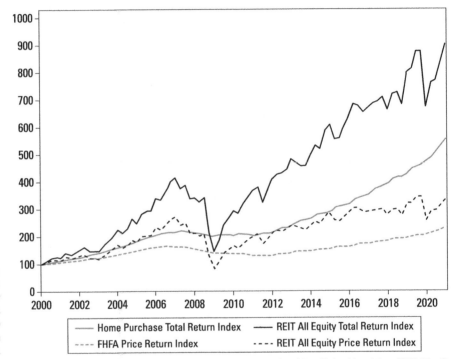

Source: Adopted from National Association of REITs (Nareit).

FIGURE 10-2: REITs versus single-family home returns from 2000 through 2021 (Q1).

Also consider how REIT returns include dividends versus homeownership's imputed rent — the money owners would be paying to rent an equivalent house. Even then, REITs have provided stronger long-term returns. As the chart in Figure 10-2 shows, investing $100 in REITs in 2000 would have turned into $902 by the end of the first quarter in 2021. That's an 11 percent compound annual growth rate.

There's also the issue of liquidity to consider. Despite what we saw in 2020–2022, homes tend to be illiquid assets. You can't click a button and see them sold in a matter of minutes. With publicly traded REITs, you can. Just log into your trading account or call your broker, and voila!

None of this information is meant to knock homeownership. It's only to show the very separate benefits of REIT ownership. Both have unique long-term benefits and possibilities. But for investment purposes, REITs just can't be beat.

The Taxation Situation

REITs run off a simple business model that's easy to understand . . . right up until you get to the question of taxes. To understand these ins and outs, you have to first be aware of three types of taxation:

>> Individual taxes, which you pay on ordinary income and dividends

>> Capital gains taxes, which you pay when you sell for a profit

>> Corporate taxes, which are made on a company's profits before it distributes income to shareholders (these are only indirectly related to your earnings but still worth considering)

As I first point out in Chapter 3, REITs must pay out at least 90 percent of their taxable income by law. Most pay out the full 100 percent. The trade-off is that they avoid corporate tax altogether. And no, it's not a loophole.

REITs are treated in the same manner as pass-through entities like limited liability companies (LLCs), partnerships, and S-corporations. This is one of their biggest advantages, and it does benefit the investor more than it burdens them. At the same time, shareholders do bear the entire brunt of the tax burden this way.

As I also mention in Chapter 3, Uncle Sam always gets his cut somehow, someway. In the case of REITs, that's through the ordinary income, long-term capital gains, and return on capital you make off them. And each one has a different tax treatment.

REITs issue tax notices at the end of each year called a Form 1099-DIV. These do indicate which is which, but it's still good to know the basic definitions of the terms you're looking at. It always is.

Ordinary income

Most of the money distributed by REITs is considered ordinary income because distributed operating profit in general falls into that category. These tax rates vary based on your income level and therefore the tax bracket you fall into.

For example, if your taxable income was $600,000 in 2022, you'd be taxed at a rate of 37 percent (if you're single) for ordinary income distributions paid that year. So if you made $5,000 in qualifying dividend payouts that year, you'd get to keep $3,150 of it.

That might not be fair, but this isn't a book about debating tax policy. It's a book about REITs; I'm just telling you how it is.

Qualified business income

I should also mention the qualified business income (QBI) deduction for *pass-through income* — the business income you report on your personal tax return. Entities eligible for the QBI deduction include

» Sole proprietorships

» Partnerships

» S corporations

» LLCs

You're eligible to deduct up to 20 percent of QBI from your taxes on REIT dividends that are considered ordinary income and not interest. Thus a 20 percent deduction on ordinary income distributions from REITs as QBI reduces the top tax rate from 37 percent to 29.6 percent. Keep in mind, the QBI deduction is slated to sunset (expire) in 2025 unless it gets extended.

Long-term capital gains or losses

Again, ordinary income generally makes up the bulk of REIT distributions and taxation. But it's not uncommon to see some portion labeled as long-term capital gain. This occurs when a REIT sells a property it's owned for over a year and chooses to distribute that income to shareholders in the form of a special dividend.

Long-term capital gains are taxed at lower rates than both ordinary income and short-term gains — currently 0 percent, 15 percent, or 20 percent in the United States, depending on your income. But they're always lower than the corresponding marginal tax rate for ordinary income.

Return of capital

Some part of a REIT's distribution could be considered a return of capital (ROC), which isn't immediately taxable. This obviously lowers your cost basis (the price you effectively paid) in an investment asset.

Suppose you pay $50 per share to buy the fictional ABC REIT, which distributed $1.00 per share as a non-taxable ROC. That means your cost basis would be reduced to $49 per share. Which sounds nice at first glance. Really nice, in fact!

Just keep in mind that this allowance could make your tax bill higher when you sell the shares, since your cost basis is lower.

Individual Retirement Accounts

Because REITs tend to have above-average dividend yields and those payouts are taxed at higher rates, REITs are perhaps the best type of dividend stock to hold in tax-advantaged accounts like individual retirement accounts (IRAs). There, you won't have to worry about dividend taxes at all each year. Nor will you have to pay taxes in the year you sell a REIT at a profit.

There are two main types of IRAs in which you can hold your REIT investments: a traditional IRA and a Roth IRA. Let's take a look at both.

Traditional IRA

In a traditional IRA, you don't owe any taxes until you withdraw money from the account. It also allows you to direct pre-tax income toward investments that can grow tax-deferred. The Internal Revenue Service (IRS) assesses no capital gains or dividend income taxes on such holdings until you make a withdrawal.

Better yet, individual taxpayers can contribute 100 percent of any earned compensation to an IRA — up to a specified maximum dollar amount, that is, depending on your age. Income thresholds may also apply, and tax-filing status and other factors could affect your contributions as well.

Traditional brokers, online brokers, robo-advisors, and financial advisors can all help you set up an IRA when and if you're ready.

The Roth IRA-lternative

Then there are Roth IRAs. These are individual retirement accounts with their own set of specific tax advantages. Holders of Roth IRAs add money after taxes, not before, which means you don't have to worry about being taxed as you withdraw — provided you're at least 59-and-a-half years old (or disabled) when you do and have had your account open for at least five years. You can also withdraw funds tax-free if you're a first-time homebuyer.

As Charles Schwab notes, this can best suit investors who expect to be in a higher tax bracket by the time they think they'll take money back out. Hopefully that pertains to the majority of you reading this who haven't retired yet. But there are other qualifications you may or may not meet. So it's best to check with a professional before trying to set up an account.

Chapter **11**

The Big Fish REIT Investors

I n Chapter 10, I lay out the REIT investment thesis for the average investor. Chances are high you fall into that category, in which case, there's no shame in it. Most people do. Even so, it's important to know a thing or two about your way-above-average counterparts: the bigger fish swimming out there in the publicly traded asset ocean. These whales — more properly known as *institutional investors* — are a big deal in more than just their size.

This chapter dives into these deep, deep waters filled with pension funds, endowments, private equity, foundations, bank trusts, insurance companies, and family offices. Collectively, institutional investors make up about two-thirds of the REIT ownership base.

Major *defined benefit plans* (programs that promise a specified paycheck per month at retirement) and *sovereign wealth funds* (state-owned investment programs) around the world rely on REITs to varying degrees. If "varying degrees" doesn't sound impressive, keep reading. Besides, these institutions want to increase their real estate allocations. According to the Pension Real Estate Association (PREA) 2022 Investment Intentions Survey, they average 8.9 percent exposure around the world . . . and want to bump that up a solid point to 10.1 percent.

Some institutional investors are content to keep their REIT portions as is, in which case they're free to do so. There are other real estate options available, of course, such as through private real estate. But enough are seeing the benefits of real estate investment trusts to make a difference, as I show in this chapter.

Why Institutional Investors Love REITs

Approximately 64 percent of the world's top 25 largest investors use REITs to boost their real estate holdings' growth potential (see Figure 11-1). These investors average about $430 billion in total assets under management (AUM), with their real estate portfolios averaging above $30 billion. Again, that's real estate in general, not real estate investment trusts in particular. But even a slice of that collective $75 billion-plus can and does make a whale-sized difference for the REITs they choose to get involved in.

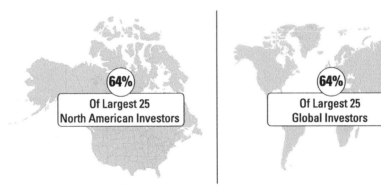

FIGURE 11-1: Percentage of institutional investors who use REITs to boost growth potential.

Source: Adopted from National Association of REITs (Nareit).

This makes sense since REITs are well known to play a key role in helping institutional investors fill their real estate allocation goals and improve their overall risk-return profiles. Take it from CenterSquare Investment Management, a global real asset manager that, together with its subsidiaries, handles approximately $13 billion in assets for major institutional and private investors alike. Uma Moriarity, a CFA and senior investment strategist there, explains how: "REITs offer investor portfolios exposure to cash flows generated through long-term leases that can withstand the impact of short-term volatility in economic conditions."

Moreover, REITs are liquid and often boast higher-quality financial data. This makes REITs the easiest way for institutional investors to add exposure to specific real estate sectors or geographies — easiest and often the most efficient.

It takes time to deploy capital into private real estate ventures. And it takes time to sell them down the road if necessary — time and even teams, which means more money spent in order to make money. REITs, however, provide a quick-and-easy liquid alternative that allows pensions to put money to work immediately and with very little effort, comparatively speaking.

All of that is, of course, why we "little fishes" love them, too. The sector offers the same exact benefits to everyone equally — just as it was designed to do.

Yes, the big guys can make more money than we do because they have more money to start out with. However, we benefit enormously from their involvement because they offer a whole new level of respectability to each and every REIT they put in their portfolios. And that respectability comes with greater liquidity and share prices appreciation. Essentially, if they're willing to give a stock the time of day, others are more likely to do the same.

In the next few sections, I discuss institutional benefits in further detail. Some of the following information might sound familiar because, again, it applies to us *average* investors as well. But as you read it, keep in mind that I'm now talking about money on an exponential scale.

The geographic diversification is "out of this world"

As I reference in Chapter 5, dozens of countries and regions have some sort of REIT law (or at least REIT allowance) on their books already. No doubt more are still to come. As of December 2022, there were 893 listed REITs with a combined equity market capitalization of approximately $2.5 trillion around the world.

All that international money may or may not be annoying (or downright difficult) for mom-and-pop investors to access due to the additional fees, currency exchange issues, and research involved. But because institutions have entire teams paid to handle those sorts of complications, it's not nearly as much of a bother for them. And it's a much cheaper option regardless compared to building an on-the-ground presence to get that global touch.

As for those countries that don't allow REITs yet, many of the ones that do also allow them to invest internationally. This means they can expand their holdings by hopping borders when worthwhile opportunities present themselves. There aren't many governments out there (at least to my knowledge) that exclusively ban already existent REITs from buying up national property, foreign though they might be. This means there are a growing number of ways for investors to tap into real estate markets. And as I show in the next section, the non-average investors are becoming increasingly aware of how they need to expand their horizons.

REITs generally do a great job of explaining their geographic footprint to investors in their quarterly investor presentation and Securities and Exchange Commission (SEC) filings. Those are available to the public and should be featured on each company's website.

REITs create a good balance between old and new

Many old-money institutional real estate portfolios are overweight on office and retail, and underweight on more "newfangled" sectors, as illustrated in Figure 11-2. If that seems odd to you considering the ongoing debate surrounding working from home (or not working from home) — not to mention the unmistakable rise of e-commerce — it should be. But you might be surprised at how slow-to-move some organizations can be. Office and retail represented the bulk of real estate assets in the past, and some people have a hard time adapting appropriately.

This is perhaps where individual investors have an edge. If you're looking to increase your exposure to newer and/or alternative economy sectors — including cell towers, healthcare, data centers, alternative energy infrastructure, and self-storage — you only need to consult yourself and perhaps your spouse or financial advisor. You don't need to take your conclusion to a board or counsel before you can act.

Boards can be both enormous benefits and sizable detriments at the same time. They're (mostly) filled with brilliant people who have a lot of experience . . . and just as significantly sized opinions on how to apply it all.

Fortunately, they're waking up more and more to their need to find wider waters with a more diverse array of assets. They're looking to increase their gains by getting with the times and accessing business trends that seem like they're here to stay. In which case, they recognize what Figure 11-2 shows: how REITs provide better access to these newer and alternative real estate sectors than their private-sector counterparts.

REITs help fill the asset allocation gaps

LaSalle Securities, a world-class brokerage firm, presented a case study from the end of 2018. It shows how REITs can dramatically affect portfolio alignment, distributing the risk much better than other real estate offerings can.

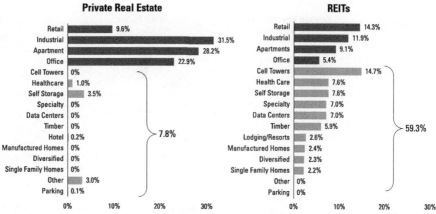

FIGURE 11-2:
Property diversification in private real estate holdings and REITs.

Private Real Estate

Retail	9.6%
Industrial	31.5%
Apartment	28.2%
Office	22.9%
Cell Towers	0%
Healthcare	1.0%
Self Storage	3.5%
Specialty	0%
Data Centers	0%
Timber	0%
Hotel	0.2%
Manufactured Homes	0%
Diversified	0%
Single Family Homes	0%
Other	3.0%
Parking	0.1%

7.8%

REITs

Retail	14.3%
Industrial	11.9%
Apartments	9.1%
Office	5.4%
Cell Towers	14.7%
Health Care	7.6%
Self Storage	7.6%
Specialty	7.0%
Data Centers	7.0%
Timber	5.9%
Lodging/Resorts	2.6%
Manufactured Homes	2.4%
Diversified	2.3%
Single Family Homes	2.2%
Other	0%
Parking	0%

59.3%

Source: Adopted from National Association of REITs (Nareit).

This was due to one of its clients, a U.S. healthcare system in the Northeast with total assets ranging from $4 to $5 billion and a real assets allocation (including real estate) of 3 percent to 5.5 percent. This group was initially invested in several private real estate funds with heavy retail and office exposure. But as the 21st century progressed, it began worrying about how its money was performing and how it would fare in the future. LaSalle's healthcare client thought it could better benefit from exposure to newer and/or niche property types. Accordingly, LaSalle (with $78 billion in assets under management) immediately got to work, assessing where the client's portfolio was lacking and what to do about it.

Figure 11-3 details the process, with the first pie chart showing just four property sectors represented. In order, that would be offices at 38 percent and apartments and industrials at 24 percent each, with 14 percent going to retail. Add in the new portfolio that includes cell towers, healthcare, data centers, self-storage, specialty sectors, triple-nets, niche residential, and life sciences, and then smash the two together. What you get is something that's much more competitive — especially going into the new decade.

This process and ultimate product definitely depended on REITs, which offer a lot more real estate diversity opportunities than private real estate. For instance, the NFI-ODCE Index tracks the largest private real estate funds, which are full of low-risk, low-leverage, stable U.S. properties — by traditional standards, that is. Less than 10 percent of its assets are outside of the four property sectors illustrated in that first pie chart in Figure 11-3.

REMEMBER

It's REITs that have been eager to get into the so-called "new economy" sectors that the 21st century runs on. You can easily see that by looking at Nareit's Equity Index. Only slightly more than a third of its allocation is to "old economy" players.

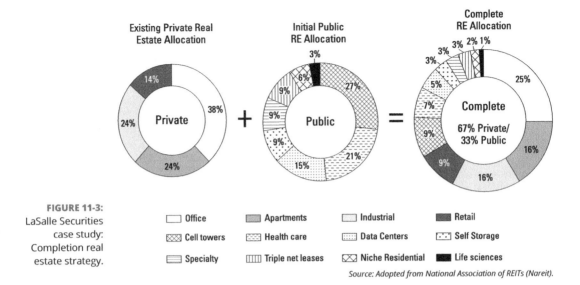

FIGURE 11-3:
LaSalle Securities
case study:
Completion real
estate strategy.

☐ Office	▨ Apartments	☐ Industrial	▓ Retail
▨ Cell towers	▨ Health care	⋯ Data Centers	⋯ Self Storage
☰ Specialty	⫼ Triple net leases	⋈ Niche Residential	▨ Life sciences

Source: Adopted from National Association of REITs (Nareit).

REITs enhance ESG attributes

Over the past decade, institutional investors have become increasingly concerned with the environmental, social, and governance (ESG) profile of their investment portfolios. I first bring up ESG in Chapter 3, touching on its pros and cons. But here I tell you that an increasing number of corporations and organizations have become more active in the space, implementing and encouraging further acceptance of it.

For these investors, REITs provide access to some of the best-in-class performers in each of the three categories. As Figure 11-4 illustrates, REITs are setting targets to address sustainability and climate change, as well as increasing disclosure around key social issues.

REMEMBER

At their core, most REITs are simple businesses that own and operate different kinds of real estate. This works in their favor here (as well as in many other areas). Think about it: It's both easier and cheaper to report on almost anything — including ESG — when you've got fewer departments to deal with. Key categories like energy consumption and health and safety are especially simpler for REITs to control, monitor, and improve compared to, say, the oil and gas industry, manufacturing, and some tech companies as well.

TIP

Certain REITs are even directly involved in ESG-specific activities. HASI, for instance, owns, operates, and finances renewable energy products.

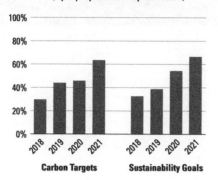

REITs Publicity Disclosing Carbon Targets and Sustainability Goals
(by equity market capitalization)

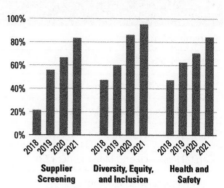

REIT Disclosure of Social Policies
(by equity market capitalization)

FIGURE 11-4:
REITs expand ESG disclosures.

Source: Adopted from National Association of REITs (Nareit).

For all these reasons and more, real estate investment trusts are looking increasingly attractive to institutional investors. I want to highlight the "more" part of that sentence for those of you who might be concerned about REITs' ESG involvement. This is not a political book, and the following is not a political statement. There are those who will agree with it and disagree with it, but the fact remains that many Republican-led states in the United States are pulling away from the concept. So you're more than welcome to wonder if an ESG focus is more of a liability than a long-term bottom-line booster.

REMEMBER

But here's the thing: REITs are attractive regardless of which political winds are blowing. It just so happens that the current trend adds to the attraction. If the ESG movement dies a sudden death tomorrow, though — as unlikely as that is — REITs will still offer plenty of appeal.

A Peek at the Top Institutional Players

REITs represented 2 percent of the commercial real estate market in 1995. Today, that amount has grown to around 10 percent. Moreover, REITs tend to pick up (or build) higher-quality properties: the newer ones with better features that conform with current expectations.

Table 11-1 lists the top 20 institutional investors in U.S. equity REITs, a few of which you might recognize. By market value, Vanguard is the largest with $176.88 billion, while BlackRock comes in second with $123.44 billion. Those two heavy hitters do admittedly make the rest of the list look puny, but I wouldn't sneeze at even UBS Asset Management's invested amount: $10.5 billion is still worth talking about.

TABLE 11-1 **Top 20 Institutional Owners of U.S. Equity (S&P Global)***

Institutional Owner	Rank by Market Value	Market Value ($B)	No. of REIT Positions
Vanguard Group Inc.	1	176.88	160
BlackRock Inc.	2	123.44	160
State Street Global Advisors Inc.	3	72.31	157
Cohen & Steers Capital Management Inc.	4	40.05	52
Norges Bank Investment Management	5	27.18	123
Capital Research and Management Co.	6	26.13	24
Geode Capital Management LLC	7	24.63	159
FMR LLC	8	21.44	150
Principal Global Investors LLC	9	19.55	148
T. Rowe Price Group Inc.	10	16.11	148
JP Morgan Asset Management	11	16.00	142
Northern Trust Global Investments	12	15.70	158
Dimensional Fund Advisors LP	13	15.57	146
Wellington Management Group LLP	14	14.53	75
Stichting Pensioenfonds ABP	15	13.39	52
Charles Schwab Investment Management Inc.	16	13.33	155
Legal & General Investment Management Ltd.	17	13.10	148
BNY Asset Management	18	11.57	151
Invesco Ltd.	19	11.11	147
UBS Asset Management AG	20	10.50	157

* Data compiled March 29, 2023. Analysis includes investor positions in equity REITs that traded on the Nasdaq, NYSE, or NYSE American as of December 31, 2022. Excludes positions held by individuals or family offices/trusts.

Most of this capital is admittedly invested in exchange-traded funds (ETFs), indexes, and mutual funds, so they're not direct deposits. But the money still makes its way to the REITs, regardless.

TIP

If you're not familiar with ETFs, don't worry. I have a whole chapter — the very next one — that discusses it and its investment cousins at much greater length. Chapter 12 gives you details not only about what they are but also actual funds you can invest in — on the cheap too.

Pension funds

Pension funds — funds designed to benefit retired members — are well-known for their real estate positions. And by *well-known,* I mean to people who pay attention to pension funds, which certainly isn't everyone. So don't feel foolish if you weren't aware of this allocation.

That aside, real estate is an asset class that pension funds recognize as something that can work — and work well. It's been a source of advancing income for them for a while. But now they're more and more realizing that REITs offer a specific brand of real estate that can boost their profit potential even more by complimenting already existent (or modified) private real estate positions.

In May 2022, BlackRock Real Assets' Raj Rehan, who heads up real estate securities, said that "the activity that we have seen in the last two or three years has really stepped up in terms of engagement and interest." His clients see REITs as a way to grow their portfolios while also hedging against inflation. And while that year did prove a rough one for REITs in the end, savvy investors understand the value of patience. It's the long-term results that count, not short- or even mid-term fluctuations.

REMEMBER

As I've said before and I'll say again, every asset class has its ups and downs. Sometimes they look good at even a casual glance. Sometimes they're under obvious pressure. And still other times, they go up but not as much as everything else. This last possibility showed in 2015–2020, when REITs underperformed broader equities, in part because there were new growth sectors that were more exciting. Figure 11-5 captures some of that data, showing REITs' larger movements over the years.

TIP

Really though, it's a matter of ratios and averages that you want to consider. Institutional investors definitely do, measuring how often the downs occur and how well the ups make up for them. These are factors that must be taken into consideration for a truly sustainable, optimized portfolio.

Take Nareit's analysis of Preqin data between 2016 and September 30, 2021. It showed that the amount of U.S. defined benefit plans invested in REITs as part of their real estate allocation was rising, growing from 55 percent to an estimated 67 percent. That same kind of jump applies to endowments and foundations, when investments jumped from 51 percent to 63 percent. And *Pensions & Investments'* 2022 annual survey found that REIT assets in the largest 200 U.S. retirement plans shot up 22 percent year over year to $34.2 billion by September 30, 2021.

That looks like an impressive number all by itself. However, I do have to point out that real estate equity portfolios grew 13.4 percent to $418.3 billion. That's a nice jump, to say the least — one that shows how much real estate-specific money is not going to REITs.

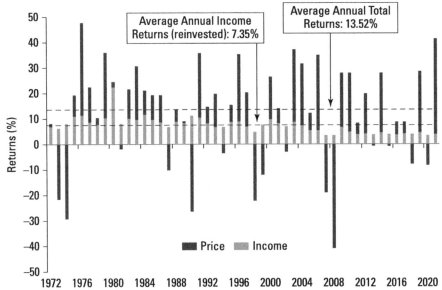

FIGURE 11-5:
FTSE Nareit All
Equity REITs
Index annual
returns
(1972–2021).

Source: Adopted from National Association of REITs (Nareit).

REMEMBER

It's also important to keep in mind how much easier it can be to grow a smaller percentage (tens of billions, in this case) than it is to make large leaps in bigger quantities. All the same, if you're looking for growth, REITs can clearly offer something substantial.

REITs roar back

Critics can point out that REITs had a very good year in 2021. The Nareit All Equity REITs Index did skyrocket 41.3 percent to post its second-best year ever. Therefore, the data — and any positive conclusions — could be seen as skewed. John Worth, executive vice president for research and investor outreach at Nareit, agrees with the first part of that commentary.

As for the second part, though, he points out that real estate prices in general were up immensely. Which is a fair point to make. Yet here's the takeaway both he and I want you to focus on: Over the five-year period through 2021, real estate in general rose 40.5 percent while REITs came in at 47.4 percent. This tells Worth that pensions aren't "selling out of REIT positions to bring down their allocation as REITs outperform." They're actually adding to them.

TIP

I spoke to Worth while working on this chapter, and he also pointed out that the real estate landscape is changing. For one thing, it's going digital just as much as everything else is these days. And REITs have been on the front edge of that innovation. I have already touched on that once in this chapter, but I especially show evidence in Chapters 6 and 7. That's where I reference the number of proptech applications within the REIT sector that have technologically enhanced marketing, leasing, property management, construction, and financial reporting. Institutional clients who are new to the REIT space are taking notice of those upgrades and the strong performances they've enabled relative to private real estate and other public securities.

Pension funds flock to REITs

Right now, pension funds typically give real estate about a 10 percent chunk of their total investment portfolio. That's too low, though, according to Nareit, which suggests 15 percent instead. And for those of you who are quick to point out that a REIT advancement group is hardly going to be unbiased on the subject, consider how it doesn't recommend putting all of that toward REITs — not even half of it, in fact. It simply recommends that no less than 25 percent of that 15 percent go toward the assets it champions.

Either pension plans are listening or they're paying attention to other sources saying the same thing. One way or the other, Nareit's Kurt Walten, senior VP of investment affairs and investor education, says that "pension plans are increasingly using REITs as a way to complement their private real estate investment." This includes one of the world's largest real estate investors, APG, a Dutch pension services provider.

Nareit notes that APG "uses a fully integrated strategy combining REITs and non-listed real estate to build and manage a portfolio of global real estate investments." As of early 2022, that meant that 60 percent of its real estate–specific funds were devoted to private real estate, while 40 percent went to REITs. That's significant — and a great example for others to consider.

I don't expect everyone to put that much into REITs, mind you. But hopefully that enormous amount makes its fellow pension funds think. It should also show that there is a lot of room for growth in this arena.

University endowments and the "Yale Model"

Let's next move on to large university endowments, particularly those from Ivy League schools. They're among the most influential, closely watched institutional investors out there. And of course they know that. As leaders in diversified multi-asset investing for decades, they enjoy a reputation for innovation and attractive risk-adjusted returns: the epitome of smart money.

AUSTIN PENSION'S 50-50 STRATEGY

Most institutional investors are going to be much more diversified, and with good reason. I've already stressed how important diversification is — one of the main reasons REITs are so attractive in the first place — one, though hardly all. But there is an industrial investor that puts a whopping 50 percent of its real estate allocation toward REITs.

The City of Austin Employee's Retirement System (COAERs) conducted a strategic review in 2019. After careful considerations, assessments, and evaluations, the people in charge reached a conclusion. And that conclusion was very much in REITs' favor. The pension fund decided to evenly split its real estate funds between REITs and private properties. And while 2020 proved to be a very difficult year for REITs, COAERS didn't falter, which meant it was able to benefit from 2021's rebound.

Altogether, it was devoting $350 million to real estate equity, which amounts to 10 percent of its strategic asset allocation.

I can also point out private sector pension fund Teachers Insurance and Annuity Association (TIASS). TIASS, a U.S.–based money pool, invests $24.2 billion in REITs. Most of that is by way of direct investments, with smaller amounts devoted to funds, both listed and unlisted.

Then there's ABP, the Netherlands' national civil pension fund. It's the world's largest public pension fund that's active in real estate. This one invests more than 10 percent of its $400 billion assets under management to direct, listed, and unlisted real estate investments.

These elite endowments do have a lot going for them, including impressive finances and state-of-the-art equipment. And that's to say nothing about the brilliant minds operating both, not only professors and students but also a wide array of alumni who don't mind helping their alma maters out. These people not only know about exclusive, top-performing investment opportunities, they also have the ability to act on them. And that can and does make an enormous difference.

Universities, of course, make money from tuition and room and board fees. They can also receive fair chunks of change from wealthy individuals who are either associated with them or want to be associated with them. And the government helps public institutions of higher education as well through various means. But we also shouldn't forget how much investments contribute to university funding. They pool the money they receive together and make more still by allocating some of it toward buying up assets of various kinds. Their typical goal is to achieve real average annual returns of 5 percent every five or 10 years.

Again, the eight Ivy League schools, especially, have the resources to make this happen. So perhaps it shouldn't be surprising that six of them rank in the top 20 of largest endowments, as shown in Table 11-2.

TABLE 11-2   **Endowment's Total Market Value in Fiscal Year 2022**

Rank	University	Total Endowment
1	Harvard University	49,444,494
2	University of Texas System	42,668,276
3	Yale University	41,383,300
4	Stanford University	36,3000,000
5	The Trustees of Princeton University	35,794,186
6	Massachusetts Institute of Technology	24,739,862
7	Trustees of the University of Pennsylvania	20,724,351
8	The Texas A&M University System and Related Foundations	18,243,191
9	University of Michigan	17,347,188
10	University of Notre Dame	16,729,299
11	Regents of the University of California	15,417,663
12	Northwestern University	14,121,488
13	Trustees of Columbia University	13,279,846
14	Washington University	12,252,329
15	Duke University	12,166,260
16	Vanderbilt University	10,206,067
17	Emory University	9,997,742
18	University of Virginia	9,858,442
19	Cornell University	9,838,198
20	The Johns Hopkins University	8,244,472

Source: Adopted fron 2022 NACUBO-TIAA Study of Endowments.

You might already be expecting something along these lines, in which case you're correct: Those top 20 and other big university endowments know the value of real estate. They have for several decades now, especially after David Swensen, Yale's chief investment officer from 1985 through May 2021, promoted the idea of alternative investments.

The results were impressive over his 36 years there. Very, very impressive, as evidenced by how Yale

>> Outperformed the average endowment by 3.4 percent per year (according to Cambridge Associates), with a 13.7 percent annualized yearly gain

>> Outperformed the traditional 60/40 portfolio (60 percent U.S. stocks to 40 percent U.S. bonds) by 4 percent

>> Booked almost $58 billion in investment gains

Those figures were more than enough to inspire copycat attempts across the higher educational field. And they're more than welcome to do so considering how Swensen literally wrote a book on the subject for public consumption, titled *Unconventional Success* (Free Press). In it, he wrote how "asset-class exposure to equity real estate produces a hybrid of equity-like and bond-like attributes, generating inflation protection at a lower opportunity cost than other alternatives."

His portfolio did include traditional stocks and bonds, mind you — but only up to a certain point. When he first took over, Swensen found himself overseeing the then typical 60/40 portfolio. But he turned it into a flourishing resource that much more focused on such asset areas as

>> Venture capital

>> Private equity

>> Hedge funds

>> Natural resources

>> Real estate

And that made all the difference.

Private equity firms

Moving down the list of real-estate-seeking institutional investors, let's discuss private equity firms last but not least. These are investment partnerships that buy up portions of companies with the intention of managing them before selling them for a hopeful profit. Contrary to their name, they can be publicly traded. But regardless of whether they are or not, they're after big money — which is why other institutional and accredited investors tend to love them.

TIP

This isn't to say that individuals don't appreciate them or can't invest in them, too. Publicly traded private equity firms are up for grabs just as long as you can afford their shares. In fact, these partnerships are very much interested in courting average investors, recognizing them as a channel of growth that hasn't been tapped nearly as much as it could be.

Private equity firms present a huge pool of investment potential for REITs. Like other institutional investors out there, they have a lot of money on hand — portions of which are assigned to real estate in general. REITs are already on their radar, and they do own shares of them to varying degrees. But that amount could be set to head higher.

Let me introduce you to one private equity firm in particular. If you follow financial news at all, you should recognize the name Blackstone, and with good reason. It's the world's largest alternative asset manager: a giant institution that boasts $991 billion in AUM. That's astonishingly close to a trillion dollars — all managed by a single entity. It's mindboggling when you think about it, if you can think about it at all. A trillion dollars is a very difficult concept to grasp considering how it's such a high number and so very, very much more than any of us will ever own. Even the world's richest people are only billionaires, with less than $300 billion to their name.

Twelve thousand is a much easier number to consider, which works for my purpose here, because that's roughly how many real estate assets Blackstone holds. It seems safe to say that real estate is a very big deal in this giant's estimate. In particular these days, it's been focusing on strong, growing, intriguing sectors within that asset class.

This global force also owns Blackstone Real Estate Income Trust (BREIT), a private, open-ended REIT you may have heard of. Being unlisted, BREIT isn't as liquid as publicly traded competitors, of course. That's something worth noting. But it's also not as volatile when volatility strikes. And being run by such a big and powerful name tends to be a big enough benefit to overcome any doubts in investors' minds.

Admittedly, market jitters meant it had a rough patch late in 2022, where investors suddenly wanted it to be much more tradable than it is. When BREIT stuck to its guns, enforcing rules it had already very clearly laid out, it ended up with some fairly bad publicity — short-term, that is.

That negative news and the uncertain economy that had prompted it didn't stop the University of California from getting involved just a few months later. In January 2023, the school agreed to put $4 billion into Blackstone for a minimum 11.25 percent net preferred return over six years, supported by $1 billion of BREIT shares.

Signs of the Times

I've already shown multiple examples of how REIT awareness is spreading among institutional investors. But let's sum it all up now.

Many institutional investors believe the current economic climate puts REITs in a great place. To quote CenterSquare Investment Management senior investment strategist Uma Moriarity, the sector is "poised to perform for investor portfolios," especially compared to "private real estate and broader equities." That prediction is based in large part on a previous enormous gap in 12-month trailing returns between public and private real estate.

As Nareit noted in February 2023, the third quarter of 2022 saw a 38 percent valuation difference between the two, with commercial real estate losing out. Since that's "one of the largest spreads on record," expert after expert believes it's bound to even out from here.

And that means there's an excellent chance REIT prices will rise as well.

If that sounds too optimistic, consider research by the ever-present Nareit and CEM Benchmarking, which provides investment insights for institutional investors. Together, they show that REIT returns have outperformed private real estate by around 2 percent per year.

Part of that is because private institutional funds usually come with management fees of 1 percent to 2 percent. Some include performance fees as well, where the investment manager and investor split profits after a certain point. REITs, on the other hand, are traded like stocks and therefore come with the same cost expectations.

REMEMBER

Fees can't explain how REITs perform during recessions and market pullbacks, though. I discuss in Chapter 2 how well they can do even in challenging times, but it's worth mentioning here as well. According to Nareit, the sector outperformed both private real estate and the broader stock market during and after each of the last six recessions.

Consider also how the Nareit All Equity REIT Index averaged 22.7 percent annualized total returns, while the Russell 1000 recorded just 8.2 percent growth and the NFI-ODCE Index — a popular private real estate index — saw a mere 5.2 percent. Institutional investors understand all of this. They also increasingly recognize that investing with REITs allows them to be more nimble and targeted in capturing gains when and where they come.

And if there's anyone out there that doesn't like the sound of that, it will be news to me.

Chapter **12**

Pressing the REIT Easy Button

You may remember the bright red Easy Button Staples introduced in its commercials almost 20 years ago. Those ads were so popular that Staples ended up selling toy versions of the button, which went on to sell millions of units. There was no doubt the idea was a hit. And with good reason: Who doesn't want things simplified in this hectic world?

Those Easy Buttons didn't do anything to actually make life easier outside of lightening the mood, of course. And I can't say there's an Easy Button to REIT investing either. But there are a set of tricks, tips, and tactics that can help simplify the big picture enormously. That's why in this chapter, I talk about simplified REIT investment opportunities such as REIT exchange-traded funds (ETFs) and other bundled packages like mutual funds and closed-end funds. These offerings allow you to benefit from multiple stocks with a single purchase — or press of that REIT Easy Button.

Easy isn't always best, of course. So let me blunt right from the beginning: Acting on the following information may or may not make your investing life more profitable. That very much depends on your situation, for reasons I outline in this chapter. Still, it's good to know that these simplified offerings exist, especially if you are itching to get started right away.

REITS: THE BEST THING SINCE SLICED BREAD

Hopefully I've convinced you by now that owning REITs is the best thing since sliced bread. As I explain in Chapter 2, there's $228 trillion of real estate in the world, with some $19.6 trillion in the United States alone. And when we narrow that number down to commercial real estate, it's still enormous at $20.7 trillion (as of the second quarter of 2021, according to Nareit). Given that immense size, I'd say it's safe to say the category plays an integral role in the global economy.

That's why investors have long since looked to commercial real estate for its attractive, wealth-building characteristics. And since 2001, global real estate securities have outperformed many other major asset classes, including the broad equity market as well as investment-grade bonds and commodities. Under the right circumstances and the right management — publicly traded or otherwise — they offer stable income streams and capital growth that are tough (and I would argue foolish) to ignore.

REITs provide a simple, liquid, inexpensive, and diverse way to invest in all of that. And you can simplify them further through the asset vehicles described in this chapter.

Give Me an E . . . Give Me a T . . . Give Me an F! Give Me REIT ETFs!

ETFs, short for *exchange-traded funds,* can be a perfect solution for average investors who are limited in the amount of time and/or money they have to build their own basket of REITs. ETFs are easily tradeable funds full of investments that fall under the same umbrella, whatever that umbrella might be. It's a big, big world out there, with plenty of connections to be made. That much is evidenced by the thousands and thousands of global ETFs you can choose from today.

ETFs can be structured to track anything and everything from the price of an individual commodity to a large and diverse collection of securities or specific investment strategies. As such, some ETFs focus on precious metals. Others offer exposure to big-cap stocks. There are bond ETFs, equity ETFs, currency ETFs, commodity ETFs, clean energy ETFs, healthcare ETFs, index-specific ETFs, country-specific ETFs, emerging nations ETFs . . . and the list goes on from there. There are even "biblically responsible" umbrellas, entertainment-oriented ones, those geared toward weight-loss pharmaceutical products and the companies that make them, businesses preferred by millennials (such as Uber, Netflix and Chipotle), and artificial intelligence.

Whatever the focus, think of an ETF as a cake with layers. You get a piece of the profit across an array of companies, products, indexes, and/or sectors, while limiting your risk. If one holding (layer) starts to struggle, all the other holdings should save investors from feeling the heat. They're essentially a portfolio in and of themselves — an umbrella-specific portfolio, but a portfolio nonetheless.

Because many ETFs are so focused, don't think that you can hold a single umbrella as your one-and-only holding and think you're good to go. You still need other forms of diversification across asset classes, company types, and focuses in your overall portfolio if you want to minimize risk.

Why ETFs are attractive to investors

ETFs are popular with retail investors for their one-stop-shopping attributes and with financial advisors because they're simple to explain to clients. Advisors can also charge additional fees on top of the ones directly tied to the fund itself. So there's that, too.

Investors can get around those extra charges by cutting out the middleman and buying ETFs themselves through online brokerage accounts.

Another (unflattering) reason they're attractive to advisors is the fact that professionals can blame any negative price changes on index movements — which ETFs are usually tied to — instead of their own stock-picking ability. And in these consultants' defense, they're not always wrong about that. ETFs do tend to perform in line with the indexes they're tied to.

With that said, there is a difference between index underperformance and underperformance from asset allocation. An ETF's portfolio value and, therefore, stock price can also falter or fall due to misallocation. Sometimes their managers give too much weight to one stock or asset over the others. For instance, if Company A makes up 15 percent of "ETF SOS," and Company A's stock comes under intense or even moderate pressure, it's going to be a lot more difficult for Companies B to Z to compensate.

Good, ethical financial advisors should and do spot that kind of problem ahead of time. Better yet, they'll help you track down the best ETFs for you. On the other hand, there's a lot of wiggle room for those who are less proficient or honest. If there isn't noticeable index underperformance in an ETF's portfolio, there's less of a chance incompetent advisors will be fired.

How ETFs can help you diversify

Many investors find that using a financial planner or investment advisor has its advantages. These professionals offer personal attention to clients, helping them figure out good investments to consider and bad investments to avoid in general, based on the individual metrics discussed in Chapter 8.

That's important. Very important, in fact. Choosing the most efficient way to gain exposure to the asset class in question is key, particularly for investors with limited funds or time available. But you want to be just as cost-effective as you are diverse — maybe even more so.

TIP

When it comes to investing in real estate, the adage about location isn't entirely true. Location is important, mind you. Again, very important. But it has to be tempered with reasonable or better-than-reasonable buy-in prices along with leverage, leasing, and management considerations. I find myself very much agreeing with Steven Schoenfeld who wrote *Active Index Investing* (Wiley, 2004). He says it's best to "invest in the right properties, with the right people at the right prices." Property, people, and price: Those "are the three components of a successful strategy."

I know this is supposed to be the easy chapter. And it is. But first let's remember why an easy chapter has to exist in the first place. Because, as Schoenfeld acknowledges, getting property, people, and price all right "is more difficult than it might seem." Moreover, this isn't one of those formulas where you can get two-thirds of the elements right and expect to still come out ahead. "Missing any one of them can easily result in losses." I couldn't agree more with that since I'm living proof of how far one can fall after failing one part of the test.

Before I became a writer, I spent two decades as a commercial real estate developer and owner — positions that allowed me to raise my net worth to over $25 million. I can't say that I handled that money as well as I should have, because I didn't. But the straw that broke the camel's back was the partnership I had in that arrangement. When that unraveled, I was left stuck with an ownership interest I couldn't liquidate. Add in bad management — also a people problem — and I lost almost everything.

That turned around after I switched my focus to publicly traded REITs. By owning them, I now have my bases covered. I have access to full liquidity and diversification across property sectors and geography. As I keep stating, everyone has their own considerations and has to make their own decisions. But in my case, I prefer my REIT benefits to come with higher total returns, which are much easier to come by through individual stock ownership instead of ETFs. It's been proven that a more hands-on approach involving research and fundamental analysis can deliver a better outcome than owning the market in its entirety.

ACTIVE OR PASSIVE INVESTING: THE DEBATE RAGES ON

Discussions about whether active or passive investing works better can turn heated pretty quickly. Everyone — professional, amateur, or otherwise — who knows about the two seems to have a strong opinion on which one is superior.

The first is, as implied, hands-on in nature. Either an individual or portfolio manager looks through available assets, (hopefully) examining them carefully to determine which ones to buy and which ones to set aside. Passive investing, meanwhile, involves funds or other investment baskets that can be bought and then largely ignored from there.

While passive investing is more popular among individual investors, there are valid arguments to be made for both. For one thing, passive investing boasts greater investment flow and money earned. Then again, active investing has a greater potential for higher gains.

The reason why so many people don't achieve that potential is multifaceted. Those who hire professionals to do it for them, for instance, face higher costs of doing business that cuts down on their returns. Then there's the power of market pressure that causes people to want to cut and run instead of waiting out the volatility or — better yet — buy smart, sustainable stocks whenever their share prices dip. This single factor accounts for so much individual investor loss that it's hard to calculate.

That's why I believe anyone with that proclivity who doesn't feel confident they'll be able to change should at least consider REIT ETFs.

With that said, I have the time and confidence (balanced with a proper amount of humility, mind you) to back my available funds. If you do too, great! But there's no need to worry if you don't. Thanks to REIT ETFs, a diversified real estate strategy is available to even the smallest, most hands-off investors.

Breaking Down REIT ETFs by Category

The earlier sections give you an idea of how many ETFs there are in general — which is a lot! But now let's get into REIT ETFs specifically. Because as of this writing, there were almost as many REIT ETFs as flavors of Baskin-Robbins ice cream.

If that sounds surprising, perhaps I should have made myself clearer when discussing ETFs in general. You can think about them this way: If a larger asset category can be split into smaller asset categories, then there's probably an investment interest in them. And if there's an investment interest in them, then there's probably an ETF to satisfy that attraction.

As such, there are REIT ETFs devoted to U.S.–only investments while another one focuses exclusively on non–U.S. developed markets. Another targets small caps, while still another invests in high-yielders. And still more ETF examples have high concentrations of REITs despite their broader real estate appeals.

I cover various ETFs in the following sections, but let's start with the plain vanilla REIT ETFs that are the larger market capitalization–weighted indexes.

Mega market cap weightings

The following are the REIT ETFs with market capitalizations of a billion dollars or more:

>> **Vanguard Real Estate Index Fund ETF (VNQ):** VNQ has $32.77 billion of assets under management, or AUM. It avoids mortgage REITs altogether, investing around 37 percent in specialized REITs, 14 percent in residential REITs, and about 13 percent in industrial REITs. While it emphasizes large-cap REITs, VNQ does hold mid and small caps as well. With 166 stocks in its portfolio, it's the big dog to beat. VNQ is passively managed with a 0.12 percent expense ratio. It aims to track the MSCI U.S. Investable Market Real Estate 25/50 Index's returns. The fund's top holdings include Prologis Inc. (7.8 percent), American Tower (6.3 percent), and Equinix (4.4 percent).

>> **Schwab U.S. REIT ETF (SCHH):** SCHH has $5.69 billion of AUM. It also avoids mREITs and similarly stays away from hybrid REITs. Instead, it has a large concentration of specialized REITs (~39 percent), residentials (~14 percent), retail (~14 percent), and industrial (~13 percent). Passively managed with a 0.07 percent expense ratio, SCHH aims to track the Dow Jones Equity All REIT Capped Index's total returns. The ETF hold 137 REITs, with its largest three being Prologis (8.8 percent), American Tower (8.3 percent), and Equinix (5.1 percent).

>> **The Real Estate Select Sector SPDR Fund (XLRE):** XLRE has $4.63 billion of AUM. It has a 0.10 percent expense fee and includes large-cap REITs (excluding mREITs) as well as other publicly traded real estate companies listed on the S&P 500. XLRE is passively managed and aims to track the S&P Real Estate Select Sector Total Return Index. There are 31 companies in it, with higher concentration levels of infrastructure (~21.5 percent), industrials (~11.9 percent), residentials (~11 percent), and data centers (~10 percent). Its largest components are

Prologis (~11.9 percent), American Tower (~11.3 percent), and Equinix (~7 percent).

>> **iShares U.S. Real Estate ETF (IYR):** IYR has $3.28 billion of AUM and 78 holdings. While all its top ten investments — which make up more than 45 percent of its portfolio weight — are REITs, it does also own shares of regular real estate companies as well. IYR is passively managed with a 0.39 percent expense ratio and aims to track the Dow Jones U.S. Real Estate Capped Index. Its top sectors are specialty (~39 percent), residential (~13.4 percent), and industrial (~12 percent). And its largest holdings are Prologis (9.6 percent), American Tower (8.1 percent), and Equinix (5.6 percent).

>> **iShares Cohen & Steers REIT ETF (ICF):** ICF has $2.27 billion of AUM. It invests in large-cap (or large-ish-cap), liquid REITs and similar stocks. ICF is passively managed with a 0.32 percent expense ratio and aims to track the Cohen & Steers Realty Majors Index. With only 30 holdings, it has significant exposure in the specialized (44.8 percent), residential (17.8 percent), and retail (14.5 percent) sectors. Top constituents include Equinix (8.5 percent), Prologis (8.2 percent), and American Tower (8.2 percent).

>> **Fidelity MSCI Real Estate Index ETF (FREL):** FREL has $1.16 billion of AUM. It isn't exclusive to REITs, though its top ten holdings do all fall into that category. It is passively managed with a 0.84 percent expense fee. And it aims to track the MSCI USA IMI Real Estate Index. FREL features 161 holdings, with its largest being Prologis (9.3 percent), American Tower (7.6 percent), and Equinix (5.3 percent).

All six of these billion-dollar ETFs are well diversified across property sectors and geographies. They're all geared toward highlighting U.S. REITs. So it only makes sense then that they share so many constituents, just with different weightings.

Speaking of weightings, VNQ puts 47 percent of its equity into its top ten holdings, while SCHH and IYR put 46 percent. XLRE and ICF have a whopping 62 percent, while FREL's figure is "just" 43 percent. You'll also see American Tower, Prologis, Crown Castle, Equinix, and Public Storage represented in each one.

REMEMBER

The bigger the ETF the more often you're going to see a solid mix of the good, the bad, and the ugly in what they hold. And I would argue that this is true of each of the ones just listed. With that said, these big players can help reduce volatility as well as investment costs since their expense fees are so low.

TIP

If you prefer the ETF route, which can be hands-off and provide diversification to your portfolio, the larger REIT ETFs can be a great low-cost option for REIT exposure.

Global REIT exposure

Again, VNQ, SCHH, XLRE, IYR, ICE, and FREL are all U.S. focused, which may or may not be what you're looking for. If it's not, there are also global REIT ETFs such as

>> **iShares Global REIT ETF (REET):** REET has $2.91 billion of AUM with 348 portfolio holdings. It features shares of publicly listed REITs in both developed and emerging markets around the world, as well as REIT–like holdings where REITs haven't yet been legalized. With that said, its top ten holdings are all U.S. based. Investors should also know that it can invest up to 20 percent of its assets in cash, cash equivalents, and more speculative assets such as futures, options, and swap contracts. REET is passively managed (0.14 percent expense ratio) and aims to track the FTSE EPRA/Nareit Global REITs Index. Its top three holdings are Prologis (8.4 percent), Equinix (4.9 percent), and Public Storage (3.6 percent).

>> **Vanguard Global ex-U.S. Real Estate Index Fund (VNQI):** VNQI has $3.59 billion of AUM and boasts 671 holdings, including publicly traded global REITs and select real estate management and development businesses. As the name implies, it does not hold any U.S. companies. VNQI is passively managed with a 0.12 percent expense ratio, and aims to track the S&P Global ex-U.S. Property Index. This index is market-cap-weighted, which means each of its components are sized according to that category's total market cap. The ETF's top holdings are Goodman Group (~2.5 percent), Sun Hung Kai Properties (~2.2 percent), and Vonovia SE (~2.2 percent).

>> **SPDR Dow Jones Global Real Estate ETF (RWO):** RWO has $1.25 billion of AUM. It invests in global REITs, including U.S. REITs with international positions. Its more than 200 holdings span multiple sectors, including commercial and residential mREITs, real estate developers, specialized REITs, and investment management fund operators. The fund tilts significantly toward commercial REITs and shies away from real estate developers. While global in nature, RWO overweights the United States with 70 percent exposure and is a bit light on Asian coverage. RWO is passively managed with a 0.50 percent expense ratio and aims to track the total return performance of the Dow Jones Global Select Real Estate Securities Index. Its top holdings include Prologis (8.9 percent), Equinix (5.1 percent), and Public Storage (3.8 percent).

These global REIT ETFs are highly diversified, even more so than the U.S.–specific ETFs I mention earlier. REET and RWO only devote 33 percent of their funds to their top ten holdings, and VNQI just 19 percent.

Keep in mind that one primary benefit of international REIT exposure is diversification, because the average investor doesn't know which countries will have greater growth. And even if they did, they wouldn't have any way of investing solely in that country's real estate.

Specialty REIT ETFs

Of course, anything easy in life can be complicated somehow, someway. And the same is true of ETFs. They may have started out with the intent to simplify investors' lives, but they've certainly gotten creative from there.

In the REIT space, that means there are a set of specialty collections under more novel umbrellas. Basically, these vehicles exist for those less-hands-on investors who still like to throw some spice into their portfolios. This doesn't mean they're not still one-stop shopping offerings. They're just one-stop shopping for a more select, off-the-beaten-path focus. Some specialty REIT ETFs include the following:

- » **Pacer Benchmark Data & Infrastructure Real Estate SCTR ETF (SRVR):** SRVR has $749 million of AUM. It holds mostly real estate companies, including REITs, in developed nations around the world that make 85 percent or more of their earnings or revenue from the data and infrastructure sectors. SRVR is passively managed with a 0.5 percent expense ratio and seeks to track total returns of the Solactive GPR Data & Infrastructure Real Estate Index. It has 18 holdings, with its top three being American Tower (~15.6 percent), Equinix (~15.4 percent), and Crown Castle (~15.3 percent).

- » **iShares Residential and Multisector Real Estate ETF (REZ):** REZ has $632 million of AUM. It holds 39 companies — including apartment REITs, manufactured home REITs, healthcare REITs, and self-storage REITs — within the U.S. equity market. Investors should also know that it can put 20 percent of its portfolio toward futures, options, swap contracts, cash, and cash equivalents. REZ is passively managed with a 0.48 percent expense ratio and seeks to track the FTSE Nareit All Residential Capped Index. Its top three holdings are Public Storage (~13.1 percent), Welltower (~9.1 percent), and AvalonBay (~6.3 percent).

- » **iShares Mortgage Real Estate Capped ETF (REM):** REM has $594 million of AUM. It invests in mortgage REITS (mREITs) — both residential and commercial — and has 33 constituents in its portfolio. REM is passively managed with a 0.48 percent expense ratio and tracks the FTSE Nareit All Mortgage Capped Index. Its top three holdings are Annaly Capital Management (~17.4 percent), AGNC Investment (~11.4 percent), and Starwood Property Trust (~9.7 percent).

>> **Pacer Benchmark Industrial Real Estate SCTR ETF (INDS):** INDS has $217 million of AUM. It holds 30 companies from developed markets that get 85 percent or more of their earnings or revenue from industrial or self-storage real estate. INDS is passively managed with a 0.55 percent expense ratio, and it tracks the total returns of the Solactive GPR Industrial Real Estate Index. Its top three holdings are Public Storage (~15.5 percent), Prologis (~14.7 percent), and Life Storage (~5.2 percent), which plans to merge with Extra Space in the second half of 2023.

>> **VanEck Mortgage REIT Income ETF (MORT):** MORT has $166 million of AUM and tracks the overall performance of U.S. mortgage real estate investment trusts. It has 26 holdings and seeks to access a wide range of asset sizes, holding small-, mid-, and large-cap mREITs at its discretion. MORT is passively managed with a 0.41 percent expense ratio and tries to replicate the MVIS U.S. Mortgage REITs Index's price and yield performance. Its top three holdings are Annaly Capital Management (~12.1 percent), AGNC Investment (~8.4 percent), and Starwood Property Trust (~8 percent).

>> **Vident U.S. Diversified Real Estate ETF (PPTY):** PPTY has $116 million of AUM. It focuses on a diverse basket of real estate companies traded on U.S. exchanges. These holdings include assets that operate in major cities but exclude externally managed businesses and those that aren't very liquid due to fewer shares available. PPTY is passively managed with a 0.419 percent expense ratio, and it tracks the USREX U.S. Diversified Real Estate Index. This index assigns fixed weights to 11 different property types: residential (19 percent), office (17.5 percent), industrial (14.5 percent), retail (14.5 percent), hotel (7.5 percent), healthcare (7.5 percent), data center (7.5 percent), diversi-fied (7.5 percent), self-storage (2 percent), manufactured homes (2 percent), and student housing (0.5 percent). Its top holdings include Prologis (~4.2 percent), Equinix (~4.2 percent), and AvalonBay (~3.9 percent).

>> **Fundamental Income Net Lease Real Estate ETF (NETL):** NETL is the first and only dedicated net-lease-focused ETF. It has $96.6 million of AUM, is passively managed with a 0.60 percent expense ratio, and seeks to own net-lease REITs that generate steady and reliable income. NETL holds 22 assets with broad diversification across multiple property types and locations, all leased to high-quality, creditworthy tenants. Its top three holdings are Realty Income (~8.4 percent), W.P. Carey (~8.2 percent), and National Retail Properties (~8.2 percent).

>> **ALPS REIT Dividend Dogs ETF (RDOG):** RDOG applies the Dogs of the Dow Theory to each REIT property segment by using the S-Network Composite U.S. REIT Index as its core pool of eligible securities. It seeks to provide investors with equal-weight exposure to the five highest-yielding U.S. REITs — a category known as the Dividend Dogs — within nine sectors. Constituents must have trailing 12-month (TTM) FFO per share that is greater than their

TTM dividend payouts per share for yield preservation. RDOG holds 45 REITs, with its top three being American Tower (~2.5 percent), One Liberty Properties (~2.5 percent), and National Storage Affiliates (~2.4 percent).

» **Hoya Capital Housing ETF (HOMZ):** HOMZ has $33.4 million of AUM and is passively managed with a 0.30 percent expense ratio. It tracks the performance of the Hoya Capital Housing 100 TM Index, which contains 100 companies meant to represent the U.S. residential housing industry. The fund is not REIT focused, as it holds 30 percent of residential REITs, 30 percent of homebuilder/construction firms, 20 percent of home improvement/furnishing, and 20 percent of home services/technology. Its top holdings include Lowe's (~2.7 percent), Home Depot (~2.6 percent), and Tri Pointe Group (~2 percent).

» **Hoya Capital High Dividend Yield ETF (RIET):** RIET has $31.2 million of AUM and is passively managed with a 0.50 percent expense ratio. It tracks the Hoya Capital High Dividend Yield Index, which follows 100 U.S.–listed real estate companies with high dividends. Each prospective holding is placed into one of three market capitalization tiers and assigned one of 14 property sectors. RIET features a 30 percent portfolio position to small-cap REITs and 10 percent to preferred stocks. Its top holdings are AGNC Investment (~1.8 percent), Services Property (~1.8 percent), and Extra Space (~1.7 percent).

Residential REIT ETF (HAUS): HAUS has $4.6 million of AUM and is actively managed with a 0.60 percent expense ratio. It invests in REITs that derive their revenue from residential properties. Eighty percent of its portfolio is dedicated to residential REITs, while the remaining 20 percent usually is taken up by U.S. real estate–related securities. Its top holdings are Mid-America Apartment (~9.2 percent), Equity Residential (~9.1 percent), and AvalonBay Communities (~9.1 percent).

Now, before you go diving into any of these specialty REIT ETFs, you do have to recognize that their expense ratios are a good bit higher (as illustrated by the graph shown in Figure 12-1):

» HOMZ: 0.30 percent

» RDOG: 0.35 percent

» MORT: 0.41 percent

» REM: 0.48 percent

» REZ: 0.48 percent

» PPTY: 0.49 percent

» RIET: 0.50 percent

» INDS: 0.55 percent

» SRVR: 0.55 percent

» HAUS: 0.60 percent

» NETL: 0.60 percent

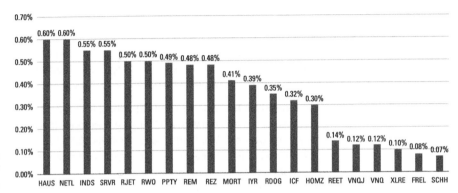

FIGURE 12-1:
Specialty REIT ETF
expense ratios.

WARNING

Keep in mind that some of these REIT ETFs offer unique risk-reward schemes, including high yields. MORT, for one, has been known to yield over 14 percent. REM has been over 11 percent and RIET over 10.5 percent. However, as I discuss in Chapter 8, make sure not to get suckered by sucker yields. Because, yes, ETFs can pack that painful punch, too.

Preferred REIT ETFs

Two additional specialty REIT ETF alternatives offer attractive yields in the form of preferred shares, something I discuss in Chapter 4. The first is InfraCap REIT Preferred ETF (PFFR). It has an AUM of $60 million, is passively managed, and has a 0.45 percent expense ratio. PFFR holds REIT preferred stock, precisely as its name indicates, and excludes shares with low yields-to-call, liquidity, and market caps.

PFFR invests in a variety of REITs, including diversified REITs, shopping centers, retail, offices, and hotels, as well as mREITs. Table 12-1 outlines how its sector weightings and yields break down.

The second specialty REIT ETF alternative is Virtus InfraCap U.S. Preferred Stock ETF (PFFA), which has $530 million in AUM. Actively managed, it has a 1.21 percent expense ratio and uses leverage of 20 percent to 30 percent to help drive more competitive returns. PFAA selects its stocks and weightings based on carefully considered quantitative, qualitative, and relative valuation factors. This unique blend has helped it outperform its benchmark, the S&P Preferred Stock Total Return Index.

TABLE 12-1

PFFR's Weight and Current Yield Breakdown by REIT Sector

REIT Sector Breakdown	Weight	Current Yield (Q1-23)
Mortgage	32.9%	9.2%
Diversified	7.7%	7.9%
Shopping Centers	8.0%	6.3%
Retail	1.3%	7.2%
Office Property	10.3%	9.7%
Residential	1.9%	6.2%
Storage	12.0%	5.5%
Hotels	10.1%	8.1%
Healthcare	3.6%	10.0%
Data Centers	12.1%	7.4%

PFAA invests in preferred shares of mREITs as well as those of diversified REITs, shopping centers, offices, and hotels, to name a few sectors. Table 12-2 outlines how its sector weightings and yield break down.

TABLE 12-2

PFFA's Weight and Current Yield Breakdown by REIT Sector

REIT Sector Breakdown	Weight	Current Yield (Q1-23)
Mortgage	19.5%	9.5%
Diversified	12.8%	8.2%
Shopping Centers	3.0%	7.0%
Office Property	1.2%	9.3%
Storage	0.0%	6.0%
Hotels	7.6%	8.2%
Healthcare	2.1%	10.8%

The ETF Game Is All About Scale

When considering whether to invest in an ETF, you should keep the ETF's operational costs in mind. Each fund could spend up to $200,000 every year for legal and administrative provisions. And then there are custodian and management costs to keep in mind as well. When everything's all added up, it takes an annual $250,000 to $500,000 to run a single ETF.

Specialty REITs in particular are generally smaller in size with less than $100 million in AUM. So they have to deal with the expenses of licensing an index, especially in their early days. As such, while fees are variable depending on the provider, these specialized indexes carry additional fees of 0.05 percent to 0.10 percent.

Another major disadvantage to owning REIT ETFs is that you have no control over the REITs being bought and sold. You also have no influence over their management teams. If you owned shares in the REITs themselves, you could at least sell your shares and vote with your feet. But that's not nearly as effective when you own shares via a third party that members of the actual companies' management are barely monitoring — if they're monitoring them at all.

TIP

Even most of the REIT ETFs based on market cap–weighted indexes won't produce the same wealth-building characteristics you can achieve through a tactical REIT basket. If you've got the time and energy to do your research and the nerve to buy and sell based on fundamentals instead of day-to-day market drama, you should strongly consider picking and choosing your own collection of REITs instead of letting someone else do the work for you. And if you ultimately decide against that option, make sure to carefully read the prospectuses of any ETFs you're interested in. That way, you can better understand all the risks involved. Because there are always risks, even for lower-risk assets like ETFs.

REMEMBER

To be clear, I'm not saying that REIT ETFs are bad. I would much prefer investors to have exposure to them rather than shunning REITs altogether. REIT ETFs might even be a better choice for certain individuals. I'm not going to say otherwise when there are always underlying personal factors to take into consideration.

REIT Mutual Funds

A *mutual fund* is a financial vehicle that pools assets to invest in securities like stocks, bonds, money market instruments, or other assets. Mutual funds are operated by professional money managers who allocate the funds' assets and attempt to produce capital gains or income for their investors.

Unlike most ETFs, mutual funds are actively managed by managers or teams who get paid to buy and sell securities. Their goal, of course, is to beat the market and help their investors profit. But because they require much more time, effort, and manpower to run, they tend to come with higher costs than ETFs. And with high minimum investment requirements, too, though that varies from example to example.

Of course I'm biased, but I consider ETFs a more optimal way to invest. One major reason for this is that they're rules-based; they're much more transparent.

TECHNICAL
STUFF

Mutual funds fall into one of two legal classifications, with open-end funds being far and away more common. They dominate in both volume and AUM. There's no limit to the number of shares this category can issue, and individual investors' share values aren't affected by the number of shares outstanding. Closed-end funds, on the other hand, issue only a specific number of shares and do not change that limit as investor demand grows.

There are many mutual funds that specialize in REITs. But a great way for investors to gain broad exposure might be through the Cohen & Steers Realty Shares Fund (CSRSX). For starters, the asset manager behind it — Cohen & Steers — is a world-class institution. Its founders, Marty Cohen and Bob Steers, are legendary for creating and managing the first mutual fund specializing in real estate securities in 1985 and then the first closed-end fund in 1988.

More specifically, CSRSX is its flagship and longest-tenured fund, with 31 holdings and $5.44 billion AUM as of February 28, 2023. Even active investors might want to invest a minimum amount in it (or something similar) in order to benchmark their personal REIT investment track records and get a window on what institutional investors are doing.

TIP

By owning shares in a top-notch fund, investors gain access to the third-largest asset class in the world (behind fixed income and equities). That's a big deal in and of itself. Plus, there's no other cost-effective way that an individual investor can gain access to such a diversified global real estate portfolio with professional management. As Evan Serton, portfolio manager at Cohen & Steers, once told me, "By allocating capital across the world, you gain access to early growth [companies] and in different stages in the economic cycle."

This isn't to say that CSRSX in particular or mutual funds in general are perfect investments. There are tradeoffs to consider, as there always are. For one thing, there's an average 1.15 percent that you have to pay of your total assets and expenses in management fees. Plus, these funds aren't customized, which means your individual investor tax profile isn't automatically aligned with the fund's strategy.

REMEMBER

As always, be careful and don't put all your eggs in one basket — even into "a basket within a basket" like a mutual fund (or ETF).

REIT Closed-End Funds

Last but not least, a closed-end fund (CEF) is organized as a publicly traded investment company by the Securities and Exchange Commission (SEC). Like a mutual fund, a CEF is a pooled investment fund with a manager who oversees it. As such, it charges an annual expense ratio to cover the costs involved before the investor begins to see performance kick in.

TECHNICAL STUFF

CEFs start out by raising a fixed amount of shares through an initial public offering (IPO). They're then structured, listed, and traded like stocks on a stock exchange, where they can make income and capital gain distributions to shareholders. And their stock prices fluctuate according to market forces, such as supply and demand, as well as the changing values of the securities in the fund's holdings.

That all sounds very stock-like, I know. Yet CEFs have several attributes that set them apart. For one thing, they represent interest in specialized portfolios of securities that typically concentrate on a specific industry, geographic market, or sector.

As of February 28, 2023, one of the largest CEFs focused on REITs was — once again — from Cohen & Steers. The almost $1.8 billion Cohen & Steers Quality Income Realty Fund (RQI) owns 207 holdings. It attempts to amplify returns through leverage, with a 27.65 percent leverage ratio as of January 31, 2023. RQI does have a high expense ratio of 1.45 percent for managed assets and 1.91 percent for common assets. On the plus side though, the dividend is paid monthly.

Cohen & Steers' other real estate-focused closed end funds include the Cohen & Steers REIT and Preferred and Income Fund (RNP) and the Cohen & Steers Real Estate Opportunities and Income Fund (RLTY). The latter is its newest CEF offering. Both funds also pay monthly dividends.

Not interested in that enormous asset manager? In that case, the Nuveen Real Estate Income Fund (JRS) is another great closed-end fund that invests in REITs. It holds a total of 80 assets, including the usual assortment of large, influential REITs such as Prologis, Equinix, and Public Storage. And despite a high expense ratio of 1.54 percent and high turnover rate of 92 percent, it has a history of being one of the safest funds around.

4

The Part of Tens

Chapter **13**

More Than Ten FAQs About REITs

E ducation is a critical part of the investing process, and investing in REITs is no different. There are plenty of whats, whys, wheres, whens, and hows that can and even should be asked about REIT investing. And while there are people who have obviously achieved the title of expert in this or that field, there isn't a single individual who can claim to be all-knowing. There's simply too much historical information to digest, with more information constantly coming in. Add in personal factors about your exact financial position, abilities, and goals, and productive analysis becomes even more complicated.

For those reasons (and a few more), I can't say I have the answers to all your questions about REITs. And don't trust anyone who says otherwise. However, I can point to concrete facts and figures as well as historical data that can help you find surer footing in your REIT investing journey. That's why in this chapter, I lay out the most frequently asked questions I hear about investing in REITs and provide useful answers to each.

How Do REITs Perform in a Recession?

I've lived through many recessions by now. Some of them were mild, others severe. REITs have survived every single one of them so far, including those that were specific to real estate. So I think it's safe to say they're battle-tested. In fact, one of the reasons I'm a writer today as opposed to a real estate developer is because of the Great Recession, which forced me to change my career.

It's easy to criticize REITs for how they performed in 2008–2009, when so many of them cut their dividends. Some of that criticism is even warranted; I'm hardly saying they're blameless. But you must remember how that financial collapse was only paralleled by the Great Depression. It saw the end of banking giants Lehman Brothers and Bear Stearns, with Citigroup and AIG almost falling apart as well. The financial markets were in utter turmoil, and there was no certainty that any REIT would have access to capital. Therefore, everyone did what they had to, including slashing their shareholder payouts when necessary.

Fortunately, most REITs learned lessons along the way that resulted in stronger and safer business models. They've also maintained solid balance sheets since then, recognizing that excessive leverage can destroy shareholder value. Yes, the COVID-19 pandemic shutdowns in 2020 did force many to reduce their dividends again. But once again, let's face the facts in full, including how it was a freak incident that nobody saw coming, and how there were still plenty of REITs that passed even that test with flying colors thanks to their previous financial practices. Most REITs — minus the lodging sector — still did pay dividends that year. Some of them had to reduce the amount, it's true. However, they still helped supplement retirees' income and contributed to non-retirees' compound interest efforts in the end, despite facing a literal plague.

Let me say it again (and perhaps more clearly): I can't say that all REIT stocks performed well during those intense downturns, nor can I say they always fare well in regular recessions. There are certain property sectors that tend to suffer more during downturns just as there are individual companies that are managed and/or positioned better or worse depending on the details.

For example, lodging REITs have greater cyclicality and very much rely on business travel to keep income flowing. That's why they tend to come under pressure when the economy turns sour. Alternatively, net-lease REITs' cash flows are driven by long-term leases that make them much more consistent and enable them to almost always keep their dividends as-is or improving.

REMEMBER

Publicly listed REITs tend to lead private real estate in both selloffs and recoveries during recessionary periods, which can lead to superior returns for those who recognize this. By understanding the leading and lagging behaviors of the larger sector and its various parts and pieces, investors can take advantage of downturns and the lower prices they offer to construct more resilient and profitable income portfolios.

Why Are REITs Good Inflation Hedges?

REITs are negatively affected by inflation. That fact needs to be stated loud and clear. Rising prices can increase operating expenses such as property maintenance, management costs, insurance, and taxes. And while some REITs in some markets can pass these higher costs through to their tenants, that's not always the case.

There's also the matter of the Federal Reserve, which acts as a watchdog for inflation. When there's a perceived threat in this regard, the Fed will raise short-term interest rates to slow the economy — which can then prompt a recession — which can then make it difficult for property owners to maintain their rental rates and occupancy levels. And even the thought of inflation can turn public perception against REITs, whether that's justified or not.

At the same time, real estate in general and REITs more specifically have definite features that can provide a buffer against inflation. For example, sectors with shorter lease durations (such as self-storage) can reset rents promptly as conditions change. And those with longer, inflation-linked rental contracts offer relatively strong and steady income growth potential. Furthermore, higher costs for land, materials, and labor mean that it's more difficult to replace or add to what's already been built. That, of course, reduces the likelihood of new competing properties popping up.

REMEMBER

Here's the main takeaway: REITs own real assets. This means the values of their properties tend to rise if overall price levels increase, and lease payments tend to rise with them. These characteristics help protect investor returns against even moderate levels of inflation as the economy accelerates.

Why Invest in REITs Instead of the Next Big Thing?

I understand this question on a very personal level thanks to my son. He loves non-fungible tokens (NFTs) — a trendy category that includes digital art, domain names, and even in-game items like power packs and weapons that gamers can purchase to make their characters stronger — as much as I love REITs. He spends a lot of time researching these modern assets, which came into existence in 2014 but really exploded into public perception after the decade turned.

In some ways, I view NFTs as an interesting asset class that offers unique characteristics no other category can match, so I do understand their appeal. But as I frequently remind my son, REITs enjoy many attributes that NFTs don't, such as

» Diversification

» Professional management

» Liquidity

» Transparency

» Dividends

There's also the fact that an NFT's value is based entirely on someone else's personal opinion of its worth in the moment, which is the reason why I call the category "trendy." Demand alone drives the price rather than the fundamental, technical, and/or economic indicators that typically influence REIT prices. So if and when demand alone sours, so do these assets — quite possibly for forever.

REMEMBER

NFTs are risky because their future is uncertain. That's always the case with the next big thing. We don't yet have a lot of history to judge their performance.

Alternatively, REITs have been around for over 60 years. So as I've mentioned, they're battle-tested and relied upon by millions of investors around the globe. Moreover, at the risk of sounding brash, my investment choice allows my son's investment choice to exist. Without data center and cell tower REITs, for instance, there would be no such thing as NFTs.

I'm not trying to pick on them alone, though. Think of other trends, such as the artificial intelligence craze. There's far too much hype and far too little substance in that field at this point, so the same arguments apply.

TIP

I can already hear the outraged responses as some of you point out one company or another that's doing very well in such sectors. So let me clarify: This isn't to say you can't make money by investing in the next big thing. There are certainly some businesses and assets that are much more likely to come out ahead than others. So go ahead and own (very) conservative positions within these spaces if you have the desire and dollars to do so.

REMEMBER

However, if you can't build a case for them standing on their own without having to rely on landlords in the process, then they probably don't deserve to replace REITs in your portfolio.

How Many REITs Should I Own at a Time?

I get this question a lot, and my standard reply goes something like this: More than one, and make sure you're adequately diversified across property sectors and geography. In other words, don't invest in a single stock and then assume that you have your REIT bases covered.

TIP

In general, I like to see investors own no fewer than ten REITs, with roughly 10 percent of their REIT-specific funds invested in each company. However, if you have 30 percent of your equities invested in REITs, I suggest you consider owning closer to 20 REITs, with 5 percent devoted to each.

As I've said throughout this book, it's impossible for me to know what your financial situation and risk tolerance look like. But in general terms, I consider 10 to 20 REIT positions reasonable. Just make sure to diversify across property sectors and geographies along the way. And consider allocating some capital to REIT preferreds and/or bonds as well.

REMEMBER

Age is also an important factor since your time horizon constitutes one of the most influential factors in structuring an investment portfolio. You can take on more risk with your investments when you're young because you have more time to recover if things go wrong. Making a costly mistake with your portfolio at age 50 could seriously set you back on your retirement journey or other financial goals, such as paying for your child's college education.

TIP

If you don't have adequate time or resources to conduct due diligence, the exchange-traded funds (ETFs) alternative (as described in Chapter 12) may be the way to go.

Does My House Count toward My Real Estate Holdings?

Homeownership may be desirable for many people, and a home can be a valuable asset over time. However, a house is considered a consumption item, not an actual investment.

Hate to break it to you if you've been thinking otherwise, but primary residences don't generate income. They consume it in the form of mortgage interest, real estate taxes, insurance payments, utility expenses, and the costs of repairs and maintenance. In contrast, REITs generate rental income that's then distributed to shareholders via tax-advantaged dividends.

REMEMBER

Furthermore, publicly traded REITs are highly liquid investments diversified across different types of properties — typically dozens, hundreds, or even thousands of them — and geographic locations. By contrast, a home is a relatively illiquid, location-specific, and individualized asset. It's highly concentrated, making it vulnerable to unexpected changes in demand within its neighborhood, whether due to shifting demographics, natural disasters, or the local business environment.

Homeownership is important, mind you, but it's not a REIT. Not even close.

Should I Invest in REITs That Just Went Public?

I'm generally not a fan of being an early investor in any company, REIT or otherwise. Why jump feet first into an unproven public position when you know it will probably offer plenty of opportunities later on? It seems much better to see how it does for a while before buying up shares. That way, it can grow into something sizable enough to attract well-known sponsors, positive attention, and profits. This all takes time — time that your money could likely be better spent elsewhere.

REMEMBER

Investors of most new companies have fewer ways of knowing whether leadership is well suited to handle what they need to handle, including facing reporters, analysts, and stockholders. The board of directors will probably have more established individuals on it, it's true. But how those individuals interact with each other for the good of that particular company will be a mystery. And employees may have been very good at handling their old job requirements, but now they have to maintain and file proper Securities and Exchange Commission (SEC) paperwork on top of it.

Some management teams have compared this due diligence to certain very uncomfortable medical procedures. (I'm sure you catch my drift.) And they're not entirely wrong in that analysis, especially in the first few years of public existence.

Basically, there are just so many unknowns that need to be sorted out and addressed. More than likely, the new REIT in question will find itself adding expenses as it brings on new personnel to deal with the new responsibilities. It will also have to come to terms with corporate governance, financial reporting controls, compliance with the Sarbanes-Oxley Act, executive compensation, and the list goes on.

If that sounds like a lot, it is. Make no mistake about it.

Now, those issues all exist after the initial public offering (IPO). When it comes to investing in the IPO itself, there are also numerous aspects for the company to consider, forms to file, and information to look over. The short list includes

>> Financial statements

>> Third-party consents

>> Investment theses

>> Human resources analyses

This is why I'm the first person to say that pursuing an IPO isn't for just any old private REIT. And the mere fact that a REIT does IPO doesn't mean it should have. This process and the statutes that come with it can be more than worthwhile for companies with the patience, stamina, and desire to make them happen. But some just don't know what's what until they experience it for themselves. Each one should carefully consider the general and specific ups and downs involved. And each investor should carefully consider those factors as well.

What Is the Best Way to Get Rich Owning REITs?

I wish there were a faster way to get rich that I could recommend. But the only sure way to success I can tell you about is to adhere to what Benjamin Graham, author of *The Intelligent Investor* (Harper Business), considered to be the essence of sound investing described. In three simple words, it's *margin of safety.*

In his classic book (which I recommend to anyone and everyone who wants to invest in general), Graham explained that the margin of safety constitutes a "favorable difference between price on the one hand and indicated or appraised value on the other." Much like the concept of buying low and selling high, REIT investors must pay close attention to quality and value.

TIP

It's impossible to eliminate risk altogether, but you can greatly minimize it by avoiding questionably run and questionably positioned companies. The same goes for those with stock prices that just don't match their business proportions and near-term possibilities. Instead, you want to buy shares of worthwhile companies that aren't overpriced. Better yet, you want to buy shares of worthwhile companies that are undervalued in the moment — with every indication that they'll be bouncing back up soon enough.

By doing so — and reinvesting your dividends to tap into the power of compounding — you'll intensely strengthen your opportunity to get rich with REITs, slowly but surely.

When Should I Dollar-Cost Average?

Dollar-cost averaging is a system that's supposed to lower the cost basis of an investment you already own by buying more of it after it has declined. Suppose an investor buys shares of a REIT at $100 per share and it then declines to $90. The investor then buys in at that price as well on the premise that the stock is bound to go up again, and the goal is to lower their net cost and accelerate their profit timeline.

Dollar-cost averaging can work out well under certain conditions. When you purchase shares over time at regular intervals or predetermined price points, you can decrease the risk of paying too much comparatively speaking. Or to put it a slightly different way, you maximize your chances of paying a lower average price over time. Finally, dollar-cost averaging helps you get your money to work on a consistent basis, which is a key factor for long-term investment growth. So clearly, there are benefits to be had.

REMEMBER

But there are also downsides if conditions aren't just right. This practice is advisable only if you're certain you have a good REIT that was undervalued when you bought it in the first place, making it even more undervalued when you buy it in the second place.

Should I Own REITs That Pay Monthly?

A handful of REITs pay monthly — a number I would like to see grow. Automatically reinvesting dividends is a benefit of dollar-cost averaging, but buying REITs with monthly dividends can be an even better choice. These steady-paying dividend checks are not only more convenient, they also allow more opportunities for compounding to work its magic. In addition, these REITs minimize market risk — specifically, the risk of reinvesting at peak prices — and opportunities for second guessing.

Here's another reason to like them. If you have to sell one, it's an easier decision to make for one simple yet significant reason: You don't need to wonder if you should wait a month or two for the next dividend to be paid. It's a matter of weeks, maybe even days.

TIP

Retirees and others who count on these checks to pay bills and cover regular expenses have additional reasons to appreciate monthly paying stocks. At the risk of stating the obvious, it's a lot easier to plan out your expenses when you have money coming in every four weeks or so than when it's coming in every three months. Basically, if there's a downside, I don't know about it.

Most Canadian REITs pay monthly dividends, as I first mention in Chapter 5. That's no doubt at least in part because of their large retail investor base. Even so, maybe U.S. REITs should follow that same blueprint. I certainly think so.

What's the Best Way to Get Started?

Well, you've already answered that question because you're reading this book. Hopefully, you now have a firm foundation to build off of in the wide world of REITs. My goal with this book is to provide you with a high-level overview of REITs that can in turn provide you with the necessary framework to construct your own dividend dynasty.

As a virtual landlord, you can now be positioned to build bond-like rental streams and equity-like residual values. REIT investors expect to generate results somewhere between expectations from the bond market and those from the stock market.

What Are Other REIT Resources to Consider?

In addition to this book, I've authored thousands of articles about REITs on Seeking Alpha (www.SeekingAlpha.com). I share a tremendous amount of my research there, as well as on Wide Moat Research at www.WideMoatResearch.com. But in case you're sick of me by now, there are also other great resources for REITs out there to explore.

One of the biggest and best resources is the National Association of Real Estate Investment Trusts (Nareit) website (www.nareit.com). This REIT–advocating, REIT–educating, REIT–expanding institution features basic information as well as a flow of articles and research to keep investors up to date about the ever-changing world of real estate investment trusts. I know it's been an enormously helpful resource for me, and I find it very hard to imagine that you won't find it helpful as well.

TIP

Incidentally, Nareit also sponsors conferences each year that are open to individual investors as well as bigwigs and the well-connected.

If you're interested in investigating specific companies at a higher level, most REITs have detailed investor relations sites where you can access company financials, presentations, and updates. These can be veritable gold mines of data just waiting to be read whenever you need them.

Other terrific websites include FactSet, S&P Global, and FASTGraphs, though I do have to warn you that they aren't free.

What's a SWAN Stock?

The REIT sector uses quite a few acronyms. Chapter 8 details terms like FFO, AFFO, and NAV, frequently used terms that are important to understand. But here's one that isn't so well known — yet. I'm determined to popularize it considering what a useful category it describes.

This would be SWAN, which stands for *sleep well at night.* I wish I could tell you I coined it but that wouldn't be true. However, I do use it often in my writing to designate REITs with the highest likelihood of being stress-free investments. This should sound good to everyone, but it will especially appeal to anyone who experienced financial adversity in the past or who's going through something right now. That includes me, because I nearly went bankrupt in 2008. It's why my new mission in life is to help investors make wise choices, avoid losing capital, make worthwhile profits . . . and sleep well at night.

TIP

Whether looking at REITs or regular stocks, the best way to practice SWAN investing is to understand that monetary success involves both playing good offense by earning money, and defense by spending as little as possible for good value. Then balance those risks and rewards appropriately. I'm living proof of how well this concept works, which is why I always close the articles I write with these following words:

Happy SWAN investing!

Chapter **14**

Ten Mistakes to Avoid When Investing in REITs

For everyone ready and even raring to get their REIT portfolio started, I'm happy to hear it! REITs are a great resource that I (obviously) endorse. But if I've said it once, I've said it 100 — even 1,000 — times: There is no perfect investment. And an investment becomes even more imperfect in the hands of an imperfect investor. Which, for the record, we all are. I'm not perfect. You're not perfect.

Acknowledge it. Accept it. Embrace it.

That's why in this chapter I discuss ten mistakes you want to avoid, both when first stepping foot into the REIT waters and after you get more comfortable. These might sound like novice rules but don't be fooled. You should never be too far along to forget them. Sidestepping these gotchas can help make you a smarter, more successful REIT investor — someone who makes better choices with better facts and figures at your disposal and accomplishes better results as a direct result.

Obsessing Over Just One REIT

Legendary investor Sir John Templeton said, "The only investors who shouldn't diversify are those who are right 100 percent of the time." And he's absolutely correct about that. Diversification is exceptionally important in portfolio construction and maintenance. It's just not wise to put all your eggs in one basket or, in this case, stock — regardless of how much you like the REIT.

In case you're not familiar with Templeton, *Money* magazine dubbed him "the world's greatest stock picker of the century" in 1999. Yet he was only right 66 percent of the time. Sixty-six percent! This should lead to the easy conclusion that your success rate will be even lower. I'm not trying to chip away at your confidence by saying so, but Templeton was someone who devoted his professional life to analyzing the stock market. He also had in-the-know connections and people working for him.

REMEMBER

If arguably the greatest stock-picker in the world — with all of that on his side — needs to be diversified to protect against losses, the average investor can surely benefit from the practice of diversification, too. So don't fall in love with a single REIT, putting too much money into it and making it your one and only position within the sector. (Really, this applies to any other category of stock as well.)

It should also be stated that you can get obsessed with one REIT (or other stock) while still holding others. Investors far too often allocate much more of their portfolio to a single position over everything else. Favoring a company in moderation is one thing. I have no problem keeping something of a hierarchy, in which some shares are deemed more valuable than others; I'm just not devoting 50 percent of my funds to just one REIT, even if it is the one to beat, because you just never know. Even the one to beat can be beaten . . . or fall altogether.

Obsessing Over a Single Sector

One of the great things about investing in REITs is how you can invest across a variety of property types and sectors. This stock-market category is extraordinary in its ability to be both so specific in focusing on real estate and yet so varied, merging with everything from medicine to retail to travel to advertisement to technology and beyond.

Some of these areas may be more impressive looking than others, especially if you're attracted to high-growth plays or high-yield plays. Perhaps you're personally aligned with a specific industry. Or maybe you got spooked by others, making you more wary about how and where you put your money. Your reasons might be very compelling and even very logical, but don't let them snowball into a mindset that has you overlooking the diversification gift that REITs offer. Although you may have particular confidence in one specific sector, it's dangerous to fall in love with it.

I always recommend exuding caution in this regard; otherwise, your portfolio can become inadequately proportioned and you could suffer more significantly the next time volatility hits. Yes, that's a possibility even if you own multiple REITs within a single sector. For example, if you put all your capital into hotels because of their higher yields, the next time the economy falters and business travel suffers, so will your portfolio. I can almost guarantee it.

TIP

This is why I recommend a balanced approach that involves figuring out sector targets based on your own personal risk tolerance. Try buying into different property types, sorting through them based on key demand drivers. If you really like technology as a larger category, for instance, you can diversify your REIT selections by owning shares of technology-driven REITs: cell towers, data centers, and industrials (warehouses). You can easily spread capital across these categories, providing good diversification while benefiting from the forces of three separate business efforts: 5G, cloud computing, and e-commerce.

Owning Nothing but REITs

As much as I like REITs, I would never recommend owning nothing but them in your investment portfolio. This is for the same reasons I caution you against hyper-focusing on just one stock or just one sector. The lack of diversification could hurt you far worse than it could help.

This isn't to knock REITs at all. As I hope I show throughout this book, this is an excellent investment category with so much to offer. Yet think about your portfolio being fully stocked with REITs during 2020. What would have been the likelihood of you holding onto your investments through the year instead of panic-selling everything you owned as the sector crashed under the weight of the shutdowns? Well, let's just say it wouldn't be very good.

A loss is really only a loss once you sell your stock, but boy! Paper losses can mess with your head, encouraging you to throw out the good with the bad when both are getting trashed in the moment. That's why you want a balanced portfolio: to keep your emotions balanced as well.

TIP

Around 40 percent of my portfolio is devoted to REITs, but that's because REITs are my job. I spend hours and hours every day interacting with them through hard-core research, analysis, and interviews. For most investors, I recommend starting with 10 percent exposure and gradually increasing that amount based on your overall risk tolerance. As I mention in previous chapters, including Chapter 13, your time horizon is extremely important. So for retirees, 20 percent exposure might be justified given the trustworthy level of dividend income most REITs generate.

Investing Too Heavily (Or at All) In mREITs

The more debt you use in any investment, the greater your potential for gain or loss. Quite simply, you're working with more money, which means there's further to rise and further to fall than if you'd stuck with what you initially had. The appeal is obvious, but the risks should be, too.

When you buy stocks on margin, you're leveraging investment returns with debt. So if the asset pans out as planned, great! But if not, you're stuck paying back that loan on top of losing out on your actual money. (That is to say, what used to be your actual money.) Some people manage that risk very well, making wise choices both in how much they borrow and what they put that borrowed money toward. Others not so much, and they end up suffering for it.

WARNING

Likewise, REITs that use excessive leverage to increase returns almost never provide worthwhile long-term value. During extraordinary periods — which, by definition, don't tend to last long — when commercial real estate is acquired at abnormally cheap prices, they can do very, very well.

TIP

But it's the REITs with modest debt and conservative balance sheet fundamentals that generate the most reliable results and therefore the greatest profits as a general rule.

I say all this because mortgage REITs (mREITs) own debt instead of property. This means it's automatically riskier to invest in them compared with other dividend-paying stocks. They benefit when interest rates come down, which serves to increase the value of the mortgages they hold. But when interest rates go up, the exact opposite happens. This is why mREIT spreads are wider and dividends are much higher than equity REITs.

Trying to Time the Market

Choosing exactly when to invest — down to the day or week — is known as trying to *time the market*. It's a very appealing idea but not a very easy one to accomplish. You can think of your probability of making real money this way as being equal to winning the lottery. It's that unlikely. Study after study after study from well-respected sources such as Charles Schwab show that this practice does not work. Yet people keep playing their chances anyway because of the mouthwatering amounts of cash that can be involved – or, conversely, how much money they might lose if they time it wrong.

When it comes to REITs specifically, I often tell investors to remember that they're investing in real estate stocks. That's important for a reason. The point of investing in income-producing real estate is to build wealth by collecting rent that leads to share and dividend appreciation. And while that does involve overall evaluations of individual stocks, including price points to buy and sell at, it does not involve pinpointing exact dates and consulting a crystal ball.

Your long-term strategy should not include trying to jump in and out of the market based on its short-term performance. Expect to see volatility. That's common for the stock market, perhaps especially so since the 2008 crash. And we've seen more than our fair share of daily hundreds-point swings since the 2020 hit. I'm sure we'll see more still.

REMEMBER

Your job is to be patient and professional when there's a sharp downturn. While you might need to sell some stocks for one reason or another before bullish factors take over again, do it only after assessing the situation rationally — knowing that shares often rebound and go right back to gaining again once the overall markets are in a better mood.

Historical data shows that this is especially true of well-placed, well-established, well-run companies. And because that description applies to so many REITs, I'm happy to say that the sector has typically outperformed over the decades. According to The Motley Fool (www.fool.com/research/reits-vs-stocks), REIT shares have returned 11.5 percent annually over the past 25 years (while the S&P 500 returned 10.2 percent in the same period) and 12.7 percent annually over the last 20 (while the S&P 500 returned 9.5 percent).

TIP

REITs can be even better when you have the patience to buy or add more shares more cheaply when other people have sold.

Again though — and I cannot stress this enough — that's not market timing. Buying quality stocks at undervalued prices is simply smart investing, just like taking into consideration your goals of enjoying a comfortable retirement, sending your children to college, buying a second home, or supporting your current lifestyle as you build and maintain your portfolio.

Buying Overvalued REITs

This mistake goes hand in hand with the last one, but it still deserves its own special mention. When prices rise and the bulls are in charge, greed can too easily lead to speculation. And speculation is where many investors get into trouble.

In this case, it goes completely against tried-and-true advice from one of the greatest investors of all time. In Chapter 10 I relate Warren Buffett's advice to Columbia Business School in 1984. But his advice is worth repeating here:

> You do not cut it close. That is what Ben Graham [his mentor] meant by having a margin of safety. You don't try to buy businesses worth $83 million for $80 million. You leave yourself an enormous margin. When you build a bridge, you insist it can carry 30,000 pounds, but you only drive 10,000-pound trucks across it. And that same principle works in investing.

TIP

I'll repeat my translation of that, too: You're much — much, much, much — better off buying shares when they dip than when they're flying high. As I stated in the previous point, this can make an enormous difference to the upside. Undervalued shares tend to correct themselves eventually, taking your investment along for the ride, just like overvalued shares tend to drop to reasonable levels sooner or later.

Falling for Value Traps

You don't want to buy up cheap stocks just because they're cheap. "One man's trash is another man's treasure" might apply well to garage sales and gift ideas, but the saying doesn't apply to the stock market. It might seem otherwise in the moment, like you're getting the bargain of a lifetime, but the long-term and often even short-term results say otherwise.

REMEMBER

Identifying these value traps can be tricky. Some of them are obvious, mind you, where a REIT is yielding 10 percent or more, as I discuss in the next section. That's almost always going to be an indication that you don't want to buy what that company is putting down. But there are exceptions when a high yield is justified. A careful fundamental analysis of any REIT can reveal whether it's a trap or a good investment opportunity. Consider its growth history, present situation, and future projects, as well as the metrics and ratios I describe in Chapter 8.

Often a company's demise can be traced to changes in the cash-generating power of its business model. That's one of the reasons REIT investors should look at past earnings in the form of adjusted funds from operations (AFFO). When that's in a consistent state of decline, it only makes sense that the business will find itself declining, too.

REMEMBER

REITs create value for their owners by investing cash (into real estate) to generate more cash in the future. The amount of value they create is the difference between cash inflows and the cost of the investments made. So a REIT's cost of capital is critical for determining value creation and evaluating strategic decisions. That's why it's important to always consider the return you expect to make on your invested capital.

And if that return on invested capital doesn't paint a pretty picture, you're probably better off avoiding it altogether.

Falling for Sucker Yields

A value trap doesn't always involve a sucker yield, but a sucker yield is always a value trap. Let me explain.

A REIT that yields 10 percent or higher almost always means (with some exceptions) that investors perceive very low growth or, even worse, a potential dividend cut up ahead. It's tempting to act on that kind of percentage, but it usually ends badly. Hence the term *sucker yield:* It makes a sucker out of the buyer. It's simply too good to be true.

WARNING

If a stock seems to pay out a dividend that's exceptionally high, investors should look even harder at the payment behind that dividend than they otherwise would. When a REIT pays a dividend beyond its earnings power, it's essentially eroding capital. It has to find money to cover its obligations, borrowing from its savings, operations, or elsewhere until it can't even do that anymore. (Or, much less likely, it manages to dig itself out of that financial hole.)

It's important to recognize that there are two ways to make money in the stock market: capital appreciation and dividends. But when the latter gets hit, the former almost always get affected too. So it's a lose-lose situation. And when you're talking about an extraordinarily high dividend yield combined with an unsustainable business model, that loss might be permanent — as in there's no stock bounce back from there.

That's why investors should always focus more on dividend safety than dividend yield.

One of the best ways to focus on dividend safety — thereby avoiding sucker yields — is to pay very close attention to the payout ratio. (In which case, keep in mind that AFFO is superior to its calculating cousin, funds from operations [FFO], in determining a REIT's free cash flow.) If a REIT earns $0.90 per share in AFFO but puts $0.30 toward managing recurring capital expenses, it has just $0.60 left to cover everything else, including dividends, savings, and expansion. And if it does, in fact, pay out that whole $0.60 in dividends, then it's going to struggle to expand even in a strong market. And if any negative news hits, expect serious trouble. That's why you want to take a hard-core pass on every sucker yield you meet.

With that said, as I state in the previous section, don't think that every high-yielding opportunity is a sucker yield. Do your homework to see what should be avoided — and what should be pounced on right away.

Considering REITs to Be Fixed-Income Investments

What makes REITs so attractive compared with other high-yield investments like bonds and utilities is their combination of significant capital appreciation potential and steadily increasing dividends. They offer exposure to equity real estate in a way that produces both equity-like and bond-like attributes. The exact mixture generates inflation protection at a lower opportunity cost than other alternatives.

So yes, REITs do offer certain fixed-income attributes (like bonds). But the important thing to remember is that their income isn't actually fixed because most REITs grow their dividends. As they profitably acquire more properties, they grow their cash flow and increase their dividends, and their shares appreciate over time.

REITs also have high dividends that provide more current income than bonds while also offering the potential for income growth and capital appreciation.

Forgetting That the CEO Works for You

In Chapter 9, I mention Benjamin Graham's and David Dodd's book, *Security Analysis* (McGraw Hill). I particularly highlight where they explain that "a stockholder is an owner of the business and an employer of its officers." This might have seemed like a simple concept at the time: something you just gloss over in a larger read. But if so, I hope you reconsider that initial impression here.

Graham and Dodd are pointing out that investors, not management, are the rightful owners of the businesses they buy into. They therefore deserve to be treated with respect instead of set aside like inconsequential children. Or here's another way of putting it: When you invest in a stock, you're also paying the salary of the management team.

REMEMBER

That means you're the boss — even of the head honcho. And don't ever forget it. Obviously, you alone can't fire the CEO, CFO, or anyone else in the company. Your fellow owners would have to band with you to make that kind of thing happen.

But you don't have to put up with any nonsense on their part either. If you don't like what they do, how they do it, or any other such thing, stop paying them. Sell your shares and invest in a management team that will meet your needs. What happens from there at the old company won't be your business — or your problem — anymore.

Warren Buffett said it this way: "The business owner's approach is so fundamental that, unless it's ingrained as part of your basic philosophy, you're going to get in trouble in life when you do investments." Never forget it.

Appendix **A**

Assessing Weighted Average Cost of Capital

Whether it's Walmart, Coca-Cola, Intel, or Realty Income, a company's overall cost of capital is essential to success. The best companies out there thrive by investing capital at rates of return that significantly exceed their cost of capital. And you want to invest in the best companies. That's why it's utterly essential to understand the way REITs grow their earnings and dividends.

For starters, having a cost advantage is key. This simply means that a company can provide goods or services at prices that undercut its rivals, which then helps it achieve fatter profit margins and sell even more. Because this is a pretty big deal, here's the formula to show how REITs generate shareholder value:

Cap Rate – Cost of Capital = Investment Spread/Profit Margin

In case you forgot, a cap (capitalization) rate is simply a ratio of net operating income (NOI) to property asset value. If the NOI for a property is $100,000 per year, and the value of one of its properties is $1 million, the cap rate is 10 percent.

Let's put this information into practice with an example. Suppose DEF, a fictional triple-net REIT, purchases a stand-alone building at a 7 percent cap rate with a 4.5 percent cost of capital. In this case the formula looks like this:

7.0% – 4.5% = 2.5%, or 250 basis points (bps)

Now you have the investment spread, or profit margin. And, for the record, 2.5 percent (250 basis points) is a very good investment spread for a net-lease REIT to achieve. In fact, any REIT would be happy to see that calculation conclusion.

Let's break it down further though to see what else there is to see.

A Textbook Example of Cost of Capital at Work

Let's consider the equity details related to spread investing, which is the deliberate act of looking for favorable spreads in order to determine what's worth buying. In which case, you'll also want to know the term *equity multiple,* which can be calculated as:

Present Value ÷ Amount Invested = Equity Multiple

Very simply, the higher the equity multiple, the lower the cost of capital. And that translates into bigger margins — which is most definitely a good thing.

TIP

You also want to know a REIT's cost of debt, which is typically a measure of its cost of issuing debt. Keep in mind that when a company uses more debt, the interest rate it is charged rises. When you include the cost of capital from all sources — such as equity cost, preferred stock (if any), and debt cost — you arrive at the *weighted average cost of capital* (WACC): the average rate a REIT expects to finance its property.

REMEMBER

WACC is critical for determining value creation and evaluating strategic decisions. It's the rate you compare with return on invested capital to determine whether a company has creative value. By aggregating projects into portfolios rather than assessing them individually, managers can often overcome excessive loss aversion.

Let's use DEF as an example again to see this in action, adding the following details into the picture:

Stock price = $70.00 per share

Funds from operations (FFO) = $3.15 per share

Equity cost = 4.5% ($70 ÷ $3.15)

Estimated cost of ten-year debt = 4.5%

Now assume that DEF has 66 percent in equity and 34 percent in debt. In which case, the 4.5 percent equity cost of 66 percent is 2.97 percent. And the 4.5 percent debt cost of 34 percent is 1.53 percent. All told, the WACC is 4.5 percent, because 2.97 percent + 1.53 percent = 4.50 percent.

(Author's Note: In reality, the WACC would actually be lower than that because most REITs use free cash flow instead of equity. And cash has a 0 percent nominal cost.)

As I mention earlier, DEF acquires a property at a 7.0 percent cap rate using the above-referenced 4.5 percent WACC. That translates into an investment spread of 2.5 percent, or 250 basis points. And that means that the REIT is a major cash cow that's generating considerable profit margins from its wide-moat business model.

Don't Be(lieve) a Sucker (Yield)

Now let's consider another make-believe REIT called XYZ and contrast it with DEF. ZYX, which is also a net-lease REIT, has a higher cost of capital. This forces it to buy riskier assets with the goal of hopefully delivering comparable investment spreads.

You can derive the company's cost of capital as follows:

Adjusted funds from operations (AFFO) yield = 7.0% (annualized estimated AFFO of $2.00 ÷ $30.00 stock price)

Estimated cost of ten-year debt = 7.5%

50% equity = 7.0% × 0.50 = 3.50%

50% debt = 7.5% × 0.50 = 3.75%

WACC = 3.50% + 3.75% = 7.25%

In order for XYZ to generate investment spreads of around 250 bps like the DEF REIT does, it would have to pursue higher-risk acquisitions at cap rates of around 10 percent. That's a lot more risk than most responsible management teams in most situations would accept because the underlying credit (of the tenant) is less stable.

Investors should likewise hesitate to invest in a REIT that's stuck with those kinds of choices. Most REITs that use expense capital to make risky investments end up having to eventually cut their dividend. That's why I call them "sucker yield" scenarios.

TIP

The key to success in the stock market in general — not just for REITs — is to always seek out companies that enjoy competitive advantages. And one of the most important advantages to consider is cost of capital (see Figure AA-1). Understanding how the company makes money is the secret to unlocking value and sleeping well at night.

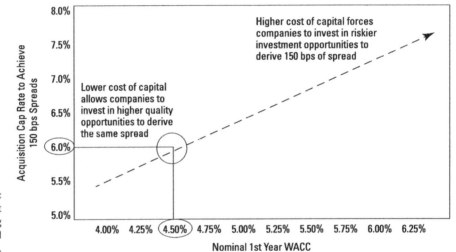

FIGURE AA-1: Investment strategy: Utilizing low cost of capital advantage.

Appendix B

Determining Net Asset Value

N et asset value (NAV) is used to assess a company's actual market value by indicating the worth of its shares. You should be warned: This metric is subjective. Make no mistake about that. All the same, many analysts and investors consider it a valuable tool when assessing REITs. In fact, it's the most common REIT valuation approach. In which case, it's worthwhile going into detail about.

Calculating NAV: A Four-Step Process

The Following is the four-step process for calculating a REIT's net asset value.

Step 1: Use NOI to determine fair market value

A number of assumptions are involved in this assessment, but the most important one is definitely determining a REIT's fair market value. Admittedly, it's also the most subjective factor. But here's how it works, nonetheless. You first research the REIT's net operating income, or NOI, as generated from its real estate portfolio. Usually, this should be on a one-year basis.

TIP

I detail NOI in Chapter 8, but the quick explanation is that it's calculated as real estate revenue minus operating expenses. Fortunately, most REITs provide NOI in their quarterly supplemental reports, which should be available on their websites. More often than not you can find them on the "Investor Relations" or some similarly named page.

Unfortunately, NOI isn't the subjective part of the formula. The subjective part is determining the capitalization, or cap, rate for each asset. This is how much yield you can reasonably expect from the REIT's property portfolio over the space of a year.

TIP

Cap rates can also be applied to single properties, especially when determining whether to make a purchase or in relating the details of a new purchase to investors.

Determining a portfolio-wide cap rate requires a significant understanding of comparable sales. You can sometimes find this in a company's 10-K filing or supplemental report. And some commercial real estate brokerages publish cap rate data for each property type and region as well.

That's not always the case, though. Sometimes the data just isn't easily available. In fact, it usually isn't. In that case, use distinct cap rates and NOIs for each region, property type, or individual property that the REIT in question holds.

Once you have a market cap rate, you simply divide it by NOI to calculate the fair market value (FMV) of the real estate:

Cap Rate ÷ NOI = Estimated Portfolio Value

Step 2: Calculate NAV

Next, add the value of the REIT's other tangible assets to the value of the properties to find the total asset value:

Real Estate Value + Cash + Other Tangible Assets = Total Asset Value

This includes cash and land held for development — items that can be found on the REIT's balance sheet. Because land itself doesn't depreciate (or generate rental income), the value listed for land held for development should be accurate.

Step 3: Subtract debt and preferred stock to arrive at NAV

The last step to calculating a REIT's NAV — though not the last step in our over-arching assessment — is to subtract the company's debt and preferred stock from the total asset value you've arrived at:

Total Asset Value – Liabilities = NAV

These liabilities can also be found on the balance sheet.

Step 4: Divide by diluted shares

To use the NAV as a valuation metric, you need to run it through one more calculation, this time to determine its value per share. After all, you don't own the whole company, only a fraction of it.

Fortunately, this is a very simple step. All you need to do is divide the NAV by the number of shares outstanding (once again, you can find that information on most companies' websites):

NAV ÷ Shares Outstanding = NAV Per Share

After accounting for potentially justifiable discounts or premiums to NAV (as described in the next section), you can then reach your own conclusions about whether the REIT's share price is overvalued or undervalued as is.

An Expert's Take on NAV

I want to point out that the highly respected real estate-specific research and analysis firm Green Street is the pioneer in analyzing NAV. It has a very good opinion of this metric, yet even it's not shy about acknowledging that REITs should never be appraised at their NAVs alone.

That's why Green Street derives a "warranted share value" by adding in other factors it believes could impact where each stock should trade. These include

>> Franchise value (management's ability to create shareholder value)

>> Balance sheet strength

>> Corporate governance

>> Share liquidity

>> Corporate overhead expense ratios

Green Street also weighs comparable REITs against each other. It doesn't deem an individual stock to be cheap or expensive in a vacuum, instead it provides general guidelines on REIT sector valuations.

It's not until then that it draws a conclusion about where shares should likely trade at when fairly valued. Overall, this particular NAV–based approach has worked well for Green Street, as evidenced by the firm's excellent track record of forecasting relative performance. With that said, it is difficult to calculate and hardly perfect.

TIP

Investors who use this analysis should develop their own criteria for determining an appropriate premium or discount, taking into account the rate at which the REIT will grow its NAV, funds from operations (FFO), or adjusted funds from operations (AFFO) relative to both its peers and a purely passive investment strategy.

Appendix C

Calculating Adjusted Funds from Operations

The following example is a derivation of adjusted funds from operations (AFFO) and funds (or cash) available for distribution (FAD or CAD) from a ficticious REIT known as Rhino REIT. Keep in mind that unlike AFFO, which deducts the amortization of real estate-related capital expenditures from FFO, FAD or CAD is often derived by deducting nonrecurring (as well as normal recurring) capital expenditures. Also, some REITs (and analysts) deduct repaymemts of principal on mortgage loans. There is no commonly accepted standard for adjustments to CAD or FAD.

For this example, I assume 1,000,000 shares:

Net Income:	**$25,000**
(+) Depreciaition and amortization:	2,000
(−) Gain from sale of assets:	(500)
Funds from operations (FFO):	26,500
FFO per share:	**26.50**
(−) Maintenance capital expenditures:	(4,000)

(–) Straight-line rents:	(500)
Adjusted funds from operations (AFFO):	22,000
AFFO per share:	**22.00**
(–) Nonrecurring capital expenditures:	(349)
Funds or cash available for distribution:	21,651
FAD or CAD per share:	**21.65**

Glossary

A

Accretion: The gradual and incremental growth of assets and earnings due to business expansion, internal growth, or a merger or acquisition. An accretive merger is one where the pro forma (post-deal) earnings per share (or funds from operations [FFO]) is greater than the acquirer's (buyer's) FFO before the deal is made. The opposite of accretion is dilution. See also *Dilution; Funds from Operations (FFO)*.

Acquisition Costs: The direct costs related to an investment purchase. Typical costs include closing costs, brokerage fees, legal fees, title insurance, and due diligence costs. See also *Due Diligence*.

Adjusted Funds from Operations (AFFO): An unofficial measure of a real estate company's operations-generated cash flow that includes industry-specific considerations that funds from operations (FFO) does not account for. AFFO is calculated as FFO – straight-lined rents – recurring capital expenditure + equity-based compensation + lease intangibles + deferred financing cost (as explained in greater detail in Chapter 8). AFFO is a more precise measure of a REIT's earnings than FFO because it adjusts for GAAP (Generally Accepted Accounting Principles) and for recurring capitalized expenditures. There is no standardized definition of AFFO; therefore, financial statement users should understand how the measure is defined by the company. AFFO is the most useful metric to demonstrate a REIT's ability to cover the dividend. See also *Funds from Operations (FFO); Lease*.

Amortization: The process of reducing a mortgage's balance or asset's cost over time through a fixed payment schedule of equal amounts each month (or other predetermined period). Part of each payment goes toward the principal and part goes toward the interest each time so that, as payments progress, the amount going toward the principal increases naturally. See also *Mortgage*.

Annualized Return: The total return made over the lifetime of a holding calculated as an equivalent return on an annual basis. Because it's calculated on a time-value basis, it is not the same as an average. The annualized return equation is [1+ cumulative return] ^ [365/days held] – 1).

Appraisal: The value of a real estate asset determined by an independent agent, typically one certified as a member of the Appraisal Institute, or MAI.

A-REIT: An Australian real estate investment trust.

Asset Class: A category of investments with similar characteristics and risk profiles. Examples include real estate, equities, and fixed income. REITs are also considered to be a distinct asset class.

Asset Management: The proactive management of capital to maximize total investment returns.

Average Daily Rate (ADR): The average rate paid for rooms sold for a single hotel, market, or the larger industry over the course of a night, week, month, or year. It's calculated by dividing room revenue by the number of rooms sold. By comparison, RevPAR is calculated by dividing room revenue by the number of rooms available. See also *Revenue Per Available Room (RevPAR)*.

B

Base Rent: The initial rent set in a contract for an initial period, which typically covers agreed-upon tenant space and standard improvements. (Any additional improvements are amortized into the lease to arrive at a final negotiated rent.) Base rent can then change over the term of the lease by (1) a pre-specified amount such as a per-annum percentage or an amount per square foot every 24 months, or (2) a variable amount based on something such as consumer price index (CPI) growth. Base rent is also called *minimum rent* or *base minimum rent*. See also *Lease; Tenant*.

Basis Point: The percentage change in the value or rate of a financial instrument, such as an interest rate. One basis point is equivalent to one-tenth of 1 percent, or 0.01 percent.

Bond: A fixed-income loan that governments and corporations offer investors in exchange for periodic interest payments as well as a complete repayment of the bond's face value — its initial established worth — at maturity.

Book Value: The historical cost of an asset plus any additional capital invested into it without factoring in depreciation. Book value is not the same as market value.

Build to Suit: An agreement to construct a property according to the unique needs and requirements of a particular tenant at a particular place. The landowner pays for construction and then leases the land and building to the tenant. See also *Lease; Tenant*.

Buyback: When a company repurchases its own outstanding shares from shareholders, usually to return capital to investors or signal confidence in its prospects. One major reason for businesses to do buybacks is that they genuinely feel as if their shares are undervalued.

C

Capital Expenditure (CapEx): An expense necessary to maintain ongoing operations. Examples of this in real estate include roof repairs and HVAC system replacements.

Capital Improvement: A capital investment that improves the competitive value of a property or significantly extends its useful life. Unlike capital expenditures, capital improvements typically have a prospective return on investment (for example, adding or upgrading the common area amenities of an apartment property, modernizing the facade at a shopping center). See also *Capital Expenditure (CapEx)*.

Capitalization Rate (Cap Rate): While there are actually five types of capitalization rates, the one real estate investors tend to mean (unless otherwise specified) is the *going-in cap rate,* which is calculated by dividing a property's or portfolio's net operating income in the first full year of ownership by its purchase price. It is used to estimate the investor's potential return on their investment in the real estate market. This can also be applied to expected earnings. See also *Net Operating Income (NOI)*.

Cash Available for Distribution (CAD): An estimate of the cash a REIT has available to pay dividends and the most meaningful indicator of dividend safety. CAD is calculated by subtracting capitalized interest expense and principal amortization payments due on secured debt — excluding any principal amounts that are maturing. These "balloon payments" are accounted for in the financing activities section of a company's Statement of Cash Flows and typically get refinanced with new debt when they mature. Another term for CAD is Funds Available for Distribution (FAD).

Cash Flow from Operations: The cash remaining from net operating income after deducting of debt service and ground lease payments, but not capital expenditure or income taxes. See also *Capital Expenditure (CapEx)*; *Ground Lease*; *Net Operating Income (NOI)*.

Cash Flow: The cash remaining after various expenses and expenditures are deducted from income. Cash flow can be defined several ways, depending on the expenses involved and how expenditures are deducted. The unqualified term usually means net cash flow.

Cash-on-Cash Return: The cash return on equity, commonly used to express the initial return on a new investment. When assessing an equity REIT's real property, cash-on-cash return is equivalent to dividing adjusted funds from operations per share by equity price per share. See also *Adjusted Funds from Operations (AFFO)*; *Equity REIT*.

Commercial Mortgage-Backed Security (CMBS): A type of mortgage-backed security that's secured by a pool of mortgage loans on (usually stabilized) commercial property. Modification of a CMBS loan (for example, restructuring, early payoff) can be more difficult than with a traditional mortgage loan provided by a bank or life insurance company since it relies on the original terms of the initial mortgages involved. See also *Mortgage-Backed Security*.

Common Area Maintenance (CAM): The operational expenses pertaining to a property's common areas, such as its parking lot, landscape, lobby and/or common restroom(s). These can either be paid for by the landlord (which typically means higher rent) or the tenants as an added expense.

Cost of Capital: The cost of raising equity (common or preferred stock) or debt capital. A company's cost of capital is critical for determining value creation and for evaluating strategic decisions. The cost of equity capital is based upon the anticipated long-term total return to the equity investor (income and appreciation). The cost of debt capital is merely the interest expense on the debt incurred. Leveraged and unleveraged returns on investment activity (acquisitions, dispositions, development, repurchases) are typically compared to the appropriate leveraged or unleveraged weighted cost of capital to determine the accretion or dilution to earnings and net asset value (NAV). See also *Dilution; Net Asset Value (NAV); Leverage.*

Covenants, Bond: A legally binding term of agreement between the issuer and holder. Positive covenants require the bond to meet specific requirements. Negative covenants forbid the issuer from undertaking certain actions.

D

Debt Service: The money required to make principal and interest payments on outstanding loans, mortgages, and/or bonds. For accounting purposes, interest payments are considered expenses, while principal payments are treated as capital expenditures. See also *Capital Expenditure (CapEx).*

Debt Service Coverage Ratio (DSCR): A measure of the cash flow available to pay existing debt obligations. It's the ratio of available net operating income to the total debt service payment. A DSCR of less than 1.0 means negative cash flow. See also *Cash Flow; Net Operating Income (NOI).*

Debt-to-Equity Ratio: A financial ratio that compares a company's total debt to its shareholder equity (total assets minus total liabilities), indicating how much of its financing is funded by debt. A higher debt-to-equity ratio generally suggests higher financial risk. A debt-to-equity ratio is calculated by dividing the company's total debt by its total equity.

Debt-to-Gross Asset Value: Conceptually, gross asset value (GAV) is the value of the firm's tangible assets after adding back depreciation, and it's used to measure the degree of leverage of the REIT. It can be used to gauge the solvency of a REIT. See also *Gross Asset Value (GAV).*

Debt-to-Total Market Capitalization: A commonly used ratio that gives a sense of how much debt a company has relative to its market value. The ratio is an indicator of the company's leverage, which is debt used to purchase assets. See also *Market Capitalization.*

Debt Yield: A company's net operating income divided by the amount taken out in a loan or loans. For example, a property with $10 million of net operating income (NOI) and a $100 million mortgage loan has a debt yield of 10 percent. Higher debt yields imply lower leverage and lower risk, whereas lower debt yields imply higher leverage and risk. See also *Leverage; Net Operating Income (NOI).*

Default: The failure to fulfill a contracted duty or discharge an obligation such as make a timely payment under a lease or loan or maintain a certain credit quality or sufficient cash liquidity. See also *Lease.*

Depreciation: An accounting expense (and tax deduction tool) that allocates the cost of an asset over its estimated useful life.

Dilution: A decrease in how much of a company each existing share is worth due to more shares being issued.

Discounted Cash Flow (DCF): An analysis of a company's value by estimating its future cash flow. The goal is to get a good idea of an investor's potential return, adjusted for the time value of money. DCF is calculated as $[CF_1 \div (1 + r)^1] + [CF_2 \div (1 + r)^2] + [CF_n \div (1 + r)^n]$, where CF_1 represents the cash flow for year one, CF_2 the cash flow for the second year, CF_n the cash flow for additional years being assessed, and r the discount rate being applied (often the weighted average cost of capital). DCF can provide a more accurate assessment of value than income capitalization when a property is operating on a shorter-term lease, particularly above or below market terms. See also *Lease; Weighted Average Cost of Capital (WACC)*.

Distributable Net Income: GAAP (Generally Accepted Accounting Principles) net income that's subjected to adjustments such as adding back depreciation, amortization, and future income tax expenses. But it excludes any gains or losses on asset dispositions and future income tax benefits. Other adjustments are made as necessary. Distributable net income is commonly used when assessing REITs. See also *Amortization; Depreciation; GAAP (Generally Accepted Accounting Principles)*.

Diversification: The practice of spreading investments across different assets or securities in order to reduce risk.

Dividend: A regular (such as monthly, quarterly, annually) or special distribution paid by a company to its stock or operating partnership unit (OP unit) holders. See also *Operating Partnership Unit (OP Unit)*.

Dollar-Cost Averaging: A strategy to manage price risk in which you purchase shares over time in smaller amounts at regular intervals, regardless of price. This decreases the risk of paying too much if or when market prices drop.

DownREIT: A joint venture between a real estate owner and a REIT that assists the real estate owner in deferring capital gains tax on the sale of appreciated real estate. Real estate owners who contribute property to DownREITs receive operating units in a partnership. See also *Joint Venture*.

Due Diligence: The process of researching and analyzing an investment's risks and rewards, including how it makes its money and what assets it owns.

E

EBITDA (Earnings Before Interest, Taxes, Depreciation, and Amortization): This measure is sometimes referred to as *net operating income (NOI)*. However, NOI typically refers to a company's property-level operating earnings, whereas EBITDA refers to them on an enterprise level. As such, EBITDA subtracts general and administrative (G&A) costs from NOI. See also *Amortization; Depreciation; General and Administrative (G&A); Net Operating Income (NOI)*.

Equity Market Capitalization: The market value of a company's entire outstanding common stock and/or operating partnership units (OP units). See also *Market Capitalization, Operating Partnership Unit (OP Unit)*.

Equity REIT: A REIT that owns and/or has an equity interest in rental real estate.

Expense ratio: A measure of the costs incurred by an investment fund, such as a REIT, in relation to its assets under management (AUM).

External Growth: The expansion of a company or organization through mergers, acquisitions, or partnerships with other companies.

F

Fair Market Rent: The amount that an off-market property would command if it were available for leasing in that moment. See also *Lease*.

Fair Market Value: The value a willing buyer would pay to a willing seller for a specific property if all material facts were known to both parties.

Fee Simple: The legal term referring to a permanent, absolute interest in a piece of property.

Floating Rate: An interest rate that can fluctuate or vary over time. Usually tied to a benchmark or reference rate.

Full-Service Hotel: A hotel with a broad range of guest amenities as well as at least one restaurant and meeting facility. Examples of full-service hotel brands include Hilton, Hyatt, Marriott, and Westin.

Funds Available for Distribution (FAD): See *Cash Available for Distribution (CAD)*.

Funds from Operations (FFO): The most commonly accepted and reported measure of REIT operating performance. According to Nareit's FFO White Paper, it's calculated as GAAP Net Income + GAAP Real Estate Depreciation and Amortization – Gains on Real Estate (in GAAP Net Income) + Losses on Real Estate (in GAAP Net Income) +/– Adjustments for Non-Controlling Partnerships + Impairments. See also *Amortization; Depreciation; GAAP (Generally Accepted Accounting Principles)*.

G

GAAP (Generally Accepted Accounting Principles): A common set of accounting principles, standards, and procedures that public companies must follow when they compile their financial statements. Private companies are not required to follow GAAP.

General and Administrative (G&A): Expenses incurred in a business's day-to-day operations that may not be directly tied to a specific function or department within the company. G&A expenses include rent, utilities, insurance, legal fees, and certain salaries.

Gross Asset Value (GAV): The market value of all a company's assets before factoring in taxes, benefits, and other deductions. This includes, but is not limited to, its real properties.

Gross Leasable Area: The total floor area available for rent plus all common areas of the building. See also *Net Leasable Area*.

Gross Lease: A lease structure in which the tenant pays a base rent and the landlord covers operating expenses (for example, property tax, property insurance, maintenance expenditures, and utilities). Gross leases are typical in the office and multifamily sector. See also *Lease*.

Gross Lease with Escalations: A lease in which the landlord pays operating expenses during the initial year or term but passes incremental expenses, or a portion thereof, on to tenants. See also *Lease*.

Ground Lease: A lease that grants the right of use for a parcel of land to the lessee, usually for lengthy periods (up to 99 years). Once that term is up, the land and everything on it reverts back to the lessor. See also *Lease; Lessee; Lessor*.

H

Hybrid REIT: A REIT that both owns properties like an equity REIT and holds mortgages on properties like a mortgage REIT. These are far less common than their counterparts. See also *Equity REIT; Mortgage REIT*.

I

Impaired Asset: A term that describes an asset with a recoverable value or fair market value that is lower than its carrying value. When an asset is impaired, a write-down on the balance sheet and an impairment loss are recognized on the income statement. Whether an asset should be impaired and how much should be impaired is determined by the accounting rules. IFRS and US GAAP apply different rules to impaired assets. See also *GAAP (Generally Accepted Accounting Principles); International Financial Reporting Standards (IFRS)*.

Implied Equity Market Capitalization: The market value of a REIT's entire outstanding common stock plus the value of all UPREIT partnership units (or operating partnership units, or OP units) as if they were converted into the REIT's stock. It excludes convertible preferred stock, convertible debentures (unsecured loan certificates that are backed by general credit instead of specific assets), and warrants. See also *Operating Partnership Unit (OP Unit); UPREIT (Umbrella Partnership REIT)*.

Initial Public Offering: The procedure by which a private firm first makes its shares available to the general public through a stock exchange.

Internal Growth: Expansion through internal means like boosting sales, improving production capacity, and creating new goods or services. It utilizes the business's current assets, skills, and market opportunities. Often referred to as *organic growth*.

Internal Rate of Return: A financial indicator used to evaluate an investment's viability and prospective return. It stands for the discount rate at which the investment's cash flows have zero net present value (NPV).

International Financial Reporting Standards (IFRS): A set of accounting rules for the financial statements of public companies that are intended to make them consistent, transparent, and easily comparable around the world. The United States uses GAAP (Generally Accepted Accounting Principles). See also *GAAP (Generally Accepted Accounting Principles).*

Intrinsic Value: Also known as *real value,* a measurement of what the company or asset is worth. In the REIT sector, one of the most common methods to arrive at intrinsic value is to utilize the net asset value (NAV) approach. Also, REITs can be valued based on other fundamental metrics including price to funds from operations (FFO) and dividend yield. See also *Funds from Operations (FFO); Net Asset Value (NAV).*

J

Joint Venture: An arrangement whereby two or more parties enter into an agreement to each contribute resources to a specific project, whether money or properties or expertise. Joint ventures are a common arrangement in development projects where different skillsets and offerings are necessary.

J-REIT: A Japanese real estate investment trust.

Junior Debt: Any secured debt that is subordinate to a senior debt obligation. The foreclosure of senior debt typically eliminates junior debt, but the foreclosure of junior debt has no effect on senior debtholders.

K

Kick-Out Clause: A lease provision that allows the landlord or tenant to terminate the lease if a specified event occurs (for example, if a sales threshold is not met). See also *Lease.*

L

Landlord: One who rents property to another party. A property owner who surrenders the right to use property for a specific time in exchange for rent paid.

Lease: A contractual agreement whereby the lessor (typically the owner) of a property grants the lessee the right to use the property for a specific amount of time in return for a stipulated rent. See also *Lessee; Lessor.*

Lease Commencement Date: The commencement date of the term of the lease for all purposes, whether or not the tenant has actually taken possession so long as beneficial occupancy is possible. See also *Lease*.

Leased Fee: An interest in land for a specified period.

Leased Rate: The percentage of units being leased (though not necessarily yet occupied) in a building, city, neighborhood, or complex.

Leasehold Improvements: The cost of improvements for a property typically paid by the tenant.

Lease Option: An agreement within a lease that provides the tenant with a right to lease additional space in the property or to extend the lease upon expiration at predetermined terms and conditions. See also *Lease*.

Lessee: A person or group that rents property under a lease. A tenant. See also *Lease*.

Lessor: A person or group that rents out property under a lease. A landlord. See also *Landlord; Lease*.

Leverage: Borrowed capital to finance the purchase of a new asset or maintain/upgrade a current one. In the context of investing, leverage enables a shareholder to buy more, which increases both potential gains and losses.

LIBOR (London Interbank Offered Rate): The most common benchmark interest rate for international banks dealing in Eurodollars to use when charging for large loans.

Lien: A claim or encumbrance against a property if a debt, charge, or other obligation isn't properly fulfilled.

Limited Partnership: A business venture undertaken between a general partner and limited partner(s). The general partner manages the partnership and is fully liable for its liabilities. The limited partners are passive investors who are only legally responsible for the amount they agreed to contribute.

Limited-Service Hotel: A hotel without restaurant or banquet facilities and with a limited range of amenities. Examples of a limited service hotel brand include Holiday Inn Express, La Quinta, and Red Roof Inn.

Liquidity: The ease and frequency at which assets are actively traded in the market, when referring to an investment; or the amount of readily accessible investment capital (cash, undrawn credit facility, or other reasonable and accessible borrowing capacity), when referring to a company.

Loan-to-Value Ratio (LTV): The amount borrowed compared to the value of the property it was borrowed for.

Long-Term Acute Care Medical Facility (LTAC): A specialty-care hospital designed for patients with serious medical problems that require intense, special treatment for an extended period — usually 20 to 30 days.

M

Maintenance Capital Expenditure: Refers to capital expenditure (CapEx) that is necessary for the company to continue operating in its current form. Examples include refurbishing an existing store (for example, adding new flooring, painting the walls, replacing the carpet). See also *Capital Expenditure (CapEx)*.

Margin of Safety: A favorable difference between the current share price and the intrinsic (or real) value of the company. The margin of safety represents a buffer or cushion that protects against unforeseen events and serves as an all-purpose risk mitigation tool. The wider the margin of safety, the lower the risk and the greater potential for gain. See also *Intrinsic Value*.

Market Capitalization: The total market value of a REIT's outstanding common stock and preferred stock plus indebtedness. Public market capitalization, more specifically, is the sum of the market value of a corporation's outstanding stock. It is computed by multiplying the current share price by the total number of outstanding shares. A company's market capitalization, or market cap, can be labeled as large-cap, mid-cap, and small-cap.

Master Lease: A lease where the tenant is allowed to sublease an area, areas, or the entire property to one or more subtenants. The sublease is then subject to all terms in the controlling or master lease and cannot extend beyond it. See also *Lease; Sublease*.

MOB: Medical office building.

Modified Gross Lease: Sometimes called *fixed cam* or *modified net lease*. A lease where, similar to a standard gross lease, the rent is set as a fixed lump sum rather than a base rent. A series of expense recoveries (as seen in a triple-net lease) are then added from there. Tenants and landlords negotiate which expense items are included in the base rental rate (for example, property tax, insurance, common area maintenance costs). If costs increase, the lease rate may not change; but if costs decline, the expense savings accrue to the landlord. Property taxes are typically excluded. See also *Base Rent; Gross Lease; Lease; Triple-Net Lease*.

Mortgage: An interest-including loan granted to purchase real property such as land or buildings in exchange for a lien against it that becomes void upon repayment. See also *Lien*.

Mortgage-Backed Security: An interest in a pool of mortgages that are purchased from lending institutions and packaged for resale to investors.

Mortgage REIT: A REIT that makes or owns loans and other obligations that are secured by real estate collateral. Commonly referred to as an mREIT.

N

Nano Cap: A small, publicly traded company with a market capitalization below $50 million. Nano cap shares are riskier due to their size, stability, and volatility. Also, these companies lack Wall Street coverage so due diligence is a must. See also *Market Capitalization*.

Nareit (National Association of Real Estate Investment Trusts): The primary trade organization and advocate of the REIT industry. Pronounced "nay-reet."

Net Absorption: A measure of demand that assesses the amount of space occupied at the end of a period minus what was occupied at the beginning. Net absorption takes into consideration space vacated and constructed during the period.

Net Asset Value (NAV): The after-deductions market value of a company's assets — including, but not limited to, its properties — after subtracting all its liabilities and obligations.

Net Leasable Area: Also called *net rentable area*. The floor space available for rent. While it can refer to a tenant's specific space or the cumulative leasable area in a building, it generally excludes common areas and space devoted to operations such as elevators, HVAC, and so on, regardless. See also *Net Rentable Area (NRA)*.

Net Lease: A lease structure where the tenant pays for some or all of operating expenses such as property taxes, property insurance, maintenance, and utilities in addition to base rent. Net lease contracts can be single, double, or triple, judging on how much additional responsibility the tenant takes on. In common parlance, net lease is shorthand for triple-net lease. Regardless, these arrangements are typical in retail (malls, shopping centers, single-tenant properties) and industrial properties. See also *Lease; Triple-Net Lease*.

Net Operating Income (NOI): A common real estate industry income metric that is calculated by subtracting operating expenses (for example, property tax, property insurance, maintenance expenditures, and utilities) from property-derived gross income (typically rent and tenant expense reimbursements). NOI does not include depreciation, income tax, or financing expenses. See also *Depreciation*.

Net Rentable Area (NRA): A measurement of a building or tenant suite upon which rent is calculated. See also *Net Leasable Area*.

Nonrecurring Capital Expenditure: An extraordinary or one-time expense that the company does not expect to continue over time, at least not on a regular basis. See also *Capital Expenditure (CapEx)*.

Nontraded REIT: A type of REIT that does not trade on a public stock exchange. Instead, it raises capital by selling shares directly to investors through broker-dealers or financial advisors.

O

Occupancy Rate: The percentage of currently occupied units in a building, city, neighborhood, or complex.

Operating Expense Ratio: A measurement of how much it costs to operate a property. Operating expense ratio is calculated by dividing operating expenses by gross income. See also *Operating Expenses*.

Operating Expenses: Payments necessary to maintain a property including management fees, common area maintenance costs, property taxes, utility costs, hazard/liability insurance, and supplies. Income taxes, depreciation, and financing costs including principal and interest payments are excluded. See also *Common Area Maintenance (CAM); Depreciation.*

Operating Lease: A lease where all the risks and benefits of ownership fall on the lessor. See also *Lease; Lessor.*

Operating Partnership: In the case of REITs, a partnership in an UPREIT or DownREIT structure that holds real property assets. Common shareholders typically hold a majority interest in the operating partnership and the operating partnership unitholders typically hold a minority interest. See also *DownREIT; Operating Partnership Unit (OP Unit); UPREIT (Umbrella Partnership REIT).*

Operating Partnership Unit (OP Unit): Interest in an operating partnership in the same way that a share is interest in a "regular" company. See also *Operating Partnership.*

Overage Rent: Additional rent for a retail or restaurant property that is equal to a predetermined percentage of gross sales over a predetermined breakpoint.

P

Partnership: An agreement between two or more entities to go into business or invest together. Either partner may bind the other within the scope of the arrangement, and each is liable for all the partnership's debts. A partnership itself normally pays no taxes. leaving the individual partners to pay personal income tax on their share of income.

Passive Income: Income from rents, royalties, interest, dividends, and gains from the sale of securities or other enterprises in which the individual is not materially involved.

Payout Ratio: The annual dividend divided by funds from operations (FFO) or adjusted funds from operations (AFFO). AFFO is a closer proxy of recurring cash flow than FFO, so it's preferable when assessing dividend sustainability. See also *Adjusted Funds from Operations (AFFO); Funds from Operations (FFO).*

Percentage Lease: A lease of property in which the rental is based exclusively on a percentage of sales volume made on premise. It usually stipulates a minimum rental and is regularly used for retail tenants. See also *Lease.*

Percentage Rent: Additional rent on a retail property that is equal to a predetermined percentage of gross sales, for example, 5 percent of tenant sales.

Permanent Financing: A long-term mortgage loan, typically obtained at the time of purchase or after completion of construction. Typically this form of financing is utilized after construction (or renovations) are completed and the property is stabilized.

Price-to-NAV: A valuation metric for REITs, similar to price-to-book value. Book value is based on historical costs and does not reflect the rise and fall of property prices; therefore, REITs use net asset value (NAV) to derive the underlying value of its properties. See also *Net Asset Value (NAV).*

Principal: Has several meanings in finance; in this book, I use the term to describe the sum put into an investment, separate from any earnings or interest accrued.

Property Management: The operation, control, and oversight of real property as a business. Services commonly include rent collection, accounting, and property maintenance, and may include leasing.

Pro Rata Share: Also called *proportionate share.* The allocated share of operating expenses charged to a specific tenant, usually based on the area of the tenant's premises divided by the total area in the building or complex.

R

Rate of Return: The income and realized or unrealized gain on an investment expressed as a percentage of the investment. Rate of return may be further segregated by source or character, such as

- *Appreciation Return:* The portion of total return produced by an asset's change in value during the holding period, whether due to appreciation or depreciation, and realized or unrealized.

- *Cash-on-Cash Return:* Cash income as a percentage of cash invested.

- *Income Return:* The portion of total return produced by income from operations.

- *Internal Rate of Return:* An implied rate of return equal to the discount rate at which the present value of the future cash flow of an investment equals the cost of the investment.

Real Estate Investment Trust (REIT): A company that owns or finances income-producing real estate (for example, apartments, shopping centers, offices, and warehouses) as long-term investments. REITs avoid paying certain taxes by meeting certain conditions, including distributing at least equal to 90 percent of their taxable income. Pronounced "reet."

Real Estate Investment Trust (REIT) Act of 1960: The federal law that authorized REITs, allowing small investors to invest in real estate partnerships with similar benefits as offered by direct ownership, while also diversifying their risks. See also *Real Estate Investment Trust (REIT).*

Real Estate Investment Trust (REIT) Investment Diversification and Empowerment Act of 2007 (RIDEA): Legislation that allowed healthcare REITs to participate in the operating income of healthcare properties just as long as a third-party manager was involved. In effect, this allows them to change their income statement transition from lease payments to operating income. To do so they first create a taxable REIT subsidiary (TRS) with a lease between the landlord and tenant entities, as hotels were allowed to do in the REIT Modernization Act of 1999. See also *Lease; REIT Modernization Act of 1999; Taxable REIT Subsidiary (TRS).*

Real Estate Owned (REO): Real estate that has come to be owned by a lender through foreclosure or deed-in-lieu transaction because of a default.

Real Return: A rate of return adjusted for inflation and calculated in real dollars, rather than nominal dollars (reflects the present value).

Recourse Debt: A debt obligation under which the lender's claim against the debtor is not limited by the value of the real property on which it is secured. A loan with personal liability.

Recurring Capitalized Expenditure: Money that must be spent to maintain the profitability of the property. Examples include leasing commissions and tenant improvements paid to lease a space, which are capitalized and amortized (averaged) over the life of the lease. See also *Capital Expenditure (CapEx)*.

REIT Index: A benchmark or collection of publicly traded REITs compiled to track the performance of the real estate industry. Indexes gives investors a way to assess the overall performance of given markets and compare/contrast them with individual asset returns.

REIT Modernization Act of 1999: A federal tax law that went into effect in 2001 (therefore sometimes referred to as the REIT Modernization Act of 2001) and allowed certain REITs to own up to 100 percent of stock in a taxable REIT subsidiary that provides services to REIT tenants and others. For example, hotel REITs were able to participate in the operating profit of the hotel provided that there was a third-party manager, whereas previously the hotels had to be held in a lease structure. See also *Lease; Taxable REIT Subsidiary (TRS)*.

Rent Commencement Date: The date on which a tenant begins paying rent. This may or may not be the same time as the lease commencement date, depending on the lease in question. See also *Lease; Lease Commencement Date*.

Rentable Space: The area of a property or suite, measured in square feet, upon which rent is collected.

Rental Rate: The periodic charge per unit (whether an entire dwelling, square foot, cubic foot, or other measurement) for the use of a property over a set month, quarter, or year.

Replacement Cost: The cost to construct a building of equal economic utility or usefulness. The cost of construction (labor, materials) and related costs such as architectural fees, permits, property taxes, and interest during construction are all considered.

Residual Value: The estimated net market value of a property at the end of its holding period.

Return on Invested Capital (ROIC): A calculation used to assess a company's efficiency in allocating capital to profitable investments. The formula involves dividing net operating profits after tax by invested capital. ROIC gives a sense of how well a company is using its capital to generate profits. See also *Weighted Average Cost of Capital (WACC)*.

Return on Investment (ROI): A measure used to assess a company's profitability. ROI is expressed as a percentage and calculated by dividing an investment's net profit (or loss) by its initial cost. ROI is a simple metric to gauge profitability.

Revenue Per Available Room (RevPAR): A term in the lodging industry used to measure nightly room revenue over a period of time for a single hotel, market, or the larger industry. RevPAR is calculated as either (1) the product of the average daily rate (ADR) and occupancy rate, or (2) room revenue divided by the number of rooms available. By comparison, the ADR is calculated by dividing room revenue by the number of rooms sold. See also *Average Daily Rate (ADR); RevPAR Index.*

RevPAR Index: A measure of a hotel's market share in its competitive set, submarket, or market. A hotel's revenue per available room (RevPAR, or ADR, or occupancy) is expressed relative to the competitive set, whereby a RevPAR index of 100 means that the hotel is capturing its fair share; greater than 100 means it's capturing more than its fair share, and less than 100 means less than its fair share. See also *Revenue Per Available Room (RevPAR).*

RIDEA: See *Real Estate Investment Trust (REIT) Investment Diversification and Empowerment Act of 2007 (RIDEA).*

ROI (Return on Investment) Project: Typically a non-leasing capital investment that improves the competitive positioning of a property or appreciably extends its useful life. Unlike capital expenditures, an ROI project typically has a prospective return on investment (for example, adding or upgrading the common area amenities of an apartment property, modernizing the facade at a shopping center). See also *Capital Expenditure (CapEx); Capital Improvement.*

S

Sale-Leaseback: A form of financing where a person or business entity sells a property and simultaneously agrees to rent it from the buyer, generally under a long-term lease. For example, Home Depot could sell a facility to a REIT and lease back the facility. This gives it an instant influx of cash and reduces some burdens of ownership. See also *Lease.*

Securitization: The process of raising funds by selling securities that represent an undivided interest in a pool of assets, such as commercial mortgage loans or property.

Select-Service Hotel: A lodging facility that offers the fundamental basic service of a limited-service hotel but includes full-service hotel aspects such as a one- or two-meal per day restaurant and a select number of amenities (for example, a fitness room, business center). Examples of select-service hotel brands include Hilton Garden Inn and Courtyard by Marriott. See also *Full-Service Hotel; Limited-Service Hotel.*

Shopping Center: An integrated complex of outdoor retail stores designed to accommodate certain shopping and service needs of a specific market area. Shopping centers are generally categorized as follows:

- *Super-Regional/Regional Mall:* The largest shopping centers, they provide a complete range of general merchandise and fashion-oriented offerings. Typically enclosed with inward-facing stores, multiple department stores, and connected by a common walkway. Often located at major highway interchanges near major urban markets. Typically 400,000 square feet or larger, with an average size of about 1.2 million square feet for a super-regional mall (three or more anchors) and 600,000 square feet for a regional mall (two or more anchors). Anchors occupy approximately 5 to 70 percent of the leasable area. There are approximately 1,200 malls in the United States.

- *Outlet/Factory Outlet:* Manufacturer and retailer stores selling brand-name goods at a discount. Historically, outlets sold last-season merchandise, production overruns, flawed products, and so on, but today most inventory is produced specifically for sale in the outlet channel. There are 250 to 350 such properties in the United States today.

Single-Tenant Building: A building made for one tenant and occupied by one tenant. Also referred to as a *free-standing property*.

Skilled Nursing Facility (SNF): A special facility that provides professional medical services from nurses, physical and occupational therapists, speech pathologists, and audiologists. Skilled nursing facilities provide around-the-clock assistance with healthcare and activities of daily living subject to federal guidelines. Also known as *nursing homes*.

Stock Compensation: When a corporation grants company shares or stock options as a reward to employees. It is often subject to a vesting period of three to four years before it can be collected and sold by an employee.

Straight-Line Rents: Non-cash revenue that occurs when a landlord enters into a long-term lease with a tenant and the lease contains contractual rent increases over the life of the lease. Based on GAAP (Generally Accepted Accounting Principles), the company must "straight line" the entire revenue stream over the term of the lease rather than recognize revenue as the cash is collected each period. The general theory of calculating straight-line rent expense: sum the total net lease payments and dividend by the total number of periods in the lease. *GAAP (Generally Accepted Accounting Principles); Lease.*

Sublease: The leasing of a property by a tenant to a subtenant. The primary tenant remains responsible to the landlord under the original lease. See also *Lease.*

Subordination: An arrangement whereby one party puts its claim against an entity after (or junior to) the claim of another creditor.

Subordination Clause: A lease clause whereby the tenant accepts the leased premises subject to any recorded mortgage or deed of trust lien and all existing recorded restrictions. The landlord is often given the power to subordinate the tenant's interest to any first mortgage subsequently placed upon the leased premises. See also *Lease.*

Sucker Yield: An unnaturally high dividend yield attached to a company's stock because that company has a flawed or vulnerable business model. Companies that feature sucker yields tend to have unpredictable and unreliable earnings histories filled with unsafe dividend payouts. When a company is paying a dividend beyond its earning power, it is essentially eroding capital.

SWAN (Sleep Well At Night): A term used (but not coined by) the author to refer to a high-quality stock that is very likely to operate stress-free and offer unbroken, ever-growing dividends.

T

Tax Reform Act of 1986: A federal law that substantially altered the real estate investment landscape by permitting REITs to not only own, but also operate and manage, most types of income-producing commercial properties. It also stopped real estate tax shelters that had attracted capital from investors based on the amount of losses that could be created.

Taxable REIT Subsidiary (TRS): A REIT–owned corporation set up to handle decisions and responsibilities that REITs can't without incurring tax and other penalties. For example, a TRS can buy and hold properties it intends to turn around quickly. Or it can manage real estate-related services, such as landscaping, cleaning, and concierge duties. Income of the TRS is taxable, and the size of the TRS is limited to 25 percent of the REIT's assets.

Tenant: A person, persons, or business entity that signs a contract to occupy a property for a set amount of time at a set amount of money that's usually paid on a monthly basis.

Tenant Concessions: Lease adjustments that either reduce rent obligations or include upfront cash expenditures or allowances from the landlord. Concessions are generally a sign of market softness and are normally capitalized, not expensed. See also *Lease*.

Tenant Fixtures: Fixtures added to leased property by a lessee that, by contract and/or law, may be removed by the lessee upon expiration of the lease. Rules vary around what is considered the landlord's versus the tenant's property. For example, items bolted to the property such as HVAC units and kitchen equipment may be considered the property of the landlord at the conclusion of the lease and can be a source of negotiating leverage for the landlord in a renewal. See also *Lease; Lessee*.

Tenant Improvements (TI): Costs incurred in making physical improvements to the space occupied by either a new or re-leasing tenant.

Tenant Sales: The gross sales of an entire retail property or specific tenant on that property. They are typically expressed on a per-square-foot basis utilizing the entire gross leasable area of the property or tenant, as opposed to just the selling area (area used by customers and excluding any back room).

Total Return: Income return plus appreciation return.

Triple-Net Lease: A lease contract in which the tenant pays operating expenses, insurance premiums, and property taxes, typically including such things as roof and structure repairs. This arrangement is commonplace in industrial and retail assets. See also *Lease; Net Lease*.

Triple-Net Lease, Absolute: A less common and more binding version of a triple-net lease where every conceivable real estate risk (for example, rebuilding after a catastrophe, paying rent despite condemnation) is taken up by the tenant. See also *Lease; Triple-Net Lease*.

U

Unsecured Debt: Financing guaranteed at the parent-company level and not on individual properties.

UPREIT (Umbrella Partnership REIT): An entity structure that allows property owners to contribute their real estate in exchange for operating partnership units that can be converted into REIT shares. The partnership units are worth the same as the contributed property. But unlike selling the property outright, this transaction is not considered a sale and therefore does not create a taxable event. See also *Operating Partnership Unit (OP Unit)*.

V

Vacancy Rate: The percentage of all space or units of a property that is unoccupied or unleased. See also *Lease*.

Value Investing: An investment strategy that focuses on identifying and buying up undervalued assets with the expectation that their value will increase over time.

Value Trap: A stock or other investment that appears to be cheaply priced because it trades at low valuation metrics but is actually cheap for disconcerting reasons that will keep it cheap for some time to come, if it doesn't fail altogether.

W

Weighted Average Cost of Capital (WACC): The average cost of a company's capital from all sources, including common stock, preferred stock, bonds, and other forms of debt. It's therefore the average rate a company expects to pay to finance its assets. WACC is critical for determining value creation and evaluating strategic decisions. It's the rate you compare with the return on invested capital to determine if the company is creating value. See also *Return on Invested Capital (ROIC)*.

Z

Zoning: The division of a municipal area into categories, each one with a specific use (such as public, office, single-family residential, manufacturing) and specific regulations concerning structure (height, setback, and so on) and sometimes architectural design.

Index

UK-REITs, 72
Umbrella Partnership REIT (UPREIT), 34–36, 260.
    See also operating partnership unit (OP unit)
Unconventional Success, 164, 192
United Arab Emirates (UAE), REITs in, 67
United Kingdom, REITs in, 67, 72
United States, REITs in, 67
university endowments, 189–192
unsecured debt, 260
Urban Air, 101

V

vacancy rate, 260
value, rental income for creating,
    25–30
value investing, 260
value REITs, 167–169
value traps, 228–229, 260
value-drivers, 147
VanEck Mortgage REIT Income ETF (MORT), 204
Vanguard Global ex-U.S. Real Estate Index Fund
    (VNQI), 202
Vanguard Group Inc., 186
Vanguard Real Estate Index Fund ETF (VNQ), 200
variable-rate debt, 144–145
Ventas, 51, 112, 157
VICI Properties, 97, 167
Vident U.S. Diversified Real Estate ETF (PPTY), 204
Vietnam, REITs in, 67, 81
virtual landlords
    about, 7–8, 12
    commercial real estate, 8
    fundamentals, 11–12
    importance of size, 10–11
    payment to, 10
    REITs, 8–10, 12–13
Virtus InfraCap U.S. Preferred Stock ETF (PFFA),
    206–207
Volk, Chris (CEO), 156

Vornado Realty Trust, 94
V-REITs, 81

W

Walten, Kurt (VP), 189
Warning icon, 4
Washington Prime, 100
Washington Real Estate Investment Trust, 32
websites
    Bahrain Bourse, 73
    Cheat Sheet, 4
    GermanReal.Estate, 69
    The Law Reviews, 73
    The Motley Fool, 227
    National Association of REITs (Nareit), 221
    REITs Across America, 85
    Seeking Alpha, 221
    Wide Moat Research, 221
weighted average cost of capital (WACC). *See also*
    return on invested capital (ROIC)
    about, 133–135, 154
    assessing, 233–236
    defined, 260
Wellington Management Group LLP, 186
Welltower, 112
Weyerhaeuser, 117–118
wholesale colocation data centers, 109
Wide Moat Research, 221
Wojtaszek, Gary "Wojo," 114
W.P. Carey, 51, 97

Y

"Yale Model," 189–192
yield to call, 53

Z

zoning, 260

About the Author

Brad Thomas is CEO and Senior Analyst at Wide Moat Research, an independent investment research firm that specializes in a broad range of income-focused investment opportunities. He's the most-followed analyst at Seeking Alpha, a crowd-sourced investment platform, with over 110,000 followers; and he's the editor of *Forbes Real Estate*. Brad is also the founder of iREIT®, a portfolio of products that include iREIT® Research, iREIT® Tracker, iREIT® Podcast, iREIT® MarketVector™ Quality REIT Index, iREIT® Masterclass, and iREIT® Investor.

Brad has extensive experience in commercial real estate investing, transacting more than $1 billion worth of projects all told. He's been a landlord to many large corporations such as Walmart, Walgreens, Advance Auto Parts, Sherwin-Williams, Goodyear Tire, PetSmart, Aaron's Rent-to-Own, Dollar General, Dollar Tree, and CVS. In addition, he's been a multi-unit franchisee for two nationally recognized chains. All told, it's safe to say he knows a thing or two about real estate.

A former president of South Carolina's National Association for Industrial and Office Parks (NAIOP) chapter, he remains a member today. In addition, he's a licensed real estate agent in South Carolina and a member of the International Council of Shopping Centers.

Brad has authored four books so far, including this one. He's also written numerous articles for and made media appearances on outlets such as Fox & Friends, Fox Business, MSNBC, Bloomberg, CNN, *Forbes*, Institutional Investor, NPR, the American Association of Individual Investors, MarketWatch, Investopedia, TheStreet, *Barron's*, The Property Chronicle, GlobeSt, *Kiplinger's*, The Motley Fool, and more.

Brad graduated from Presbyterian College with a major in business and economics, playing college basketball and participating in ROTC for his four years there. Today, he's an adjunct professor at NYU and guest lectures regularly at Penn State University, Cornell University, Clemson University, the University of North Carolina at Chapel Hill, and Georgetown University (all about real estate, of course).

A South Carolina man, born and bred, Brad was raised by a single mother, Louise Thomas, who worked and invested in real estate for over four decades. His maternal grandfather was also a real estate investor who developed motels during the 1960s in Myrtle Beach, South Carolina. So, properties are in his blood.

Brad is married to Stephanie Thomas, with whom he shares five children (Lauren, Lexy, Nicholas, Riley, and AJ) and ACE, the dog. Plus, he's the recent grandfather of the ever-impressive Asher, who was one year old at the time of publication of *REITs For Dummies*.

You can view Brad's profile at www.linkedin.com/in/rbradthomas/, www.wideemoatresearch.com, and www.ireitinvestor.com, and you can follow him on Twitter @rbradthomas and check out his author's page at www.amazon.com/stores/author/B01H3ZLZJ4/about.

Dedication

This book is dedicated to legendary REIT tycoon Sam Zell (1941–2023).

The son of Jewish immigrants from Poland who fled to America in 1939, Zell amassed a fortune assembling one of the nation's largest portfolios of apartments, offices, and other pieces of commercial real estate. Along the way he was nicknamed "the gravedancer" for snatching up distressed properties at wide discounts, and he inspired so many others to try to follow in his ever-impressive footsteps.

Zell, considered to be a founder of the modern REIT era, was chairman of Equity Commonwealth and created several REITs as well. These businesses included Equity Residential and Equity LifeStyle Properties. Another one, Equity Office Properties — a company Zell sold to Blackstone for $39 billion in 2006 — was the first REIT named to the S&P 500 Index in October 2001. And Equity Residential followed a month later.

I was fortunate to know Sam Zell. He will be greatly missed by many, including yours truly.

Author's Acknowledgments

One of the great things about being a Wall Street writer is that I get to meet regularly with management teams. Over the years, I've soaked up far more knowledge from them than I could have ever gained at an Ivy League university.

As I reference in this book, management plays a critical role in the REIT sector. So I'd be remiss if I didn't thank people like Tom Lewis (an early mentor), Craig Macnab, Ed Pitoniak, Ben Butcher, Bobby Taubman, Taylor Pickett, Joey Agree, Brian Harris, Barry Sternlicht, Sumit Roy, Debra Cafaro, Jason Fox, Owen Thomas, Don Wood, Paul Pittman, David Gladstone, Conor Flynn, Wendy Simpson, David Simon, Steve Tanger, Chris Volk, and the list of REIT and real estate-related executives goes on.

Then there's Ralph Block, who was an unforgettable friend, mentor, and legend in the REIT sector. I'm not sure that anyone can carry the torch for him, but I am hoping that when he reads this book in heaven, he'll be proud of my efforts to keep the fire burning.

Other legends worth noting include Mike Kirby, cofounder of Green Street; Marty Cohen and Bob Steers, cofounders at Cohen & Steers; and Stephen A. Schwarzman, CEO and cofounder of Blackstone. These individuals helped popularize the REIT sector, which has led to significant liquidity for small and large investors alike, myself included. And I'd be remiss if I didn't thank the industry heralds at Nareit for their assistance over the years, especially Steven A. Wechsler, John D. Worth, and Jeanne Arnold.

These were just a few of the teachers in my life, both intentional and inadvertent. Other mentors include Chuck Carnevale, Eva Steiner, Norman Scarborough, Dr. Brad Case, Dr. Sam Chandan, Tommy Holt, DJ Horton, Brad Watt, Ricky Chastain, Joe Jackson, Kyle Cerminara, and Shelby Pruett.

I owe a tremendous thank you to the folks at Seeking Alpha as well. This investment-focused platform allowed me to publish an article on their website in 2010 — an article that began a journey of over 3,500 writeups in 13 years. David Jackson, its founder and CEO, had the vision to create a unique do-it-yourself stock research site that was the launchpad for my publishing career. That's something I won't be forgetting anytime soon.

I also want to thank my team at Wide Moat Research who inspired me to write this book. Without their support, I would never have been able to make it happen. So another huge thank you goes to Stephen Hester, CFA; Adam Galas; Nick Ward; Frances Popp; Shakila Choudhry; and Justin Law. And behind Wide Moat Research is its parent publisher, Legacy Research, where I want to thank cofounders Ryan Markish and Fernando Cruz for having confidence in our talented team.

Moving on down this VIP list, I can't say enough about the For Dummies team at Wiley. Stated simply, they've been magnificent. I can honestly say that Tracy Boggier's and Katharine Dvorak's skillsets are unmatched in the book industry.

There's always one person who's the glue when it comes to writing a book, and that person is my primary editor, Jeannette Boca. She was instrumental in this work as well as with my previous book, *The Intelligent REIT Investor*. I also needed a technical editor for *REITs For Dummies* — someone who was skilled in the sector. And I couldn't have found a better editor than Mark Decker, Sr., who has also been a mentor to me over the years. Another notable editorial voice I need to mention is Josh Cohen. He started out as a subscriber to one of my services years ago, and he continues to remind me to dot my I's and cross my T's today.

Every summer my iREIT team also hires college interns. This year I want to thank five of them for helping me with this book: Ethan Delves, Maha Malik, Connor Graham, Kirby Ryan, and Nicholas Thomas.

Almost last — but hardly least — I'm very grateful to my family who have allowed me to work at my office for many a long weekend. My wife, Stephanie, should be credited as a coauthor since she has to listen to me talk about REITs seven days a week.

And finally, I want to acknowledge the "Average Investors" — the thousands of readers and subscribers who inspired me to become the so-called "King of REITs." All of us are dummies at one time or another, whether we want to admit it or not. But hopefully after reading this book, you've graduated to become an intelligent REIT investor ready to crunch some numbers and make some money with the best of them!

Publisher's Acknowledgments

Senior Acquisitions Editor: Tracy Boggier

Managing Editor: Sofia Malik

Development and Project Editor:
Katharine Dvorak

Technical Editor: Mark Decker

Production Editor: Saikarthick Kumarasamy

Cover Image: © VideoFlow/Shutterstock

Printed and bound by CPI Group (UK) Ltd, Croydon, CR0 4YY

05/09/2023

08109013-0001